SENATOR
TED KENNEDY

By Theo Lippman, Jr.

Senator Ted Kennedy
Spiro Agnew's America
Muskie (with Donald C. Hansen)
A Gang of Pecksniffs by H. L. Mencken (Editor)

SENATOR ED KENNEDY

Theo Lippman, Jr.

W. W. NORTON
& COMPANY, INC.
NEW YORK

Copyright © 1976 by W. W. Norton & Company, Inc.

First Edition

Library of Congress Cataloging in Publication Data

Lippman, Theo.
    Senator Ted Kennedy: the career behind the image.

    1. Kennedy, Edward Moore, 1932–   I. Title.
E840.8.K35L56   1975   328.73′092′4 [B]   75-28347
ISBN:978-0-393-33526-2

Published simultaneously in Canada
by George J. McLeod Limited, Toronto

Printed in the United States of America

2 3 4 5 6 7 8 9

For Susan

CONTENTS

AUTHOR'S NOTE

In April 1974, assuming that Senator Edward Kennedy was probably going to be a candidate for his party's presidential nomination in 1976, I proposed to Evan W. Thomas, my editor at Norton, a book that would take a detailed look at Kennedy's Senate career. I have been a frequent visitor to the Senate Press Gallery since 1961, the year before Kennedy entered the Senate. I did not know Kennedy, but I knew a little about his work. I knew that he was an active and hard-working senator, involved in a fairly wide range of endeavors. I believed he was at least as skillful as most of his colleagues. And I believed that insufficient attention had been paid to this aspect of his life. It seemed to me that if he were a presidential aspirant, there would be plenty of studies of his character, his personality, his integrity, his family—as there should be—but I suspected that much of what he had actually done as a senator might be overlooked. A man's career, particularly when it is long, as Kennedy's has been, deserves at least equal billing with what Kennedy refers to as "the color in my life." What happened during several hours on Chappaquiddick Island tells us something about what kind of person Ted Kennedy is and, perhaps, what kind of president Ted Kennedy would be. But what has happened in thousands of hours on the Senate floor and in committee hearings tells us more, I believe. This is essentially a book about *those* thousands of hours, a study of Edward M. Kennedy's career, work, accomplishments as a United States senator.

In the course of a year's work on this project, I came to the conclusion that Senator Kennedy's career in the Senate to date had been full enough to be worthy of study whether he is a presidential candidate or not, this year or later. As this book shows, I also came to the conclusion that his career has been as commendable as it has been full. Whether readers agree or not, they will still find it instructive, I think, to learn what priorities Ted Kennedy has set, what goals; how he has gone about trying to achieve those goals, and how close he has come to achieving them.

Perhaps a word about how I proceeded is in order. After I told Senator Kennedy of my plans, he agreed to a series of interviews. I always found him straightforward and responsive in those interviews. Kennedy also agreed to let members of his staff answer my questions. I gather he told each to cooperate as he or she saw fit. Some staff members opened their files to me. Some showed me any material from their files I knew enough to ask about. Some were more selective still. Some were willing to talk but not provide documents. I discerned no pattern. *All* were generous with their time, to the point of sacrifice. Kennedy staff members are very busy people. I am sure that many of them worked late at their own jobs on many nights because they had spent too much time during the day answering my questions. I won't attempt to name all who helped me, for the list is so long that I would surely make a careless and embarrassing omission. What is true of staff members is also true of former staff members. Many members of the Senate and House who have been involved with Kennedy over the years were also considerate of my requests for their time. Many staff aides of Senator Kennedy's friends, adversaries, and competitors were most gracious and helpful as well. The bulk of this book is drawn from interviews, from official documents, such as the *Congressional Record*, from committee hearings and reports, and from speeches and press releases. I also have drawn heavily on reports and comments in the Boston *Globe*, the Washington *Post*, *the New York Times*, the Baltimore *Sun*, *Congressional Quarterly*, *Facts on File*, and

National Journal Reports. I am indebted to Robert L. Peabody of the Political Science Department of Johns Hopkins University for giving me an advance look at the chapter of his book on Congress dealing with the 1969 and 1971 whip fights. I drew on three earlier books on the Senate: William S. White's *Citadel,* Donald R. Matthews's *U.S. Senators and Their World,* and Ronald Ripley's *Power in the Senate.* I also made use of a Ralph Nader study, *The Judiciary Committees,* written mostly by Peter H. Schuck.

There is an enormous literature dealing with the Kennedy family. I found the following helpful: *John Kennedy,* by James McGregor Burns; *The Kennedy Neurosis,* by Nancy Clinch; *The Kennedy Case,* by Rita Dallas; *The Kennedy Promise,* by Henry Fairlie; *Times To Remember,* by Rose Fitzgerald Kennedy; *Joseph P. Kennedy, a Life and Times,* by David E. Koskoff; *Johnny We Hardly Knew Ye,* by Kenneth P. O'Donnell and David F. Powers, with Joe McCarthy; *The Heir Apparent,* by William V. Shannon; *A Thousand Days,* by Arthur Schlesinger, Jr.; *The Kennedy Legacy,* by Theodore C. Sorensen; and *On His Own: RFK 1964–1968,* by Milton Gwirtzman and William J. Vanden Heuvel. The following books about Ted Kennedy himself were valuable: *Ted Kennedy, Triumph and Tragedies,* by Lester David; *The Education of Edward Kennedy,* by Burton Hersh; *Ted Kennedy, Profile of a Survivor,* by William H. Honan; *Kennedy Campaigning,* by Murray B. Levin; and *The Bridge at Chappaquiddick,* by Jack Olson.

No one except the author is responsible for anything in *Senator Ted Kennedy,* of course.

Columbia, Maryland, July 1975

SENATOR
TED KENNEDY

1. IN THE FORUM
OF THE STATES

June 18, 1964. Midafternoon. The filibuster droned on, but its end was near. The great debate had been going on for eighty-two days. The issue was an omnibus civil-rights bill, the most sweeping ever proposed. Unlike most civil-rights bills, this one was going to pass the Senate—and without being watered down to meaninglessness. President Lyndon Johnson had pledged it as a tribute to his predecessor, the slain John Kennedy. Senator Edward Kennedy sat in the presiding officer's chair in the Senate as Senator Richard Russell of Georgia, leader of the Southerners opposing the bill, made his last speech. Russell's time was almost up. The Senate had voted cloture—limiting debate to one hour per senator—for the first time ever in a civil-rights fight. Russell and others believed that the Senate was a unique forum of the sovereign states, and that no limits of any kind must ever be applied to a senator's right to speak. So June 1964 was a turning point in the history of the institution that had been called, not only in jest, the South's revenge for Appomattox. Russell was characteristically a courteous gentleman, even in defeat. But not today. His last speech was full of invective and bitterness.

He had often said that there was nothing as terrible as being "taken off one's feet." As his hour ran out—he would be the first senator to use up his full time—his bitterness increased. He stood at his strategically located desk on the aisle in the second row, just behind the majority leader's desk, and spoke rancorously of the bill and its sponsors. He watched as the young presiding officer nervously fingered the handleless gavel that he would soon use to silence Russell and take him off his feet.

Richard Russell had been elected to the Senate the year Edward Moore Kennedy was born. Then, at thirty-six, he was the Senate's youngest member. In 1964, with thirty-two years' experience and seniority, he was the most powerful member of the Senate. He was chairman of the Armed Services Committee and of the Defense Appropriations Subcommittee. For years committee chairmen, almost all of them Southern and conservative, had dominated the Senate. They had institutional control. In the late fifties and early sixties that control began to weaken as the number of Northern and Western Democrats increased—and as the influence of the majority leader, in eclipse for years, brightened up the Senate. That majority leader was Lyndon Johnson, now the president. Johnson had run for party leadership in 1953 only after Russell turned down his suggestion that *he* take the job. Russell recommended Johnson for the job. Johnson took it on the condition that Russell sit behind him on the floor to tutor him. And so he had.

Russell continued his harangue. The galleries were full of spectators, unsympathetic to him and his new lost cause. Russell stared at Kennedy as he paused for breath and the minutes ticked away, as if daring him to call time on him. Kennedy seemed lost in thought. He toyed with the gavel.

The Senate that was dominated by Russell and his colleagues was best described by journalist William White, in *Citadel*. White talked about the need for senators to conform, to serve a long apprenticeship, to help others if they asked you, to specialize, to defend the institution. Don't assert yourself, don't look for a career beyond the Senate. Ted Kennedy read the book before he was elected to the Senate in 1962. He took its lessons to heart. His brother John, who was a senator from 1953 through 1960, gave him the same advice. Ted had visited the Senate many times during

John's tenure. He decided on his first visit in 1953, he said later, that he would like to go into public life, though it was a few years later before he decided on the Senate itself. John Kennedy's advice also included the need for preparing oneself for debate. At John's insistence, Ted read through David Brewer's ten-volume *World's Great Orations.* Floor speeches were not that important in the Senate, at least not then, at least not for a back bencher. Too many speeches and the elders would become hostile. But then John Kennedy was not the best tutor on how to get ahead in the Senate. He had not been a good senator. "Too young, too liberal, too outspoken," is the reason given by his aide Theodore Sorensen. Also, he was never there. Earlier he was out with his bad back a lot. Later he was always off running for president. He never had time for menial Senate chores for his elders, who expected that as well as deference.

Ted Kennedy was different. He came to Washington expecting to like the Senate and to be accepted. The first day there he called on the new majority leader, Mike Mansfield of Montana, and on Russell. He had met Russell as a child. Russell and his father had been friends. "Dick liked Joe," a friend says, "and always liked the boys, too, because of his early friendship with the father." Russell and Ted and John Kennedy were all Civil War buffs, and the three had occasionally visited Virginia and Maryland battlefields in the presidential helicopter with a professional historian in tow.

Ted Kennedy was a genius at getting along with older men. "Ninth-child talent," a friend put it. His mother said, "As the last child, handsome and robust, he expects to like people and expects to be liked." Kennedy knew that Russell respected those who did their homework. So he prepped himself on Russell's career. At the meeting in Russell's office, Kennedy steered the conversation around to the fact that he had been criticized for seeking the Senate seat when he was only thirty years old. "But you were a youngster, yourself, when you were elected," Kennedy said. And Russell snapped back, still friendly but in harsh syllables: "That's right, son, but I'd had a little seasoning first. I was the county attorney of Barrow County, a member and Speaker of the [State] House of Representatives for ten years, and governor of Georgia."

Kennedy began to put that ninth-child talent to work on his peers. He called on Senator James Eastland of Mississippi, the chairman of the Judiciary Committee, to which he had been assigned. They drank bourbon in Eastland's suite and became and remained friends. Eastland is twenty-eight years Kennedy's senior. He is also one of the worst racists in the Senate, and a man who has enriched himself with farm subsidies from programs he helped to enact into law. He is probably the most disreputable senator in the eyes of the people who most respect Kennedy; that is, liberal Democrats. Some contend that Kennedy, who often mimics Eastland's corn-pone accent and manners, really dislikes Eastland and only uses him to advance his own career on the Judiciary Committee. But a close friend of Kennedy's who once worked for him in the Senate says, "His relationship with Eastland is genuine. They giggle together like children. It is beyond explanation, except chemistry." Kennedy in 1963 and 1964 always "sirred" Eastland and his other elders. But he never made them feel he was a child or a person who did not belong in the Senate. Senator Stuart Symington, who had children older than Kennedy, told a friend in 1963 that he had never seen a new senator learn his job—become a peer—so rapidly.

The Senate clock's minute hand moved past 3:15, and the timekeeper's addition showed that Russell was at the end of his hour.

Contrary to legend, Russell did not give Kennedy a lot of detailed advice on that first-day session in his office. About all he told him was, "You go further if you go slow." And slow Kennedy had gone. He had not asked for any specific committees, fearing it would put the Democratic senators who make assignments on the spot. He didn't want to be the president's brother. He asked only that his state's industrial characteristics and his own interest in social issues be taken into account. He wanted the Interstate and Foreign Commerce Committee. He got Judiciary and that liberal bastion, Labor and Public Welfare. The latter committee was also a presidential-nomination launching pad. John Kennedy, Hubert Humphrey, Richard Nixon, Robert Taft, and Barry Goldwater all had served on it. Kennedy's "maiden speech" was about Massachusetts. He made his office suite (431 Old Senate Office Building) a little bit of home away from home, with bookcases, rugs, and furniture from Massachusetts manufacturers. There was also an 1802 Simon Willard banjo clock, a Worcester M-14 rifle, a model of a Grand Banks cod-fishing schooner.

Joan Kennedy picked out a house in Georgetown, on 31st Street. (After one move in Georgetown, they moved to a $500,000 house in McLean, Virginia, in 1968, the design and construction of which Joan oversaw. The house was near Robert and Ethel Kennedy's Hickory Hill.) Their 31st Street neighbors were the Hugh Auchinclosses, Jean and Stephen Smith, Chester Bowles, G. Mennen Williams. When he wasn't wearing his new-boy-in-the-Senate costume, Kennedy was wearing his New-Frontier-social-lion one. He had jumped into a swimming pool fully clothed before his election, and his reputation always included that story— outside the Senate. It did not seem to intrude into the chamber of the Senate. Kennedy was doing and saying the right things in the precincts of Capitol Hill. "The normal tendency is to be seen and not heard, and that makes sense," he would say, just at the right time to cancel out any negative effect some other public statement might have on the Senate elders. For instance, whenever Kennedy spoke to public audiences around Washington, the emphasis would be on jokes about his age and his famous brother. He was going to use a rocking chair in the Senate, he would say, that piece of furniture having become associated with the President. He was still using greasy kid stuff on his hair, he would say, a reference to a hair tonic commercial about young "unsophisticated" beginners. Demeaning to a *senator*, perhaps. But "he kept his mouth shut," as one senator put it, about the Senate. He didn't complain in public about what was wrong with it, or gush flattery, apple-polisher style, about its giants. He did his chores, such as presiding over boring debates.*

Because his name was not plain Edward Moore, Kennedy knew, he was being subjected to a more careful and continuous scrutiny than other freshmen senators. He

*He was presiding on November 22, 1963, when the first bulletin from Dallas arrived.

was a cautious legislator. He vowed he would make no mistakes. His staff was ordered to check and recheck press releases, speeches, proposals for the most minor legislation. This meant longer-than-usual hours and, according to some memories, a less-than-happy ship. Kennedy seemed determined to be his own man, not his brother Jack's, not his staff's, not the public's. He was cautious about giving his name or his boundless energy to causes. A frequent question asked by him of staff or friends who proposed legislation was, "Are you sure it can become law?" He told a number of people in 1963 and 1964, "I'm not going to support something that is going to fall on its face." The fear that he would have to again hear criticism that he had heard in his campaign that he was not qualified seemed to have made him a perfectionist—and thus a reluctant participant in much of the Senate's business. His elders interpreted this as evidence that he would mature slowly (the only way) into one of them, and they approved. Before Edward Kennedy had been a senator a year, one or another senior senator was allowing to the press that someday young Ted would be a member of that "inner club" presided over by the ageless Russell.

At 3:20 Russell's time was up. But the presiding officer let another minute, then two, then eight tick away. Russell glared at the presiding officer as he talked on, and the first rapping of the gavel was tentative, barely audible. Then louder. Senate rules are inflexible, time is finite, history is oppressive—and Russell was taken off his feet. He went in a final volley of complaints and abusive criticisms at all around him. "I had no feeling that this was a historic moment," Kennedy said later. It was. The conservative forum of the states was entering a new phase in which liberals would dominate and debate would almost routinely be cut off when minorities tried to exercise control. Ted Kennedy would become one of the most powerful figures in that new Senate.

2. "IF HIS NAME WAS EDWARD MOORE"

When John Kennedy was elected President of the United States in 1960, it became necessary for him to resign from a Senate seat he had just been reelected to in 1958. He had to resign before January 20, 1961, when he was to take the presidential oath of office. The timing of his resignation was a matter of some interest and planning. When a senator resigns his office, the governor of the state appoints a replacement, who serves until the next statewide election. In this case the governor was a retiring and repudiated Democrat who had no real love for John Kennedy. The president-elect naturally insisted on choosing his own successor. John Kennedy had never taken much interest in the Democratic party of Massachusetts, except a selfish interest. Some Massachusetts Democrats would say sourly that there were two Democratic parties in the state, the *Democratic* one and the *Kennedy* one. Outgoing governor Foster Furculo had presided over so many scandals during his term of office that he had not been renominated. He had an old grudge against the Kennedys. In 1954 Furculo had run for the Senate seat held by Republican veteran Leverett Saltonstall. John Kennedy, a newly elected senator himself, gave Furculo no help. Furculo suspected him of attempting to head off any Saltonstall support of a Kennedy opponent four years later.

In 1960 Furculo's only source of strength in negotiating with John Kennedy over the coming vacancy was that his successor was going to be John Volpe, a Republican, elected to office in Massachusetts despite the big Democratic vote that turned out for native son Kennedy. Furculo did not believe Kennedy could deny him a say in the nomination by threatening to stay in the Senate until after Volpe took his oath on January 1, then negotiating with the Republican. Kennedy told people privately he would do that, however, and in a confrontation with Furculo in the senator's Georgetown home, the power of the ascendant president easily overcame that of the discredited governor. Furculo agreed to name the man Kennedy wanted, the senator's old college friend Benjamin Smith II, whose public career was limited to municipal offices in Gloucester. His lack of experience was believed at the time to be matched only by his lack of ambition. The Massachusetts and Washington rumor mills immediately ground out the story that John Kennedy wanted a two-year senator to keep the seat warm until 1962, when Edward Kennedy would be old enough to meet the constitutional requirement for the Senate (thirty years).

That is exactly what happened, though it is difficult to prove today that such was the intent from the start. Ted Kennedy said many years later that he was not a certain candidate in 1960 or even in early 1961. One member of the Kennedy family says that John Kennedy almost put one of two Massachusetts colleagues from the House of Representatives—Torbert McDonald or Edward Boland—in the Senate. Neither would have been likely to quit without a fight two years later. Edward Kennedy would certainly not have had a chance to seek a Senate seat so soon if another prospect for the appointment had not turned it down. That was Robert F. Kennedy. Kenneth O'Donnell, who had been a Kennedy worker for years and would soon become White House Appointments Secretary, proposed that Robert Kennedy take the job, then run for reelection in 1962. Kennedy refused, accepting instead appointment as attorney general. He told O'Donnell that he would not serve in Congress unless elected.

So late in December, just before Furculo's term expired, Kennedy resigned his Senate seat and Smith was appointed. He took his seat in the 87th Congress, assisted in his chores by a staff helpfully selected for him by the Kennedys. A few weeks later Edward Kennedy, still a full year shy of the magic age of thirty, took off on a "fact-finding" tour of Africa with three senators, whom he upstaged at every stop. On his return he became a $1-a-year assistant prosecutor in the Suffolk County (Boston) District Attorney's office. He was one of twenty-six such junior D.A.'s. His boss, Garrett Byrnes, called him a potentially "great" trial lawyer. The other assistants and the lawyers who practiced in the local courts generally liked and respected Kennedy. Few thought of him as competition in their world. He very soon made it clear that his ambition led in another direction. The courthouse closed at 4 P.M. Kennedy would dash from there to meet with people—voters—at meetings all over the state. From the start of his career in public service, he was putting in sixteen-hour days. As a senator his reputation would come to be based on hard work and long hours, but even so, *sixteen*-hour days in the Senate are rare. But in 1961 Kennedy was really holding down two jobs—prosecutor and candidate. He even had two offices, Room 801 in the Courthouse and the three-room suite at 122 Bowdoin Street that John Kennedy had used. Edward and Joan Kennedy began the year living in a fourth-floor apartment in Louisburg Square. In May they moved to a townhouse at 3 Charles River Square. Kennedy often walked from home to work.

Ben Smith and some other Massachusetts Democrats still believed that Ted might not run in 1962. Smith found he liked the job of senator, and was working hard enough at it to be in position to run in 1962 if the President allowed it. The Democrat most interested in Ted's plans was Edward McCormack, the state attorney general. A popular and influential politician in his own right, experienced at thirty-eight, McCormack also had been sustained by the reputation of his uncle, Speaker of the House John McCormack. Young McCormack had his eye on the Senate nomination. He felt that the facts of his family connections and his past successes in elective office made him the best-qualified Democrat in the state to keep the seat for the party. It would not necessarily be easy, even with John Kennedy in the White House. Massachusetts voters had been voting Republican with regularity. Registration in mid-1961 was 800,000 Democrats, 650,000 Republicans—but 1,200,000 independents. Dwight Eisenhower carried the state in both 1952 and 1956. Volpe was elected governor in 1960. The same scandals that had hurt the state party in that election were regarded by some as harmful to a McCormack candidacy in 1962. But he had not been tarnished personally, and others felt that fact made him a stronger candidate. Some anti-Kennedy forces in the state believed that the biggest roadblock in Ted's way was his family ties. Some presidential advisers argued that the White House would inevitably be involved—and openly so —in any Ted Kennedy effort. Thus the issue of "too many Kennedys" that had arisen when John named Robert attorney general would be made more intense, and possibly more damaging to the President. That would be the case if Ted won. If Ted lost, the results would also be damaging to John Kennedy, argued O'Donnell and others. The nation would think of the 1962 Massachusetts election as a referendum on the President and his policies (since Ted could hardly run an anti-JFK campaign). John Kennedy would be starting his own reelection campaign with a very visible scar.

But the problem was, a Kennedy candidacy seemed to be the best hope of the party. Polling in 1961 suggested that any other Democrat—even McCormack—would lose to a good Republican candidate. In the late summer of that year, some fifteen or sixteen leading Democratic politicians and managers met to discuss the problem in President Kennedy's home at the family compound at Hyannis Port. Most were opposed to Ted's candidacy. "I wouldn't even vote for him," said one. "Then who would you vote for?" asked O'Donnell. There was a long silence, as O'Donnell knew there would be. An anti-Ted man originally, O'Donnell had become convinced by the polls that he was the best choice. O'Donnell interrupted the silence to argue that Senator Smith and all the other potential Democrats were not good enough candidates to assure that the seat would remain Democratic. Though Ted had practically no credentials as a *senator*, he had extraordinary credentials as a *candidate*.

To begin with he was the brother of the President of the United States and his chosen representative in their home state. This was a significant fact for Democratic politicians in the state, whose support was naturally of great importance. In their view there couldn't be too many Kennedys in Massachusetts. The first step for Ted was getting the party's endorsement at the state convention. Politicians deliver such endorsements. The second step would be getting out voters in both a primary election and a general election. Politicians deliver much of that vote. What Kennedy had to offer the politicians first of all was his control of federal patronage. John McCormack had controlled Democratic patronage in the state, but there had been none in the eight Eisenhower years. Ted Kennedy was going to control it in the future. He would make that clear in dealing with Democratic politicians and delegates to the 1962 convention. "Win or lose, Teddy Kennedy, not Eddie McCormack, is going to control patronage in this state," Kennedy agents broadcast in 1962.

In the second place, there were the Irish, who regarded the Kennedy successes as proof of Irish equality with the Yankees. The Boston Irish were an important part of McCormack's constituency, but they loved "the Kennedys."

In the third place, Kennedy was a good campaigner. He loved politics. His first exposure to it came early, when he was six or seven, and he and his grandfather, John Francis Fitzgerald—Honey Fitz, the mayor of Boston before World War I—who was then in his mid-seventies, would tour Boston together. The old man would point out the city's famous historical landmarks, and in between he would talk about long-ago political battles. Later as a teen-ager and young adult Ted would often take the overnight train down from Boston to Washington to visit his brothers. John was a representative, then a senator; Robert was an attorney on Senate committees. The youngest brother got an eyeful and earful of politics and government from them.

It was in 1958, though, that Ted Kennedy really felt the grip of politics, and knew that for him the family imperative of "public service" was going to mean political office. He was a student at the University of Virginia Law School that year. John Kennedy faced an easy reelection campaign. He chose Ted as his manager. The manager worked much harder than the candidate. John Kennedy had no opposition in the primary. He wasn't even in the country to vote on primary election day. Little money was spent in the ensuing campaign against Republican Vincent J. Celeste. The candidate only spent seventeen days in the state. The rest of the time he toured the country, aiding other Democrats and picking up IOU's for 1960. Meanwhile, the manager was touring the state morning and night. On a typical day he would meet with reporters in the morning ("They would give me a fairly objective view of local opinion"), meet with Democratic leaders in the afternoon, then speak to a public gathering in the evening. He told one reporter, "I'm getting a good exposure to politics this year, and I like it."

Two stories demonstrate how hard Kennedy worked in his brother's campaign. Two small communities vote early in Massachusetts, at opposite ends of the state: Washington in the Berkshires and Mashpee on Cape Cod. Their results—a possible influence on later voters—are published in the afternoon papers. Both communities were Republican strongholds. Against the advice of O'Donnell and David Powers ("Mao Tse-tung could win on the GOP ticket there!"), Ted invested a lot of time in Washington and Mashpee. He allegedly visited every home in both towns. He boasted on election eve that he had the votes there sewed up—and he did. John Kennedy ran two to one ahead of Celeste in both towns. The second story about Kennedy's political instincts concerns bumper stickers. Joseph Kennedy came into the Boston headquarters one afternoon to complain that he didn't see very many bumper stickers. Ted grabbed an armful himself and went to the entrance of the Sumner Tunnel. There he greeted commuters on their way home with, "I'm Ted Kennedy. Do you mind if I put a bumper sticker on your car for Senator Kennedy?"

It all paid off. John Kennedy defeated Celeste by better than two to one. His margin of nearly 900,000 votes was the best showing of any U.S. senator in 1958, and the best ever in Massachusetts. It was an exhilarating experience for Ted. (And for John. At the last rally of the campaign, with a great victory certain, he displayed a rare political exuberance by climbing up on a table at the G and G Delicatessen in Dorchester to join in a chorus of "Heart of My Heart" with Ted and Robert.)

In 1960 Ted's campaigning was less effective. He worked in the Mountain and Pacific states, first fighting for convention delegates in what was regarded as Lyndon Johnson territory, then seeking votes in what was regarded as Nixon country. He displayed the qualities of the political animal. Kennedy lived in the west for nine months. He estimated he made fifteen to twenty speeches a day in one ten-day stretch. (That interprets "speech" loosely.) He impressed some politicians with his style. One later remarked that when John Kennedy came to his small Wyoming town, he was obviously ill-at-ease and out of place. Ted appeared genuinely to like the place and its people—and they reciprocated. Although the '60 campaign was not as successful as the '58 effort had been, *some* Mountain delegates were won away from Johnson. Colorado gave Kennedy the nomination on the roll call. (The exact number of Colorado delegates won was not known in the Kennedy convention headquarters as the roll call progressed. When Colorado was reached the candidate and his campaign manager, Robert Kennedy, knew it was all over when they saw a grinning Ted on the television screen in the midst of the Colorado delegation.) But in the fall, Nixon carried every Western state but three. Robert Kennedy worried about that election night. He told O'Donnell that he was afraid "Jack will kid him [Ted]" about the losses, and hurt his feelings. Ted told some interviewers later he would have moved to the West and sought his political fortune there if John Kennedy had lost in 1960. That has been interpreted as an indication that Ted felt he had something to prove in the West. Maybe. On the other hand he did like the West, as the Wyoming politician said, and if John Kennedy had remained the senator from Massachusetts, Ted would have had to go somewhere as long as his goal was elective office. It was sound political thinking, psychology aside.

But John Kennedy didn't remain the senator from Massachusetts. And so in 1961 Ted Kennedy began preparing himself and particularly the Massachusetts electorate for his possible candidacy in 1962. Just before he settled into his job as assistant district attorney and began campaigning around the state, he went off on that African tour. A candidate for the Senate was expected to have a foreign policy, too. It was a quickie tour, only two weeks. But upon his return to Boston, he began making speeches about what he had seen. The speeches didn't go over too well. On one of his weekly calls to John Kennedy in the White House, to report on his trips around the state, he mentioned that he thought the forty-five-minute standard "Africa speech" was boring his audiences. The President suggested cutting the talk to fifteen minutes and taking questions from the audience the rest of the time. Ted did that, and found he got a better reception.*

He found time to visit Europe and South America later in 1961 and in early 1962. It was pure politicking, and some of the recipient nations seemed to resent it. Ted's visit to Dublin drew a rebuke in the local press. A visit to Israel produced headlines, but not about any substantive event or remark—Ted took a wrong turn on a tour. Everything he did was closely watched. Almost no one seemed to be taking his globe-circling seriously. A Foreign Service Officer who served as Kennedy's "control" in one foreign capital said years later that all he remembered was the "fun" part of the trip. Kennedy was a great man for night life, he said. Then he added that Kennedy also had impressed him as a very hard worker during the day. If nobody else was taking the fact-finding seriously, at least Ted was. Which does not mean he didn't know that the essential goal of the tour was political. When he went to South America for a lengthy visit in November 1961, he sent postcards saying "Best Regards, Ted Kennedy" to every delegate to the three previous Massachusetts Democratic conventions.

The next month Joseph Kennedy had a stroke that left him a cripple for the rest of his life. Up until that time Benjamin Smith still believed he might be allowed to seek reelection. He was campaigning in the state as if he were a candidate. Up until that time, according to Ted Kennedy today, no decision had yet been made by any of the Kennedys on what Ted would do. A popular story is that in 1960, after John won the presidency, Joe Kennedy told John and Robert that now it was Ted's turn, he had to get the Senate

*When Ted made a speech to the Young Democrats of Palm Beach, Florida, during an Easter vacation, White House Press Secretary Pierre Salinger called a reporter present to ask about Ted's speech-making ability on behalf of "you know who."

seat. Ted Kennedy says that is not true, or at least that he never heard his father say that. It is true, however, that he believed his father wanted him to run for the Senate; any hesitancy on his part was probably washed away by the stroke. Only he knows if that is the case. His mother later wrote that for his father's sake he went "beyond all out" to win in 1962. Just after his thirtieth birthday on February 22, 1962, Ted called on Senator Smith in Washington and told him he was a candidate. In March, he announced to the public that "I begin today a campaign—on the issues— pledged to build the future of Massachusetts." He could not have been more wrong. The issues took a back seat to a single question—the qualifications if any of Edward Kennedy. *He* was the issue.

The first hurdle for Kennedy was the official party nomination. A candidate who did not get that spring nomi- nation could still go directly to the people in a late summer primary. But the convention's choice not only had the party organization behind him, he also had the top spot on the primary ballot. Edward McCormack announced, too, with a blast at Ted as a man whose candidacy would be a joke if his name were not Edward Kennedy. But he apparently knew even then that his own chances were not good. The Kenne- dys were getting ready to mount the kind of well-organized convention blitz that they had made famous at Los Angeles two years before to win the presidential nomination for John Kennedy. Furthermore, Ted's campaigning around the state had paid off, according to some polls. Delegates who could not be intimidated by the power of the presidency could be persuaded by the suggestion that a Kennedy can- didacy was more likely to lead to victory than a McCormack one. A poll done for Kennedy that spring showed him ahead of McCormack everywhere in the state but Boston. His- torian Francis Russell has observed that the Kennedys were the delight of the middle-class suburban Irish, who had out- grown the "oafishness" of such old-timers as Ted's grandfa- ther, Honey Fitz, and Ed's father, the 300-pound Knocko McCormack. That was working in Ted's behalf, too. Kennedy had enormous resources. The President had stated that no members of the Administration would be available to Ted in the primary. Repeating that pledge at a Gridiron

Club dinner in Washington, the President joked, "Of course, we may send up a few training missions . . . [and] all I can say is, I'd rather be Ted than Ed," playing on two popular phrases of the day. In fact, John and Robert Kennedy were helping Ted with briefings. So was Milton Gwirtzman of Senator Smith's staff; he was a former John Kennedy campaign aide. At least one middle-level executive department official, William Hartigan, quit his job in Washington to work for Kennedy in Massachusetts. He was rehired as soon as the election was over; it was a de facto leave of absence.

If to McCormack the Kennedy candidacy was a near joke, to a large group of an important Massachusetts constituency it was an outrage. That was the liberal intellectual community. Mark DeWolfe Howe, professor of constitutional law at Harvard Law School, fired off a 900-word letter to 4000 colleagues across the state calling Kennedy's decision to run "preposterous and insulting." The scholars in Kennedy's corner definitely represented a minority of the community. Samuel Beer and Robert Wood of Harvard and James McGregor Burns of Williams worked for Kennedy, in return for a pledge that he work for a strong programmatic state Democratic party.

That the central issue in the campaign was Kennedy himself was apparent from the start. Kennedy acknowledged this with his campaign slogans—"He Can Do More for Massachusetts" and "He Speaks with a Voice That Will Be Heard." The first slogan, a theme John Kennedy had used in his 1952 senate race, was a double-edged reminder to the voters that this Senate candidate was following in prestigious footsteps. The second slogan was a reminder that his predecessor was now in a position to listen. One of McCormack's slogans turned the theme inside out: "I Back Jack But Teddy Isn't Ready." A less successful one was "He Has Done More Than the Man Next Door." (The Kennedy and McCormack campaign headquarters were side by side on Tremont Street.) Amateur anti-Kennedy signs sprouted, such as this one seen at the convention in June: "Mommie, Can I Run for Senate?"

Stephen Smith, Kennedy's young brother-in-law, came to Massachusetts from New York to run the campaign. For the first phase, the preconvention period, Smith ordered detailed biographies of the 1700 delegates. If he found a delegate was a Little League fan, say, he would send a Kennedy supporter who was influential in Little League to call on him. And so forth. Smith ordered "coordinators" to call on each delegate each day once they began arriving in Springfield for the balloting. As in Los Angeles, the Kennedy floor men communicated with each other and Smith and Kennedy with walkie-talkies. Most of the delegates knew Kennedy personally. By one count he had visited an estimated 1300 of them at a series of delegate parties in March, April, and May. McCormack had delegated assistants to do his calling. The Kennedy forces were also working on the politicians who had influence with delegates. Several state senators and some thirty young state representatives, who were believed to control 650 delegates, were won over early. By the time the convention opened on June 8, McCormack probably knew he was not going to win the delegates' support, though he would not say so. He told one reporter that a variety of federal rewards, such as postmasterships, were being offered to delegates. "When you analyze them [all], they add up to pressure. But the amazing thing is we are still ahead." Ted Kennedy pointed out in rebuttal that there were not that many postmasterships, or any other kinds of federal job, that could be offered state party delegates. (One federal job that could be offered to McCormack was an ambassadorship. Stories that the Kennedys did attempt to buy him out of the race with such a job, or with lucrative new business for a Boston or New York law firm, were widespread, but never substantiated.) Whatever pressure there was, it is safe to say that Kennedy won delegates primarily by the force of his campaigning, not any offer of favors. His aides were predicting a two-to-one convention victory, and seemed heading for that when McCormack conceded and announced that he would fight it out in the primary instead, campaigning as "The Qualified Candidate."

Judged strictly as a *candidate*, Kennedy was the qualified one. He had that awesome organization, with unlimited money. He far outspent McCormack. He purchased more television time than McCormack and his later Republican and Independent opponents combined. He had twenty offices in Boston and in most other large Massachusetts towns. The organization published an eight-page, two-color magazine, "The Ted Kennedy Story." In his behalf, 300,000 telephone calls were made, 1,500,000 pieces of mail sent. Throughout the summer campaigning leading up to the primary election, McCormack made Kennedy the issue, which helped his candidacy. And Kennedy the candidate had that personal dynamic appeal that brought out crowds, whether at suburban shopping centers or factory gates.

McCormack believed that the way to overcome the organization and appeal was to force Kennedy to debate him on television in a situation in which both men would be on their own, where there would be spontaneous thrust and parry with little use of prepared statements. McCormack issued such a challenge, which the Kennedy forces ducked as long as possible. Finally, more than a month after the challenge was made, the two candidates met in a high-school auditorium in South Boston for the first of two debates. Ted was briefed intensively by a troop of aides from Washington. The strategy line was for him to be deferential and wise. His opening statement was low key. McCormack's strategy line was different. He attacked Kennedy in blistering personal terms: "What are your qualifications? You graduated from law school three years ago. You never worked for a living. . . . You are not running on qualifications. You are running on a slogan: 'You Can Do More for Massachusetts.' . . . and I say, 'Do more, how?' Because of experience? Because of qualifications? I say no! This is the most insulting slogan I have seen in Massachusetts politics, because this slogan means: Vote for this man because he has influence, he has connections, he has relations. And I say no!" McCormack continued in that vein, calling the slogan an insult to the President as well as to Massachusetts. Then he turned to Kennedy's voting record. He pointed out, still in personal and biting phrases, that Kennedy had not voted on thirteen of the sixteen occasions he could have since 1963. He concluded his opening statement with, "the office of United States Senator should be merited and not inherited." They loved it in South Boston. The audience in the auditorium broke into loud and frenzied applause.

The middle part of the program was devoted to questions from a panel of newsmen. The candidates did not display significant differences of opinion in discussing tax policy, nuclear stockpiles, the United Nations, and such issues. Kennedy did display a better talent for making use of a briefing than did McCormack. He seemed to know more. He also avoided personal attacks on McCormack. McCormack looked for excuses to return to the attack. He had expected his attacks to cause Kennedy to lose his temper. Kennedy had a famous one. But the tactic did not work. Kennedy's closing statement showed no anger. McCormack's closing statement came next. There would be no answer to it, of course, and therefore the situation hardly called for continuing the attack. But McCormack was even more vicious than before. His voice became shrill as he said, "If his name was Edward Moore,* with his qualifications, with your qualifications, Teddy, if it was Edward Moore, your candidacy would be a joke."

As McCormack finished, and as his supporters in the school auditorium cheered, Kennedy turned ashen. He left the debate scene convinced that he had been shattered. He refused to talk to reporters. He and some aides drove straight to his Charles River Square home. He called John Kennedy in Washington to tell him of the debate. The President asked for Gwirtzman, who told him that "on points" McCormack had won, but that some people might have been offended by his attack. President Kennedy ordered him not to be so objective about the "points" when discussing the debate with Ted. "Bad for candidate morale," he said.

Morale was down all around. Then the reaction to McCormack's attack began to come in. The first of it was in the form of "little ladies" calling in to a Boston radio talk show complaining of McCormack's "rudeness." That perked the candidate up some. The next morning's papers were also on his side. He was up early campaigning at a factory. A worker approached him and, referring to one of McCormack's accusations, said, "Teddy, me boy, I hear you never worked a day in your life. [Pause] Well, let me tell you, you

*Kennedy was named after his father's longtime assistant and personal secretary, Edward Moore.

haven't missed a thing." Or so the story goes. Labor union officials in the state claim that their polling at the time did show that workingmen and women did not resent the fact that a man like Kennedy could start at the top of the political ladder without working.

McCormack's charge that Kennedy had not voted in most of the elections for which he was eligible had a second dimension that could have been harmful to Kennedy. Kennedy *said* he had voted in every election in the state since he turned twenty-one. McCormack produced the records to show he had not. Kennedy then said he had been misquoted. McCormack then produced a tape recording of his making the false statement. Kennedy's truthfulness could have become an issue, particularly because of a college cheating scandal that had become public knowledge very early in the campaign, raising precisely the question of Kennedy's honesty and integrity. In 1950, when he was a freshman, Kennedy arranged for a fellow student to take an exam for him. When this was found out, the college asked both students to leave school. Kennedy served two Korean War years in the Army in Europe. Harvard accepted him back and he graduated in 1956.

Stories about the cheating incident were common currency in Boston as the 1962 campaign loomed. John Kennedy and White House aide McGeorge Bundy, a former Harvard professor, gave Ted's records to Robert Healy of the Boston *Globe* about the time Kennedy entered the race. They negotiated with him on how the story was to be broken. They wanted it played down. It wasn't. However, few delegates to the convention in Springfield seemed upset about the revelation. McCormack never mentioned it in public, before the convention or in the campaigning before the primary. The public apparently looked on the cheating incident as an indiscretion. More important in the Kennedy supporters' eyes was the fact that he redeemed himself at Harvard. One Kennedy delegate to the convention said that the fact that a millionaire like Kennedy still sought out an education proved he had character. Once again Kennedy's wealth was a plus for his candidacy. Robert Kennedy had perceived all along that this would be so. In a briefing before the McCormack debate, Ted had asked his brother what he should say about why he wanted to be senator. Robert said he should say he wanted to make a contribution to the public welfare "instead of sitting in some office in New York."

A second McCormack debate, in September, was a pale version of the first. Kennedy was again as calm and unruffled as before. McCormack was equally calm this time. Between the two debates, and in the two weeks that remained in the campaign after the second one, Kennedy's style and Kennedy's organization made it almost a one-man campaign. Before the end of the campaign period, Kennedy's self-assurance was so great that he was clearly no longer just the President's little brother. *His* magnetism was drawing the crowds to his speaking dates. Stewart Alsop of the *Saturday Evening Post* (one of more than 200 out-of-state reporters who came to cover the contest) wrote, "Even if Edward Moore Kennedy had been born plain Edward Moore, he would have been no joke as a politician. He would have run for high office—although doubtless not quite so soon—as inevitably as a river runs into the sea."

What a Boston editor called "the most glamorous" primary in the state's and maybe the nation's history ended on a brilliant Indian-summer day. A record number of voters, over 1.2 million, turned out. Two-thirds voted in the Democratic half of the election, and Kennedy defeated McCormack, 559,303 to 247,403, a landslide by any measure. Republicans that day nominated another young member of a well-known political family, George Cabot Lodge.

Kennedy's first campaign had become a succession of anticlimaxes. Everyone waited through 1961 to see if he would seek the Senate seat, assuming that if he did become a candidate that would assure his winning the party's nomination at the convention. When he won at Springfield, it was taken for granted that he would win the primary. When he won the primary, it was assumed that he would win in November with ease. He did win, with 57 percent of the two-party vote.

Lodge was the son of Henry Cabot Lodge, Jr., Eisenhower's ambassador to the United Nations, a Yankee whose family had clashed with the Kennedys before. Henry Cabot Lodge, Jr., lost to John Kennedy in a fashion in 1960 when he was Richard Nixon's running mate. He had lost in a direct way in 1952, when John Kennedy ousted him from the Senate. The '52 race settled an old score—Henry Cabot Lodge, Sr., had defeated John Francis Fitzgerald in a Senate race in 1916.

George Lodge was a tall, lanky, former Department of Labor official. He was thirty-four, and could not make the argument that he was more qualified than Kennedy with the certitude of Eddie McCormack. (Considering what had happened to McCormack, why should he, anyway?) The Kennedy-Lodge race was low key and gentlemanly, not even enlivened by the presence of a premature peace candidate, Harvard professor H. Stuart Hughes, who forecast the issues and concerns that a decade hence would be Kennedy's, but won only 50,000 votes out of nearly 2,000,000. Hughes had as much a legacy from past generations as Kennedy, Lodge, and McCormack. His grandfather was Charles Evans Hughes, who ran unsuccessfully for president in the year Honey Fitz was losing a Senate race to the senior Lodge. (The Kennedys rented Charles Evans Hughes's house in Scarsdale when Joe was a New York commuter.)

The issues of the day were duly debated by the candidates, but again there was not that much difference between the candidates. (Between Kennedy and Lodge, that is; Hughes took quite different positions—which would come to be known as dovish ones—which were ignored.) The main issue was Kennedy. Lodge accused the Kennedys of arrogance and callousness, to which Kennedy replied that he admired the Lodges for their similar inclinations and contributions. Lodge said that if his father had been elected vice-president, he would not have run for the Senate. At no time did the debate approach the personal conflict of the early Kennedy-McCormack battle. "Ivy league all the way," is the way S.J. Micciche of the *Globe* summed up a candidates' debate in Worcester. "Polite" was the word an out-of-state reporter used. Once when only Lodge and Hughes met in a debate they, too, were Ivy League and polite—as they discussed Kennedy.

In a sense, all those high-level briefings with high-powered Washington assistants (including some who took time out from managing the October Cuban missile crisis) were for nothing. What Kennedy said in distinction to what his opponents said on any single issue probably did not sway a single vote. However, the fact that he appeared so knowledgeable on so many issues undoubtedly swayed many voters. Certainly those independent-minded voters who had to be shown that Edward Kennedy was not just a dumb, fresh kid were impressed by the results of the briefings. Kennedy showed early a trait he would later be celebrated for. He was a good listener with a good memory. "Talk over the audience's head," one adviser (brother Bob?) told him. So he spewed back all those statistics and facts and quotes, and the people of Massachusetts sent him to Washington to become the youngest senator in over a decade.

3. EDDIE AND ROBBIE

What Kennedy won was two years, the unexpired third of the term his brother John had begun in 1959. His performance in the two years is barely visible in any records of government activity. Instead he spent the time demonstrating to his peers that he would grow into a good senator, and campaigning for reelection. Any effort to "do more" was compromised by the special needs of a man serving a two-year term. And in the first year of that term his brother was assassinated, transforming politics in the nation, if not Massachusetts. Shortly after the assassination, Ted Kennedy turned to politicking with a grief-born intensity even greater than he had shown in 1962. For twenty-seven straight weekends he flew to Massachusetts to campaign for reelection, speaking to groups of workers, to business and civic clubs, to many high-school audiences (a favorite exercise of his still; he says he gets a sort of distant early warning of important new issues). He was also mending fences with the local politicians. He left nothing to chance, took nothing for granted, though the possibility that Massachusetts voters would turn their back on the young brother of the martyred native son president was unthinkable. Even though the two years were almost barren of the least sort of significant accomplishment.

Or year and a half. A year and a half into the term,

on June 19, 1964, Kennedy made his last campaign, fence-mending, or what-have-you flight to Massachusetts for that year. That was the day after Richard Russell's ungraceful silence began. All the other Southerners began running out of time that day—literally. The Senate galleries were packed that afternoon, almost entirely with supporters of the civil-rights bill. Outside, in the soft, bright, late-afternoon Washington sunshine, hundreds more who supported the bill waited for the liberal senators who were their heroes to come out to speak to them once the historic bill was finally passed. Ted Kennedy was waiting impatiently as the afternoon dragged on. The Massachusetts Democratic party's convention, at which he was to be renominated for the Senate, had opened in West Springfield. Joan was there holding the fort, but the faithful wanted Ted there in person. The minutes of the filibuster slipped away. At 7 P.M. Ted called West Springfield. His voice was relayed over the public-address system: "I want everyone to know that I am a candidate this year even though I'm hundreds of miles away. We are now fifteen minutes away from the vote for civil rights." It was just over thirty minutes later when the roll call began. Nine minutes later it was over. The bill had passed 73–27, and while senators Everett Dirksen, Hubert Humphrey, and others went out on the Capitol steps to receive the applause of the tourists, senators Kennedy and Birch Bayh of Indiana fled to Washington National Airport for the trip to Massachusetts.

Bayh was to be the keynote speaker at the convention. His wife, Marvella, was with them for the flight. So was Kennedy's forty-one-year-old administrative assistant, Edward Moss. The plane they made the trip in was an Aero Commander C-7, owned by a Massachusetts businessman. The pilot was Edward Zimny, also of Massachusetts. They were headed for Barnes Municipal Airport at Westfield, Mass. Some three hours later they arrived in the area to find a fog blanketing the area. Visibility was less than two and a half miles, which made even an instrument landing a marginal undertaking. Kennedy had lost a brother, a sister, and a brother-in-law in airplane crashes. He himself had had some close calls in planes, including one in the family plane *Caroline*. But he was casual as the plane descended through the fog. He loosened his seat belt and was half standing as the two senators discussed the speeches they would make on arrival at West Springfield. At approximately 11 P.M., less than three miles from the Westfield airfield, the Aero Commander crashed into an apple orchard with great force, ripping off an engine, bending a steering wheel 180 degrees, crushing the nose of the plane backward and the rear compartment forward. Moss was killed. Kennedy was severely injured. Bayh and his wife were scared and hurt, but not as badly as Kennedy. They dragged him from the wreckage and then walked to the road and flagged down a car, which took them to call police and ambulances.

Word of what happened was promptly relayed to the convention. Joan rushed to meet her husband and the other injured at the hospital in Northampton. She was joined there within hours by Robert Kennedy and Jean Smith. Birch Bayh had suffered serious muscular trauma; Marvella Bayh had fractured two vertebrae. The first statement from officials at the Cooley Dickinson Hospital said, "Senator Kennedy was in deep shock when he was admitted. His pulse varied a great deal; his blood pressure was almost negligible." X-rays showed three fractured vertebrae. His right hand was split open. He also had fractured ribs, a punctured lung, a severely bruised kidney, massive internal hemorrhaging. His condition was listed as "serious." Though there was little apprehension that he might die, there was concern that he might have suffered irreversible and crippling damage to his spinal cord. He was strapped into a Stryker frame (later in a larger Foster frame, later in a Stryker again), which immobolized him between two canvas slings. There he would remain, for a week at Cooley Dickinson, then for over four months in New England Baptist Hospital in Boston. Army doctors from Walter Reed wanted to operate on his back. Joe objected and his wishes were respected. Three weeks later the surgeon-in-chief at New England Baptist, Dr. Herbert Adams, announced that the healing process was progressing so well that no operation would be necessary. But whatever instruction the reelection campaign might have provided for Kennedy or the voters of Massachusetts was now clearly not going to be provided.

There was not going to be a campaign. The nearest Kennedy came to it was when he waved and smiled at people through the large windows in his ambulance as he was taken from Northampton along the Massachusetts Turnpike, Route 128, and Route 9 to Boston and New England Baptist. There he would remain strapped in, not even sitting up for the first time until late November, not taking his first step until mid-December.

There would probably not have been much of an educational campaign anyway. The kid brother of the assassinated president was going to win reelection in a walk. He had not even counted on that sympathy vote. He had been working to get reelected—those twenty-seven weekends. And Republicans had not put up a really serious opponent. That party's nominee for the Senate seat was Howard Whitmore, a balding fifty-nine-year-old Yankee with little flair, He moved through the state powered only by decency and loyalty to party. He supported Goldwater, called for a balanced budget, complained that the state had lost jobs in the past two years. When a campaign official in western Massachusetts suggested he seek votes by charging that an injured Kennedy could not perform his duties, Whitmore replied, "My opponent is flat on his back, and from a gentleman's standpoint, I can't campaign against that."

Joan did the Kennedy campaigning. She put in long, routine days, breakfasting early on cold cereal and instant coffee (no servants at Charles River Square), then made speeches that reported on her husband's recuperation. No issues. Sometimes she showed a movie of her husband and children. She polkaed at a Pulaski Day fete, rode in a Columbus Day parade, spoke quietly and briefly to Young Democrats and to civil-rights groups. She always wore bright colors, "to boost my morale," and almost always ate lunch at the hospital with her husband.

The candidate had set up an office across the hall from his fifth-floor room at New England Baptist, where senatorial and campaign responsibilities were met. Mostly he read or watched television (with special prism glasses). He also collected seventy essays about his father, reminiscences of family and friends, so that "the grandchildren would know what he was like before his stroke." The edited essays were privately published as *The Fruitful Bough*. John Kennedy had once prepared a similar book about Joe, Jr., the eldest brother, who was killed during World War II. As he became less a prisoner of his physical ordeal, Ted began to paint some. He copied in oil *First Snow* by Dodge McKnight, a gift for his father.

He held a press conference in October. President Johnson paid him a postmidnight visit during his own campaign tour of New England. A movie about Kennedy was shown on television as a campaign event. Without trying to or needing to he was dominating the campaign. On election night he watched his running mates lose the state races, while he defeated Whitmore by a margin of 1,200,000, the greatest margin by any candidate for any office in Massachusetts history.

But probably the most significant thing candidate Kennedy did during that fall in the hospital suite was to think about becoming a good senator and preparing himself for it. Many days and nights were devoted to discussing in detail issues that loomed ahead on the national scene. The others in these conversations were experts from Harvard and M.I.T. whom Kennedy invited to brief him. Jerome Wiesner, John Kenneth Galbraith, Samuel Beer, Robert Wood, Charles Haar, and others came by to prepare Kennedy to speak with confidence for the liberal side on defense, education, tariff policy, and the like. He wasted no time. The good start he had made toward acceptance and influence in the Senate was not going to be slowed down by a broken back. He vowed he would walk down the aisle in January to take his oath of office. He was as determined to be prepared for what came after that as for the symbolic act itself.

The man who would accompany him down the aisle was his brother Robert, who was elected to the Senate from New York that fall. The day after the double Kennedy victory, Robert came to New England Baptist to visit his brother. Reporters joined them in the suite and on the porch where the injured Kennedy often was wheeled, even in the coldest weather. The brothers cracked jokes. They jibed at each other. "Is it true you are ruthless?" Ted asked. Photographers took over from reporters. At one point, Bobby's shadow fell over Ted. A photographer said, "Watch your shadow, it's in the way." Ted said, "It will be the same way in Washington."

The joke about the shadow of Robert falling over Edward was not pointless. The seniority system of the United States Senate would have less to do with their relationship than would the Kennedy family's famous primogeniture. "Just as I went into politics because Joe died, if anything happened to me tomorrow, Bobby would run for my seat in the Senate," John Kennedy had said back in the fifties. "And if Bobby died our younger brother Ted would take over from him." When Robert Kennedy got back to Washington after the postelection-day visit to New England Baptist, he sent his brother a print of the Justice Department's main entrance. Across it he scrawled:

> *For Eddie*
> *It's out of this*
> *building into yours*
> *move over!!*
> *Robbie*

And move over he did, not as a senator but as a national political leader. The Senate remained "Eddie's building." Almost from the minute he was sworn in as junior senator from New York, Robert was impatiently looking for greater, different challenges. He wasn't a legislator. He was a potential leader (later the actual leader) of a government-in-exile, as it was called, waiting, chafing as the New Frontier became the Great Society of Lyndon Johnson. The only thing the election to the Senate gave him was the forum and the freedom to say what he wanted to say, do what he wanted to do. That "only thing" was quite a bit, of course. Edward Kennedy had seen at once that as an elected official he had more freedom of movement and more influence than he would have had in any appointed post. In early 1964 he had urged his brother to seek a Senate seat rather than the vice-presidency. He had supported earlier suggestions that Robert seek the governorship of New York or Massachusetts.

Usually newly elected senators are sworn in in groups of four, in alphabetical order of the states they represent, but the first pair of brothers to serve in the Senate simultaneously since 1803 was sworn in together, accompanied only by their senior colleagues, Leverett Saltonstall and Jacob Javits (who, naturally, were not taking an oath). The packed galleries were appreciative of the history and drama of the moment, as Ted, all smiles, limped awkwardly in wearing a back brace, and leaned heavily on a cane to receive the oath from eighty-seven-year-old Carl Hayden, president pro tem of the Senate. When the two Kennedys were sworn in, the galleries burst into applause. The brothers were warmly received by their colleagues, with much handshaking all around. Edward threw a reception in his Old Senate Office Building suite, where there were yarn spinning and, as always, jokes. Bobby probably won honors with his remark about the four "rumble seats" added to the back of the Democratic side of the Senate floor which he and three other freshmen occupied. "I had better seats for *Hello, Dolly,*" he said.

Robert Kennedy got a good office suite assignment, 1205, on the first floor by the main entrance of the new Senate office building. The brothers' offices were linked by a special "hot-line" telephone. They talked every day. They also competed, according to a number of staff men and senators who were there then. If so, it was a special kind of competition. "Eddie" never gave the appearance that he was seeking to demonstrate to his brother or his colleagues or the public that he was the more *effective* senator (much less the more effective politician) of the two. Edward deferred to his brother on highly visible issues. When he thought his activities in any arena might be in even the least way harmful to Robert's future—his future outside the Senate, at any rate—he always cleared his plans with Robert. This went beyond just brotherly or senatorial good manners, and Robert did not clear anything he did or said with Edward.

The competition was keen on the staff level. One member of the Edward Kennedy staff in those years recalls that there was always pressure for what he called "toppers." When the brothers were involved with the same legislative matter, each demanded staff research that would provide him with greater knowledge about the subject or the Senate politics involved. "It was loving competition between them," a staff member said later, "but it was tough on us." Edward Kennedy could be hard on staff members who let him down. He called several staff members together once to complain, heatedly, that "My brother tells me this bill is coming up today. You told me it was not. How the hell does he know?" The brothers often were involved in working on the same bill. Robert had been assigned to the Labor and Public Welfare Committee, too. Once at a hearing on Veterans Administration hospitals, Edward's time to question a witness came first. Using the "homework" his staff had prepared for him, he brought the witness to the point of an important and damaging admission, but was unable to press further. Then Robert began questioning. His homework had been much more thorough. His insistence was greater. Edward Kennedy seemed to be embarrassed by the contrast. The aide he considered responsible was soon let go from his staff.

Another member of the staff, David Burke, who also became a close personal friend of the family, says the brothers were competitive only in a tension-relaxing sense. "It wasn't real. Jokes. Passing notes back and forth at committee hearings. Ted Kennedy might say to Bob Kennedy, 'I'm going to introduce an amendment today. I want you to stay off the floor because I need some votes.' Once Bob was trying to explain an amendment in committee that he didn't understand, and Teddy interrupted him to say, 'Just keep talking, you understand it if no one else does.' "

This teasing was above all else brotherly. Jack Kennedy, fifteen years older than Ted, was, in Ted's words, "almost a combination father and brother." He was, in fact, Ted's godfather. But Robert was only seven years older. "I did more things with Bobby." Ted meant quite a different thing than Robert's critics did when he referred to him as "big brother."

The senior Kennedy in the Senate tried to help the senior Kennedy in the family become a good senator. It was a hopeless task. "They only take about one vote a week here and they never tell you in advance when it is going to be so you can schedule other things," Robert complained to a journalist in 1966. "If I am not going to be working here, I want to go somewhere I can do something." Suggesting that the Senate schedule its business for the convenience of freshmen would have been blasphemy a few years before that. In 1966 it was only foolish—which was progress, a tide of sorts. Edward Kennedy could see that drift and ride with it, not disturbed by its slowness. "Is this the way I become a good senator—sitting here and waiting my turn?" Robert, impatient to fly to New York, whispered to Edward at a committee hearing one day. "Yes." "How many hours do I have to sit here to be a good senator?" "As long as necessary, Robbie." Another time Robert complained that a senator offered to vote with him on an issue he was interested in if Robert would do him a favor by speaking in his home state. "Is that what you have to do to get votes?" "You're learning, Robbie."

Ted Kennedy could endure the long hours in hearings or on the Senate floor, and eventually that would pay off for him in the Senate. The incident Bob complained of is of a rare sort. Politicians seldom ask for a favor so directly when their votes are sought. Senators—all officeholders—know what to expect and what not to, what is implied by a request and by an answer. Robert Kennedy never learned to live by those rules. A friend described him: "abrupt, aloof, shy, a poor speaker, not the sort who could put his arm around another pol at a party; he stiffened when others did it to him." Ted Kennedy *liked* his peers. The freshman senator from Massachusetts often would show up at informal affairs Speaker John McCormack gave for those machine Democratic representatives from big cities. Going home after one such meeting, a boisterous and shallow party, Ted Kennedy remarked, sincerely, "That's really a great bunch of guys, isn't it?"

A magazine reporter interviewed a number of senators in 1966, asking them about Ted Kennedy. One of the comments she most often heard was that Ted Kennedy would never embarrass an opponent. Bobby was not concerned about that. Once when Ted and Senator Carl Curtis of Nebraska, a plain, small-town conservative, got into an argument on the floor, Kennedy was a model of the proper and respectful junior senator. About the same time Robert Kennedy and Curtis got into an argument during a hearing at which Ralph Nader was a witness. At one point Curtis said he had no objection to Nader's statements, "but he loses me——" "With big words?" Bobby interrupted sarcastically.

So Robert Kennedy began immediately in 1965 to use the Senate as the base from which he would soon lead his crusade. And solely for that. Ted Kennedy began flexing his senatorial muscles that year, having decided that he was going to put in many years there.

4. BAR MITZVAH
IN THE SENATE

The Senate that Ted Kennedy limped into on January 4, 1965, would not ordinarily have maintained the liberal Democratic superiority that had prevailed the previous six years. A number of Democrats were elected from normally Republican states in the recession landslide of 1958. Some should have been defeated at the end of their first terms. But Lyndon Johnson's coattails, the public's sense of debt to the martyred John Kennedy, the ineptitude and extreme views of the Republican presidential candidate Senator Barry Goldwater, had all combined to bring about a Democratic landslide in 1964. The Senate in the 89th Congress was even more lopsidedly Democratic than it had been in the 88th. Kennedy was one of sixty-eight Democrats in the 100-member Senate, a gain of two by the party. In the House of Representatives the Democratic gain was thirty-eight, to make the line-up 295–140. These margins were the largest in a generation. Democratic superiority was such that, combined with Johnson's ambitious Great Society vision, the 89th Congress would pass so much new liberal domestic legislation that it would be compared favorably with Franklin D. Roosevelt's first-term Congress, the 73rd, and Woodrow Wilson's first-term Congress, the 63rd, both heavily Democratic, active, and adventurous.

Ted Kennedy was given his first leadership assignment early in 1965. Perhaps "stewardship" would be a better word. Kennedy was named manager in the Senate for a new immigration bill. The bill was a Johnson Administration bill, but Kennedy asked for the chance to handle it and Johnson agreed. So did Senator James Eastland, the chairman of the Judiciary Committee and of the Immigration and Naturalization Subcommittee that had jurisdiction over such legislation. Kennedy was a junior member of the subcommittee, but Eastland agreed to allow him to preside at the hearings and to handle the bill once it got to the floor. Eastland went along with this arrangement, even though he opposed any changes in immigration legislation and had, in fact, in years previous been able to keep such reform legislation from being debated in the Senate. Whether his change of mind was a result of Lyndon Johnson's arm twisting, or of regard for Kennedy, or of simple recognition of the fact that *that* year in *that* Congress there was going to be new and more liberal immigration legislation, only Eastland knows. Actually the more crucial structural difference in 1965 was that the chairman of the Immigration Subcommittee of the House Judiciary Committee was no longer Francis Walter, proud author of the then existing immigration law. Walter had died in the 88th Congress, to be replaced by Representative Michael Feighan, a supporter of a new law.

At any rate Kennedy asked for and was given the assignment, and by all accounts discharged it with professionalism.

The existing law, the McCarren–Walter Act, had been passed in 1952. It was based on a quota feature that took into account the ethnic make-up of the United States at the time. Over two-thirds of the quota numbers were assigned to Britain, Ireland, and Germany. Those and some other Western European nations never filled their quotas, but they could not transfer them to southern European, Asian, and African nations with long waiting lists of would-be Americans. The bill enacted in 1965 abolished national origin quotas and allowed immigration on a first-come-first-served basis, with skills and family ties to United States citizens taken into account.

Kennedy's reasons for wanting to push the bill were

many, no doubt, but two are interesting because they recur often in his career. One was that the legislation had been a John Kennedy goal. The other was that being for liberalized immigration law was good politics in Massachusetts. The idea of finishing what John Kennedy started was then an important mission in Ted Kennedy's life. This sense of family mission is even stronger now that Robert Kennedy, too, has been slain in mid-career. As for the popularity of the particular crusade in Massachusetts, that state and Hawaii have the largest percentage of citizens who are foreign born or the children of foreign or mixed parents—in Massachusetts 33.3 percent. Many of those Massachusetts "ethnics" are Irish, not harmed by the old law, but almost as many are of Polish extraction, and there are far more Italians than Irish in the state. Both of those groups wanted new law.

Kennedy managed the hearings with grace as well as professionalism. That wasn't always too easy. One member of the subcommittee was Sam Ervin of North Carolina, who was not, in 1965, the liberal hero he would become in 1973. Ervin opposed changes in the law precisely because he liked the existing ethnic—and racial—balance in the United States. If anything it wasn't "western" enough for him. His objections to some Kennedy decisions and his sharp cross-examining of witnesses made for some heated arguments among subcommittee members. When Robert Kennedy testified in favor of the bill early in March he and Ervin argued bitterly, in personal terms. Whatever damage that might have done to the legislation's chances were probably small, however, and were washed away by Ted Kennedy's good-natured flattering of Ervin. On St. Patrick's Day, which fell a few days after Bobby testified, Ted made an elaborate show of pinning a shamrock on Ervin's lapel, and the bill proceeded on its course. Ervin managed one victory. He and other Southern conservatives objected to the existing practice of allowing unlimited immigration by citizens of independent Western Hemisphere nations. He proposed a limit on such immigration of 120,000 a year. Kennedy, Johnson, and almost all proponents of reforming the law opposed this, on the ground that there was a tradition of "neighborliness" in the hemisphere. Ervin, Senator Everett Dirksen, who was also a member of the subcommittee, and Attorney General Nicholas Katzenbach—but not Edward Kennedy—met in

Dirksen's office and agreed that the 120,000 hemispheric limit would go into the bill. The House voted down the limit the same day the meeting took place in Dirksen's office, but the Senate kept it, and subsequently in a House-Senate conference the representatives went along with Ervin and Dirksen. As a face-saver of sorts the conservatives agreed to set up a special commission to look into the problem of Western Hemisphere immigration. Kennedy was named a member.

The legislation passed the House in its initial form 318–95 in August, the Senate 76–18 in September. Ethnic and nationality groups were asked by one magazine what had brought about the victory. They listed the 2–1 Democratic majority, the President's determination, the replacement of Walter with Feighan, and the evidence of public-opinion polls that Americans were no longer very suspicious or fearful of non-Western European immigration. Ted Kennedy was not mentioned. Nonetheless he did play a modestly significant role.

One last word on the immigration act. Like much Great Society legislation written in 1965, it was greatly oversold. When Lyndon Johnson signed the act into law at the Statue of Liberty in October of that year, most supporters of the bill probably thought that with the exception of the situation regarding Western Hemisphere nations, a permanent, fair, workable program for immigration had been launched. Yet within a little over two years, Ted Kennedy was telling an audience in Chicago that immigration "needs" were going unmet, that the law was not "flexible" enough, and that he would fight for reforming the 1965 act. He has in fact proposed immigration-reform legislation since then, but out of deference to his chairman, Senator Eastland, who is particularly opposed to allowing more immigration from Latin American nations, Kennedy has not pushed it. The House has passed updating legislation to no avail. Senior senators like Eastland are less powerful today than they were in 1965, but they are still powerful. It may be that a meaningful reform of the reform of 1965 will come in the 94th Congress. Or it may await the day when Kennedy himself, or someone of like views, sits in the chair Jim Eastland sits in today.

By the time Johnson went to the Statue of Liberty,

Kennedy had been through one other legislative battle and was concluding still another, in which he played larger roles than he had played in the immigration fight. One battle he won and one he lost. The one lost was probably the most rewarding to him. It was in it that he came of age as a legislator.

The one Kennedy won was the fight to get a national Teachers Corps established. In 1959 the public schools of Prince Edward County, Virginia, had been closed by officials opposed to an order to desegregate. The schools stayed closed for five years, as legal efforts to force them open dragged through courts. Robert Kennedy at the Justice Department sent his special assistant, William J. Vanden Heuvel, to see what could be done. Vanden Heuvel proposed that a private free-school system be set up with federal aid and private funds. Such a system operated for a year, until the Supreme Court required the reopening of the public schools. One of the principal problems Vanden Heuvel and the Attorney General ran into in operating such a school system was that many children who came from poor homes (and particularly those who had been out of schools for several years) needed the sort of professional teachers and educational specialists that poor rural counties such as Prince Edward could not provide in any setting, public or private.

Ted Kennedy was asked, either by his brother or by Vanden Heuvel, to look into the question of federal aid for helping poor rural counties and poor urban slum-school districts overcome this inadequacy. In the early 1960s generalized federal aid to public schools was still strongly opposed by many influential groups. Even specialized aid was often controversial; Kennedy's legislative aides thought the idea was not worth much. He overruled them to the degree that he began seeking advice from some of the specialists Vanden Heuvel had recruited for Prince Edward County, as well as from educators from around the country. Such specialists began trekking through the Kennedy senatorial office almost in a parade. Kennedy came to feel that the need for specialized teachers was demonstrably greater in the rural and slum districts, where no such teachers existed, than in the well-to-do or at least comfortable suburban districts, where there were often many such teachers employed. Furthermore, the other lesson taught by the Prince Edward experience and the interviews with other school men and women was that while those expert teachers in the suburbs might not be willing to give up their comforts for a career in the poorer schools, many were willing to spend a year or two on such faculties.

On February 26, 1965, Kennedy went before a Senate committee to propose that a national teachers corps be authorized. He offered an amendment to that effect to the Johnson Administration's revolutionary general aid to elementary- and secondary-education bill. What Kennedy wanted was a twofold attack on the problem. Some federal funds would be used to support teachers who volunteered to work in poverty areas; other funds would be used to provide fellowships for students who would specialize in the needs of poverty area students and work in such areas as teaching interns. This proposal was rejected, but Kennedy and Senator Gaylord Nelson of Wisconsin, who also favored a corps of teachers to be used for this purpose, then began to fight to get the bill added as an amendment to another Administration bill dealing with federal support of colleges.

Support for the idea began to grow, or so it seemed. Almost any liberal legislation had a good chance of passage in 1965—if President Johnson favored it, that is. Whether the Teachers Corps would have become law then without Johnson's support is hard to say. At any rate it got his support. He co-opted the idea and in July proposed a Teaching Professions Act, the heart of which was the Teachers Corps. The LBJ proposal became a title in the Higher Education Act and passed the Senate in September. The House of Representatives passed its version of the college-aid act in August, with no Teachers Corps in it. The Senate version had gone somewhat beyond what Kennedy originally envisioned. He had told the Senate Education Subcommittee that he thought the costs the first year would be between $25 and $30 million. The Senate authorized $36 million for fiscal 1966 and nearly $65 million in each of the four years thereafter. These increases were made with Kennedy's support and in response to his public championing of the concept.

A conference committee could not bring its House

members beyond a much more modest start—$10 million in fiscal 1966 and $13 million in each of the next two years. Even that was too strong a dose of federal intrusion into local affairs for most Republicans in the House. Republican members of the conference refused to sign the report. A Republican-led effort to strip the entire Teachers Corps title from the bill failed on the floor by a vote of 152–226. Republicans got their revenge the next day by helping kill the appropriation of a single penny for the program in fiscal 1966. Later funds were provided, and the Teachers Corps survives today unnoticed but supported by some $37 million a year. It is a Great Society legacy, but also a Ted Kennedy legacy. The President may have gotten the law enacted by supporting it, but the senator from Massachusetts was the one who put it on the agenda of the Senate and the agenda of the public, with several speeches prior to Johnson's conversion. Nothing spectacular, nothing flashy, just a good workmanlike job by a quiet, ambitious senator. Ted Kennedy, by the way, was not a member of the Education Subcommittee. Robert Kennedy was. William Vanden Heuvel does not remember that there was any great significance to the fact that Ted, not Robert, was the Kennedy to get the Teachers Corps through Congress. "I do remember," he says now, "that Robert said then, 'Ted knows the legislative possibilities better than I do.' "

The legislative battle Kennedy lost in 1965 had to do with the poll tax. That fight demonstrated several important characteristics the young senator had acquired that have turned out to be lasting.

It was the first fight he undertook in the Senate aware in advance that he would probably lose. "I don't want to introduce a bill that isn't going anywhere," he often said to staff members and friends in 1963, 1964, and 1965. But he knew his poll-tax plan faced great odds. More and more as his career in the Senate has proceeded he has shown a willingness to fight losing battles.

He used fully for the first time the old John Kennedy technique of preparation for battle: He invited in a number of experts in the field of voting-rights law and constitutional history to educate him at length. Today a number of senators use this technique (as some always have), but Kennedy probably has easier access to a broader range of legitimate nongovernment experts than any other elected official except the president—any president—and, perhaps, Vicepresident Nelson Rockefeller. In the poll-tax fight Kennedy demonstrated an ability to learn everything there was to know about a complex subject and retain what he learned long enough to make use of it in Senate debate. He became the expert. This surprised some scholars and senators.

Kennedy demonstrated that he understood that a Kennedy can generate an enormous amount of publicity when he engages in a campaign or crusade or fight. He made a headline issue of the poll tax, which should have been a minor, secondary item of interest, briefly noted then disposed of in a drama of much greater importance—passage of the Voting Rights Act of 1965, a law that would alter the face of Southern politics at last and for all time.

The Voting Rights Act of 1965 was a bold and imaginative stroke to end the Southern practice of preventing blacks from exercising the most basic civil right. Principally by use of the literacy test, which could be and often was used to find that a black Ph.D. was illiterate and a white citizen with little ability to read and write was not, and by use of simple threats and terror, voting registrars in the Deep South had kept millions of blacks disfranchised. In 1964 in the eleven Southern states 73 percent of all eligible whites were registered to vote, but only 43 percent of the eligible blacks were. In Louisiana the percentage for blacks was 32. In Alabama the percentage for blacks was 23. In Mississippi it was 6.

In January 1965, the Reverend Martin Luther King, Jr., began a series of protests in Selma, Alabama, to dramatize to the nation the failure of existing law and government activity to deal with the problem of wholesale disfranchisement of blacks. By March there were the familiar headlines and pictures in the papers and on television again: state troopers wielding nightsticks . . . tear-gas plumes . . . a black shot and killed, a white civil-rights marcher clubbed to death. . . .

On March 15 President Johnson appeared before a joint session of Congress to announce that he would push for a bill to end discrimination in voting. Two days later (the day Kennedy was pinning the shamrock on Sam Ervin), Johnson submitted his bill to Congress. What he proposed was that literacy tests be suspended and federal registrars be sent to supervise registration and voting in states in which fewer than 50 percent of voting-age residents were registered or voted in the 1964 presidential election. It was a "trigger" set to catch the Southern states of Virginia, South Carolina, Georgia, Alabama, Mississippi, and Louisiana, and part of North Carolina.

The President's bill was changed some as it moved through Congress. In past civil-rights struggles legislative leaders had by-passed the Senate Judiciary Committee with some parliamentary sleight of hand. Eastland had a way of never calling hearings, never reporting a bill back once he got his hands on it. This time the voting-rights bill was sent to the committee with orders that it be reported back within fifteen days. Kennedy demonstrated during those fifteen days that he took a more than normal interest in the legislation, with a sharp, well-prepared series of questions. But what made his elders sit up and blink was when he suddenly introduced an amendment to the bill that would prohibit a state from requiring the payment of a poll tax as a requisite for registration and voting. More than that, he got the committee to approve the amendment. (He almost lost it when Eastland began preparing a procedural ambush, but Senator Ervin inexplicably helped Kennedy along.) This was a milestone event. For thirty years, beginning in 1932, liberals in the Senate had sought to ban the poll tax in federal elections only, by passing an amendment to the Constitution. Practically no one even speculated that such an intrusion into a sovereign state's affairs could be done by simple statute. Fewer still believed that local elections could be covered. The House approved the constitutional amendment five times but the Senate never—until 1962. This amendment was ratified in 1964. But four states, Alabama, Mississippi, Texas, and Virginia still imposed the tax as a condition for voting in state and local elections.

President Johnson and many advocates of the voting-rights bill were opposed to Kennedy's effort. They feared that the amendment was unconstitutional and might cause the entire bill, once it became law, to be declared defective.

The House Judiciary Committee finished its hearings before the Senate committee did. It approved a poll-tax ban, too, and later the full House would approve that ban. But not the Senate. The President, Senate Majority Leader Mike Mansfield, and Minority Leader Everett Dirksen worked out a substitute for the Senate Committee version that did not ban the poll tax. Kennedy chose to make an issue of it on the floor. He lobbied other senators in the cloakrooms and their offices; studied at home with experts from the universities, including Mark DeWolfe Howe, the Harvard scholar who had so opposed the Kennedy candidacy of 1962; got lawyers in private practice as well as at law schools to express support of the Kennedy amendment in order to pressure their senators. He called on other outside pressure groups. In his lobbying Kennedy demonstrated an almost un-Senate-like persistence. Almost, but not quite. An aide of the senator's at that time remembers "several" scenes in the cloakroom where a senator not yet committed in the fight would flee when Kennedy approached him, saying, "I don't want to talk with you about the poll tax again." Kennedy kept a poster-sized chart in his office with each senator listed for, against, or undecided. He had himself briefed by a battery of legal scholars and held a mock court debate of the issue the way he had heard Thurgood Marshall had prepared himself for his Supreme Court arguments in the school desegregation cases. And all the while he was courting the press to make sure that the poll-tax fight was presented as the most absorbing drama in the voting-rights bill struggle (as in fact it was, if a drama requires an uncertain outcome; it was beyond doubt that some form of voting-rights law was coming).

All of this—applying pressure through the national Kennedy constituency of lawyers, civil-rights groups, unions, and the like; making the issue a national story of importance; appealing to senators face to face and in one-to-one meetings—was no doubt helpful to Kennedy's cause, but in the final analysis, it was of secondary importance to the way Kennedy handled himself on the floor when his amendment was debated. "He handled Sam Ervin on the Constitution, he handled Spessard Holland's sniping," an aide of that period later recalled. He profited by the expert advice he had gotten on those long night and early-morning sessions with the experts, not only in the sense of being able to make a persuasive presentation of his point of view, but also in the sense that in the give-and-take of debate he "won" arguments, or at least points. He did not overwhelm his colleagues, either. Senator Mansfield was the principal spokesman for the administration. He is not a lawyer, nor a particularly effective floor debater. Kennedy did not exploit his lack of preparation.

On May 11 Kennedy lost by a vote of 49–45. He had the satisfaction of at least forcing the senators supporting the administration to write into the bill later in the debate a congressional declaration that local poll taxes infringed on the right to vote, and to instruct the attorney general to file suit against the tax—a declaration and instruction lifted right out of the Kennedy proposal. (The Supreme Court ruled that the tax was unconstitutional when the suit reached it.) More important, Kennedy had the satisfaction of proving he was the kind of senator who commands respect of his peers. By one good count Kennedy had fewer than twenty supporters when he began the fight. Most of the twenty-five he added joined him because he convinced them he was right. He proved to them he was right about the poll tax—and he proved to them that he could become an expert on a complicated subject. Later that would make his efforts in behalf of legislation dealing with such disparate subjects as refugees, health, and military weaponry more credible. His new reputation would forever precede him. He must have known this on May 11. He certainly did not behave as if he had been defeated. His wife, sister, and sister-in-law were in the gallery for the final debate and vote. Robert Kennedy presided. They were enthusiastic and happy. Ted sat in the front row of the Senate in an all-business blue suit. Still carrying a cane, he was the picture of a winner. A number of senators congratulated him on his performance after the vote. Watching the happy scene from the press gallery, Mary McGrory of the Washington *Star* likened Kennedy's experience to a senatorial bar mitzvah. "He earned the right not to be called 'the kid' anymore," she wrote.

Forty-five votes is a lot in the United States Senate when the opposition includes an administration headed by an arm-twister like Lyndon Johnson joined by an arm-twister like Everett Dirksen. Just before the vote Dirksen boasted that he was winning votes among senators who had been persuaded by Kennedy's arguments. How? "You have to know . . . what to remind them of." Dirksen and Johnson had much, much longer Senate memories than did Kennedy. Among other things those forty-five votes symbolized was that the Senate was changing. Long memories were just barely enough.

In the area of government-supported health care—which Kennedy would later make his own best-known specialty and become the leading champion of—1965 was the year of Medicare. Kennedy was a member of the Health Subcommittee of the Labor and Public Welfare Committee and of the Special Committee on Aging. Medicare legislation, because it involved federal financing, was written in the House Ways and Means Committee and the Senate Finance Committee. However, Kennedy did prevail on the Senate to add an amendment to the bill not in either committee's version, which would allow a person to appeal administratively and to the courts a disallowance of benefits when the amount was at least $100. (The committees preferred that the minimum be $1000.) This was an obvious attempt to aid the poorer of the Medicare beneficiaries, and was thus more "liberal" than the committees preferred. Kennedy won only a partial victory—the conference committee agreed to appeal to administrative but not judicial review of claims between $100 and $1000.

The 89th Congress passed the most far-reaching housing act since 1949, but housing was Robert's specialty, not Ted's. Ted Kennedy's only contribution to the housing act was an amendment providing federal aid to preserve historic structures that could be relocated in urban renewal areas.

Ted Kennedy's most newsworthy Senate battle in 1965 involved his unsuccessful attempt at year's end to have an old family friend named to the federal bench. The man was Boston Municipal Court Judge Francis X. Morrissey.

John and Robert Kennedy as president and attorney general
had been afraid to push their father's friend for a judgeship,
because he was patently unqualified. The American Bar Association had opposed him in 1961. Again in 1965 the ABA
was opposed, a spokesman making the official charge that
there had never been a nominee so lacking in the proper
training, experience, and ability. Ted Kennedy insisted on
pushing the nomination, however, apparently out of a sense
of loyalty to his father. He might have won the Senate's
confirmation, too, but for the revelation that Morrissey
either shaded the truth or lied about his career in his testimony before the Judiciary Committee. That, plus the concentration by Everett Dirksen* on torpedoing Morrissey,
turned an otherwise shabby but routine patronage case into
a national *cause célèbre*. Kennedy *still* might have won.
Some aides and friends said years later that Kennedy be-

---

*In one face-to-face confrontation in Dirksen's office, in response to a
charge by Robert that "you hate the Kennedys," the Minority Leader told
the Kennedy brothers he had "loved" John Kennedy and there was nothing personal regarding the brothers in his opposition to Morrissey. But
this fight and the earlier one on the poll tax were but the first of many
seemingly personal conflicts between Dirksen and Ted Kennedy. In 1967
Ted was the principal figure in a successful attempt to keep Dirksen from
writing into the law what would have amounted to an annulment of the
Supreme Court's one-man, one-vote rulings in regard to congressional
districts. In one important debate only Ted, Robert, and Dirksen were on
the floor as the two brothers made a legislative history that would have
made the bill vulnerable to judicial assault even if it had become law. In
1966 Dirksen tried and failed to move a federal facility from Massachusetts to Rhode Island. In 1968 Kennedy heartily endorsed a lackluster
Democrat running against Dirksen. In 1969 Dirksen attacked Clifford
Alexander, chairman of the Equal Employment Opportunity Commission. Kennedy came to his defense with a counterblast at Dirksen, though
Alexander was not Kennedy's protégé, but that of Dirksen's deputy, Hugh
Scott. The same year Kennedy led the effort to hold up the nomination
of Dirksen's pet Otto Otepka to the Subversives Activities Control Board.
Dirksen was also the most outspoken critic of Ted Kennedy's later antiwar
speeches. Dirksen resented the young Kennedy's rapid rise to influence
in the Senate (and resented the fact that freshmen could rise so rapidly),
according to other senators and Senate aides. In 1974, six years after
Dirksen's death, I asked Kennedy if there was a personal feud. "No," he
said, with neither affection nor rancor. "Ev was a professional." But he
was also a dinosaur, and Kennedy epitomized the coming to power of a
new species.

lieved he could have won. He had President Johnson and Vice-president Humphrey working hard for him (despite some stories to the contrary). What finally resolved the issue, however, was that he didn't have his brother working for him. The junior senator from New York decided the damage the effort was doing to the Kennedy name was too great a price to pay for the piddling rewards. At a meeting at Ted Kennedy's house, Robert announced the decision, brushing aside Ted's now weakened assertion that "We owe Frank . . ." with a brusque statement that the Kennedys owed Morrissey *"nothing!"* On October 21 Ted Kennedy, with tears in his eyes, asked the Senate to send the nomination back to committee, where it would die. The Senate finished its work the next day and adjourned.

It had been a remarkably productive session, but already the war in Vietnam was reaching a point where its costs were beginning to interfere with other Great Society desires. The "guns and butter" argument that would almost immobilize that huge liberal Democratic majority of the 89th Congress in its second session was intruding into priority setting. It was becoming clear to some Democrats that their President might have to be abandoned (or taken on), might become an unpopular adversary rather than the landslide-winning leader of the months just ending. Perhaps Robert Kennedy saw that, and felt that the Morrissey fight was creating a Kennedy weakness or burning up Kennedy energies that would be greatly needed in the years just ahead. Robert Kennedy would soon become a leading opponent of the President over the conduct of the war, even seeking the presidency in 1968. But before that came about it was Ted Kennedy who began creating in America a public opinion that would ultimately conclude that the war was an enormity not worthy of American support. He did that first by indirection, as *the* American expert on the war's impact on the people of Vietnam. Kennedy became expert by using an instrument that had been ignored for years by his colleagues, a minor Senate subcommittee dealing with refugees.

5. ON REFUGEES

One of the ways the Senate began to change in the 1960s was the proliferation of subcommittes. The more sub-committees there were, the more chairmanships and staff could be awarded to younger senators. Under Senate Majority Leader Mike Mansfield, committee chairmen were encouraged to diffuse power this way. The Judiciary Committee led the way in creating new subcommittees. Eastland sometimes seemed to feel that the growing number of liberals on his committee could be neutralized on important questions if they were kept busy with peripheral subcommittee obligations. Whatever the reason, eight of the eleven Democratic members of the committee were chairmen of subcommittees in 1965. Kennedy, in only his third year in the Senate, at thirty-three, was chairman of the "special" subcommittee on Refugees and Escapees. This subcommittee had been chiefly concerned with political refugees, mostly European and anti-Communist ones, in the past. But it had a good, eager, and imaginative staff member in Dale de Haan, and when Kennedy discovered that there were refugees in South Vietnam, he was in a position to do something about it.

"What about that war we keep hearing about?" Kennedy asked David Burke, his administrative assistant, one day early in 1965. "Not many people were talking about the war that early," Burke recalled later, "but an awful lot of people from Massachusetts were coming down to see us." It was a case of a special constituency. "Dove" and "hawk" were not in the national political vocabulary in early 1965, but the division the words imply was already beginning to occur in Massachusetts. This was a result in part of the 1962 campaign. Dr. Hughes campaigned on the peace issue, and as the Boston *Globe* presciently said at the time, created the beginning of a peace constituency of sorts that would influence Kennedy and every other political figure in the state for a decade.*

"That war" was already causing refugee problems. De Haan told Kennedy as soon as he became chairman of the subcommittee in early 1965 that there were reports from representatives of voluntary agencies such as the International Red Cross that a growing number of civilians in South Vietnam were being forced away from farms and hamlets. The South Vietnamese government denied there was a problem. So did the State Department for most of 1965, even though stepped-up military action that winter and spring led to what one observer there called an "inundation" of refugees.

After the Senate vote on Frank Morrissey, Kennedy flew to South Vietnam, to look at the new refugee camps the government had at last established. It was not a very rewarding trip. The State Department arranged it. Kennedy was joined by Senator Joseph Tydings of Maryland, a member of his subcommittee, plus two old college friends, representatives John Tunney of California and John Culver of Iowa. Much of the trip was devoted to visiting U.S. military camps. A *New York Times* reporter on the scene compared the visit to a campaign tour, with large crowds of the curi-

---

*In 1966 Hughes was the subject of a State Department–initiated FBI investigation because of his liberal views and associations. That staunch cold warrior of the Passport Office, Frances Knight, asked for the investigation when Hughes began preparations to go to London and Moscow to teach and write. She was later told by a superior not to initiate such inquiries without next-level-higher approval. Kennedy learned of this and raised a public stink. Secretary of State Rusk then announced a new policy which limited to very high officials at State and Justice the right to ask for and carry out such investigations.

ous, many photographers, speeches, banter, but little apparent work. At one village, Kennedy joked with a soldier who asked him if he had ever been to his home town of Malden: "I got seventy-six percent of the vote there!" At one of the few visits to a refugee camp, Kennedy played soccer with some children. On another stop Kennedy asked an Agency for International Development official what the biggest problem there was. The official put the trip in perspective. "To be blunt, sir, if we had fewer people coming out here. . . . In the last forty-five days we've had thirty-five groups. Each demands the twenty-five-cent tour. It takes up my time. It takes up the province chief's time."

It was a naïve trip, all in all, and Kennedy displayed a naïveté of another sort when he departed, forgetting, or not yet comprehending, what that small but growing constituency back home in Malden and elsewhere in Massachusetts was trying to tell him. He said he was "hopeful" about the war, and was sure "the people in the United States are going to make a long-term commitment to freedom and democracy." He was shortly to be disabused of that notion. But not for a while. In the summer of 1965 Kennedy's first Vietnam speech had called for aid to refugees for "humanitarian reasons"—but also, seemingly mostly, "to make South Vietnam secure." At that time, even armed with information from his first subcommittee's first investigation into the refugee problem, Kennedy was blaming the Viet Cong for all those refugees streaming out of battle areas. His Vietnam trip, if it did nothing else, taught him that there was more to it than that. He went to Geneva in December 1965 to talk about refugees to the Conseil International des Agences Benevoles. He again defended United States policy in Vietnam as "perhaps necessary to preserve the independence of South East Asia," but he also conceded for the first time that, yes, U.S. and South Vietnam military actions were also creating some of the refugees.

This beginning of wisdom also led Kennedy to turn against the policy before long, but for the next two years his doubts were somewhat muted. The reason was that Robert Kennedy's flank had to be protected. Robert feared that his future as a party leader and a national leader would be jeopardized by his challenging President Johnson on a war that was still not unpopular with the majority of the public and that was, as President Johnson kept reminding everyone, something of a John Kennedy legacy to the nation, anyway. "He felt some restraint," Dun Gifford says of Ted Kennedy. Gifford was a legislative assistant in Kennedy's office at that time, and also a social friend of the Kennedys. At some point in 1966, Gifford says, Kennedy told him he had come to oppose the war "totally," but he didn't say so in public because of his concern for what such a statement might do to his brother's career. It wasn't just that he might undercut Bob. It was that he might undercut or fractionalize the slowly growing antiwar political effort. Or so some of his advisers rationalized. David Burke, Ted's administrative assistant, argues that point: "There was some inhibition on his part . . . because he always had to watch where his brother Bob was, because Bob was looked to by many people in the Democratic party as the fellow who should express the political objections to the war." The two brothers talked often about the war, and according to some second- and third-hand accounts of those talks, Ted cleared his public statements with Bob in advance, but Bob never cleared his with Ted. Publicly in 1966 Ted Kennedy was saying things like "I am eighty-nine percent in favor of the Johnson Administration's policies in Vietnam," then turning to specific peripheral refugee and other humanitarian concerns. His discomfort with his situation showed. Meg Greenfield recalled 1962 and noted the irony of the development in *The Reporter*. "There are inhibitions on his ability to maintain a separate political identity. There would be more time, fewer pressures, and surely greater room to maneuver and to move around if his name were Edward Moore."

It wasn't, so he began his war against the war on a separate front. His subcommittee had held hearings in 1965, but these did little more than alert the political genius Johnson to what was coming.* In 1966 Kennedy planned a second set of hearings, and he indicated in a speech that he would be a little tougher this time. "We must move against the

---

*Meeting with South Vietnam leaders in Honolulu in February 1966, Johnson said, prematurely, "[the refugee issue] is just as hot as a pistol in my country."

social ills of the nation with the same determination that has marked our military activities," he said. That was in March. He also said at that time that he wanted the bureaucratic capability to handle refugee problems upgraded. Just before the hearings opened in July, the administration reacted to his past and anticipated future proddings. Secretary of State Dean Rusk announced that a new post would be created to handle the problem, a special assistant to the Secretary of State for Refugees and Migration Affairs. Beginning about then Kennedy became one of the principal forces for providing assistance to the civilians in South Vietnam. His speeches began to hammer home such themes as "Battles won by the military will be hollow indeed unless the Vietnamese people can be inspired with confidence and hope that the future will bring a better way of life." Everybody was beginning to talk that way by the end of the year. The President had launched the effort to "win the hearts and minds" of the Vietnamese people. Kennedy's growing expertise in the area of refugee affairs and his chairmanship were worth a lot more than his rhetoric.

The price he was willing to pay to become an expert was fairly high in terms of time devoted to it. Before 1965, the subcommittee had been "moribund," to use a word chosen by a State Department official who worked in the area of refugee problems. In 1965 Kennedy chaired thirteen days of hearings, in addition to making the trip to South Vietnam. In 1966 he held a one-day hearing on Vietnam, five days of hearings on Cuban refugee problems, and ten days of hearings on the United States government's role in dealing with refugees worldwide. Many of the latter hearings were devoted to the problems in Vietnam (where American aerial bombing had resumed, creating some additional refugees). During 1966 and 1967, with Robert becoming increasingly critical of the war policies, Ted Kennedy's advisers on the subcommittee staff and on his senatorial staff were urging him to join in with public attacks on the refugee problems and the failure of the State Department to deal with them. But for some reason Kennedy was relatively low key in his criticisms and prodding. One friend said later Kennedy believed that President Johnson, Secretary Rusk, and Agency for International Development officials were sincere in their stated desires to give refugee and other civilian problems a higher priority. One member of the staff at the time said later that Kennedy just feared that his taking a more prominent public role would politicize the refugee issue, the way the war issue was being politicized.

He "went public" vigorously in the fall of 1967, probably because he no longer had any faith in the President's intention of dealing with the problem. Kennedy and State Department officials had been engaged in a sort of duel. In late 1966 and early 1967 subcommittee aides interviewed some sixty physicians who had served in Vietnam. On the basis of these interviews, the staff decided that there was a need for an enormous increase in the number of hospitals for civilians. Kennedy told the Administration of his staff's conclusions, and said that if the building program were undertaken he would make no public criticism of policies. And if the program were not undertaken? Then he would have to hold public hearings, he replied. In April of 1967 the Agency for International Development announced that three new military field hospitals costing $15 million would be built. Civilian war casualties could be treated there, too. It was an arrangement Kennedy found inadequate.

Kennedy then stepped up his pressure on the Administration to send a team of American civilian physicians to South Vietnam to provide an objective report on the situation. Six doctors made the trip in August. In September they returned with a 100-page report, which was marked by a critical and urgent tone. But AID officials, fighting to win the hearts and minds of Americans, issued a press release that put the report in an entirely different light. This followed a meeting of the doctors and the President at the White House. The doctors then went to the Hill to meet with Kennedy in an executive session of the subcommittee. He excoriated them for the press release, but soon shifted his anger to the Administration and agreed to hold the long-delayed hearings. The hearings would not have the neutral title of previous ones, but would be called "Civilian Casualty, Social Welfare and Refugee Problems in South Vietnam." The hearings not only focused more public attention on the fact that there may have been many more casualties than the Administration was admitting, and on the fact that a growing number of such casualties were victims of U.S. and South Vietnam actions; they also stressed another question, that of whether in fact the war was even being won.

The hearings were held on October 9, 10, 11, 13, and 16. Kennedy opened them by charging that for two years he had attempted to get Administration officials to increase their efforts to help civilian victims of the war. They had refused to, showing "lack of concern," so, he said, he hoped public exposure of the situation in the new hearings would spur them on. He certainly got the issue before the public. Four of the five meeting days the story was prominently displayed on page 1 of the Baltimore *Sun,* and drew one editorial of support in that paper. *The New York Times* also covered the story thoroughly, as did many other newspapers. So did the networks.

Kennedy came prepared, with staff studies and a scathing report by the General Accounting Office. He also came with a witness list calculated to make coverage of the hearings an assault on the Administration. Kennedy's own statements were harsh enough to be newsworthy in themselves, but the hearings also provided:

Monday, October 9: Dr. F.L.B. Blasingame, chairman of the study group that visited Vietnam in 1967, and executive director of the American Medical Association, said that fifty civilian hospitals were needed instead of the three military ones proposed by the Administration.

Tuesday, October 10: James R. Dumpson, dean of Fordham's School of Social Service and head of an AID study in Vietnam, said that failure to handle displaced persons was "destroying the effort at nation building." Don Luce, who had resigned as director of International Voluntary Services in Vietnam, said that most refugees were fleeing American bombs, not the Viet Cong.

Wednesday, October 11: Kennedy made headlines with the charge that American policies regarding refugees and medical care were "a scandal." The witnesses were from the Government Accounting Office, there to present the critical report.

Friday, October 13: Roger Hilsman, Assistant Secretary of State for Far Eastern Affairs in the Kennedy Administration, charged that U.S. strategy was not working, making more enemies than friends.

That's where the matter was allowed to rest over the weekend. The Administration had been accused of conducting a war that was by tactics and strategy both inhumane and counterproductive. On the following Monday, the Administration was allowed to come in to rebut the previous week's accumulation of criticism. AID Administrator William S. Gaud and William P. Bundy, who now held the post Hilsman had held, argued with Kennedy, occasionally bitterly, over his interpretation of the GAO study and a study Kennedy quoted to show that Viet Cong recruiting was increasing, not decreasing, as Bundy testified. Bundy was trying to offset remarks Kennedy had made during the previous week's hearings to the effect that the war effort was failing to win support from the South Vietnamese people. Bundy had a U.S. study to contradict the study Kennedy quoted from. Kennedy revealed that he was quoting from a classified Department of Defense study leaked to him. Bundy was flustered, lost his suavity. Later the Pentagon sided with Bundy, charging that Kennedy and his staff overlooked a footnote that put the figures on their document in perspective. Kennedy's credibility was probably greater than the Pentagon's by then.

These hearings were almost a one-man show; at least a one-senator show. Kennedy alone of the four members of the subcommittee sat through the five days of hearings. He was the only senator present for any length of time any day.

The antiwar tide had become a flood by October 1967. Dozens of senators were criticizing the brutality and lack of success of the war effort. Students had taken to the streets. Eugene McCarthy would shortly announce his intention to run against Lyndon Johnson because of the issue. If there was a difference between Ted Kennedy's criticism and that of the others it was that he continued to focus on the humanitarian aspects of the war, rather than the global politics of it. And he was regarded as one who *knew*. Much of the criticism now being voiced was an echo of that Kennedy had made a year or more earlier from his subcommittee pulpit. He was being quoted. He had become the expert, in the traditional Senate way of specialization and long hours of hard work in committee sessions. In a small way, at least, Kennedy helped create the antiwar movement. His forcing

into the American consciousness the bloody, tragic details of
the side effects of the political struggle in Vietnam made the
public that much less willing to support either the effort or
the goal.

In some quarters Kennedy has been criticized for
this. He is said to have intended this effect. He is said to
have lacked the courage to fight President Johnson and
the supporters of the war effort head on, to have tried
rather to undermine the war effort by demagoguing
about the casualties. (A similar charge was made about
Kennedy's concurrent criticisms of the draft, about which
there will be more discussion in chapter 7.) He certainly
knew that his horror stories were hurting the American
war effort, were undermining the President's appeals for
national unity and support. But I doubt that he was playing some clever game with the war. He is simply drawn
by instinct to so-called "people problems." David Burke,
who was writing Kennedy's antiwar speeches then, says,
"He has a natural inclination to the humanitarian side.
I'm not saying he is such a wonderful fellow because he's
a humanitarian, but for some reason he is drawn into that
—[animatedly quoting now] 'People are getting hurt! Oh
my God! Have you seen them? Isn't it terrible!'—especially when it comes to children."

Making the war itself a secondary issue was not a
tactic that could continue. Before long Robert Kennedy followed McCarthy into the race for the presidency and Lyndon Johnson announced that he was not a candidate for
reelection. The Tet offensive of February 1968 would demol-
ish the optimistic official claims that the Viet Cong and
North Vietnamese were not able to mount any sort of major
attack. But before that, Kennedy saw at first hand just how
bad the war had become and just how hard American officials were trying to keep the facts hidden. In December
1967, he decided to go to Vietnam for another tour. Perhaps
still uncomfortable about his own role in that guided tour of
1965, he decided that *he* would control his trip and what he
saw. He sent Burke and three Washington lawyers, Barrett
Prettyman, John Nolan, and Tom Powers, ahead of him. "It
was almost like an advance," Burke recalled later, "except
that our jobs were substantive rather than political. We went

there to find the things he knew existed.* Then when he got there and asked to see Can Tho and they [U.S. officials in Saigon] said, 'There's nothing in Can Tho,' he said, 'There is something at Can Tho. Tom Powers has been there and he saw it.' "

Kennedy refused the official welcoming briefing for Washington VIPs. He stayed in Saigon only two days, then went to the provinces for over a week of touring. What shocked him the most was, again, the impact of the war on civilians, and the seeming indifference of U.S. and Vietnamese military leaders to what they were doing. In one visit to a disputed area, Kennedy found South Vietnamese officials casually approving destructive attacks in areas where civilians could not help but be killed and wounded. He returned to Saigon then for the initial briefing. "And then he just tore it apart," Burke said later. "Just tore it apart. The poor majors and captains and colonels. They would say something and he would say, 'How can you tell me that, I was just there, that's not true!' " Following the briefing, Robert Komer, who was in charge of the pacification program that was meant to make the countryside secure for civilians, took Kennedy into his office and sharply criticized his investigation. "You're sticking your nose into something that is much larger than refugees," Komer said angrily. He belittled Kennedy's concern for civilian casualties, and told him he was hurting the war effort. There was a stormy exchange.

When Kennedy returned to the United States, somewhat more attention was paid by him and his audiences—to remarks about policy generally. In a Boston speech a week before Tet he said to the World Affairs Council, "I am forced to report to you, and to the people of the Commonwealth, that continued optimism cannot be justified." Just after Tet he told another audience that the United States government should present the Thieu

---

*I told a State Department official who was in Vietnam then of Burke's phrase, which suggests that Kennedy wasn't very objective in advance of his trip. The official criticized Kennedy for often taking such an approach. But he added that he was making efforts then to "spruce up" the things he knew Kennedy would be wanting to look at.

regime in Saigon with an ultimatum: "[Become] an ally worthy of our efforts and our lives," or lose all U.S. support. That was in February. In March Robert Kennedy entered the presidential race and Kennedy was swept up into that. He held only one more day's hearings on refugees that year, in May, a month before Robert was assassinated. After that tragedy, Ted Kennedy more or less dropped out of the fight until the fall. When he returned to the war, it was as one who felt that he had a role to fulfill that made the war itself the principal focus of his attentions. But he never put aside his insistence that whatever happened in the policy area, he still had the responsibility to press for medical and other humanitarian needs. The subcommittee held two more days of hearings on civilian casualties in 1969, a day's hearings on refugees and civilian casualties in Laos and Cambodia in 1970, further hearings (preceded by staff investigations on the scene and followed by staff or Kennedy reports) on the same topic in "Indochina" in 1971 and 1972. After the cease-fire the subcommittee held extensive hearings on "relief and rehabilitation" of casualties in all of Indochina, including North Vietnam, in 1973, 1974, and 1975. The My Lai massacre was made public in 1969. U.S. Army troops had methodically killed more than 100 South Vietnamese civilians. Commentators and public officials were almost unanimous in denouncing what happened. Many saw it as an aberration or an unavoidable accident of war. For others, including Kennedy, it was a symbol of the war. Kennedy said the slaughter "dramatizes . . . the extent of [the war's] toll among civilians." There had been one million civilian casualties in South Vietnam, he said, a third of whom died, most of whom were victims of U.S. and South Vietnam military actions.

Meanwhile, Kennedy and his subcommittee staff had been pressing the State Department for information on the refugee situation in the rest of Indochina. In March 1970 Kennedy sent a list of questions about it to Secretary of State William Rogers. In April Rogers replied that there had been a dramatic increase in the number of refugees since the fighting became intense in Laos at the beginning of the year; that the United States acted in response to Laotian govern-

ment requests; that more funds would be needed for AID-
administered relief programs. Kennedy accused Rogers of
not being "fully responsive," basing his charge on press reports and other information developed by his staff. He felt
that considerably more funds were needed than did the
State Department, and that the number of refugees—"often
deliberately generated by our bombing"—was much
greater than the State Department admitted. In the one-day
hearings, top-ranking AID and State officials defended policies, up to a point. A former AID official, Ronald Rickenback,
testified that bombing of population centers was carried out
"indiscriminately." William Sullivan, former ambassador to
Laos, and another State Department official, Dennis Doolin,
both testified that there were elaborate rules and procedures that served "to prevent" civilian casualties. But how
effective were they? Kennedy pursued. Doolin said he
couldn't answer that in public.

Those particular hearings did not generate the
publicity they might have ordinarily. They came at a
time when the nation, particularly its campuses, were in
an unprecedented uproar. President Nixon had sent U.S.
troops into Cambodia, touching off violent demonstrations, and on two campuses students were killed by police or national guardsmen, touching off even more
demonstrations. The headlines were of those events, as
well as of the war in Cambodia itself. But the 1970 subcommittee hearings served another purpose. "Answering
Kennedy's questions made us go through an intellectual
exercise that was helpful," said a State Department official who was involved in this general area of responsibility then. "Preparing ourselves to go down to Kennedy's
hearings is helpful to us. Bureaucracy tends to continue
doing what it has been doing. Only when it is pressured
to stop, pause, review and articulate policy is it likely to
change." How much policy was changed in Indochina because of the necessity to prepare for Kennedy's now annual hearings is a difficult question to answer. No State
Department official I asked that question of in 1974 answered flatly that Kennedy had had a compelling direc-
tion-changing effect on policy, but all expressed the view
that he had influenced the decision-makers at the point

of contact—that is, the assistant secretaries and deputy assistants who did not set policy but carried it out. And some believe he influenced policy *above* the Secretary of State level. That is, his potentiality as presidential candidate was a factor presidents Johnson and Nixon took into account.

Not all State Department officials who believe Kennedy has influenced policy implementation believe his influence has been helpful, or that he is a responsible critic of foreign-policy decisions relating to refugee problems. An assistant secretary of state, who asked not to be quoted by name (as did all State officials I interviewed; one explained, "This man may become president"), gave this assessment: "Kennedy is a light weight and his staff is irresponsible. The staff often takes at face value briefings and intelligence from peace groups. In 1971 they were told the air war in Laos was being conducted in an irresponsible way. We demonstrated that it was carefully controlled, but unfortunately the charges had already been given a lot of publicity. The staff just unduly influences him."

One State Department official who feels the same way and who has not minded being quoted in the press is Graham Martin. Martin was ambassador to South Vietnam in 1974. In March of 1974 he charged that the "remnants" of the peace movement in the United States were trying to influence journalists and "particularly . . . susceptible Congressional staffers," with the aim of assisting North Vietnam. He meant specifically the subcommittee staff. Kennedy attacked the Martin statement as irresponsible innuendo, and wrote a letter to Secretary of State Kissinger asking him to answer a series of questions about U.S. obligations to the countries of Indochina. Martin sent a confidential cable to Washington suggesting that the State Department not answer Kennedy's questions.

I think it would be the height of folly to permit Kennedy, whose staff will spearhead this effort [to reduce aid to South Vietnam], the tactical advantage of an honest and detailed answer to questions of substance raised in his letter. While, as an individual senator, he has the right to raise them, they are not questions that fall within the pur-

view of his subcommittee. . . . The list of questions is clev-
erly drawn to thoroughly mix apples and oranges. Any
substantive answer would permit another calculated campaign of distortion that would pre-empt the attention the
presentation of the Administration's case [to the Foreign
Relations Committee] should receive.

A copy of that cable was sent to Kennedy's office in
a plain envelope, apparently by a sympathetic State Department aide. When Kennedy confirmed that it was legitimate,
he assailed Martin in a Senate speech for an attempt at
"deception." Kissinger answered the original Kennedy
questions in detail. For he knew, if Martin didn't, that while
the subcommittee had no legislative responsibility in the
area of foreign policy, it had become, under Kennedy, enor-
mously effective and influential in exercising oversight of
the department.

So a decade after he became chairman Kennedy
was making State Department officials, particularly those
at AID, "stop . . . pause . . . review" policies that might
otherwise have generated an irresistible momentum despite their worth. And the fact that he was always there,
applying pressure, meant that AID officials who agreed
with his aims were more effective within the establishment than they would otherwise have been. "A lot of
times I was able to win an argument for a better system
of helping refugees and civilians, and even for a higher
level of expenditures, not by saying that *I* wanted us to
do this or that, not by saying that it was the smart thing
to do or the right thing to do, but by saying that if we
did it, Kennedy wouldn't be able to criticize us," a middle-level State Department official told me in 1974.

The level of humanitarian aid, in dollars, was
higher then indirectly because of Kennedy's chairmanship of the subcommittee. Congress authorized and appropriated funds on the basis of the information Kennedy
and his subcommittee developed and publicized, but year
after year the actual figures in the bills were someone
else's. The reason for that was partly structural. The Senate Foreign Relations Committee drafted all foreign-aid
legislation. The reason was partly that Kennedy wanted

more for humanitarian uses than Congress was willing to spend. On a number of occasions in the decade after he became chairman of the subcommittee, Kennedy would offer floor amendments raising spending. These would either be cut back or defeated in the Senate or, later, in conference with the House.

At the very end of the Vietnam War, Kennedy came the closest he ever came to directly determining for Congress how much aid would go to refugees and how it would be spent. In March 1975, as the South Vietnamese government and army collapsed and refugees began streaming south by the hundreds of thousands, Kennedy introduced a bill to internationalize humanitarian aid to the tune of $100 million. That is, American dollars would be given to the United Nations and similar organizations, for use in South Vietnam and Cambodia. Senator Hubert Humphrey, a member of the Foreign Relations Committee, took the Kennedy bill, increased the figure to $200 million, and added language giving the president authority to use force to withdraw American citizens and their dependents from South Vietnam. The committee cut the money to $100 million. As the situation in South Vietnam deteriorated by the hour, the various international agencies estimated that at a minimum some $140 million was needed. Senator Dick Clark, also a member of the Foreign Relations Committee, and Kennedy then jointly introduced an amendment to the Humphrey version of the bill when it came to the floor, raising the figure for aid to $150 million. That passed the Senate by voice vote. Then the House-Senate conferees changed the language regarding the use of international agencies so that when the compromise came back to the Senate, Kennedy voted against it, the first foreign-aid proposal he ever opposed.

In those same hectic weeks, Kennedy supported efforts to provide government and voluntary assistance for settling South Vietnamese who came to the United States. He did that not with legislation but, again, by using subcommittee hearings as a means of applying pressure and bringing public opinion to bear upon State Department officials charged with assisting those refugees. He sent his staff aides, Dale de Haan and Jerry Tinker, to Guam, where the refugees were being processed before coming to the United States, and kept firing off press releases, making statements, and otherwise attempting to influence public opinion and the bureaucracy.

Kennedy's chairmanship of the Subcommittee on Refugees and Escapees had another dimension in the middle and late sixties and early seventies. Says a State Department official who disagreed with much of what Kennedy sought in Vietnam: "Kennedy made that subcommittee the custodian of moral values in foreign policy." He did that, according to this critic's view, by being "selective" in what he chose to publicize from staff investigations—that is, information about South Vietnamese or U.S. military activities that had resulted in casualties was used in a speech, while information about North Vietnamese or Viet Cong activities that resulted in equally barbarous atrocities was ignored or played down. "Policy-makers have to be more realistic," the State official continued, arguing in effect that the custodianship of "moral values" in foreign policy had to be relinquished to someone like Kennedy—someone without real responsibility. But he grudgingly admitted that Kennedy had done "a masterful job" of it.

Certainly the decade in which Kennedy was chairman of the subcommittee was one in which "realpolitik," "hard-nosed," and similar words were more often used as modifiers for American policy in South Vietnam than words like "humane" or "compassionate." And certainly the subcommittee had become the source of much of the justifying data for those men and women in public life who were concerned about the nation having a moral foreign policy. Whether Kennedy's design was to make the moral issue his own for his own purposes or to use it as a more coercive spur than expert argument on the politics of the situation would have been I don't know, and I doubt if anyone knows.

What is known is that beginning in the last year of the Johnson Administration and continuing through the years in which the Nixon Administration was waging war in Vietnam, until the cease-fire and withdrawal of American troops in January, 1973, Kennedy was no longer just talking about the refugees and the civilian victims.

6. FIGHTING
THE WAR

I come here today to Worcester, to the heart of my home,
a state that has supported the efforts and shared the sor-
rows of my life. . . . For the last ten weeks I have not been
active in public life. I have concerned myself with my
family. I have spent much of my time with the sea, clearing
my mind and spirit, putting the past behind, opening a way
to what lies ahead." . . . On August 21, 1968, Ted Kennedy
entered the lists as a foe of the war, with no special qualifications. He had long since given up the idea that the war,
though wrong, was necessary, and now he was making it
clear that he was no longer just concerned with the effects
of the war—that he just wanted a different kind of war, one
in which "innocent" victims did not bear the brunt of the
effort. "Today I resume my public responsibilities to the
people of Massachusetts," he said. "Like my brothers before
me, I pick up a fallen standard." What he wanted, he said,
was "an end to this war. . . . And the end must be not five
or ten years from now . . . but as quickly as it is physically
possible to reach the essential agreements, and to extricate
ourselves from this bottomless pit of our dreams." Specifically Kennedy called for an end, unconditionally, to all
bombing of North Vietnam; a negotiated mutual withdrawal
of all U.S. and North Vietnamese troops with Hanoi; political
and economic aid to South Vietnam; unilateral reduction of

U.S. forces and a decrease in military activity on the ground in South Vietnam as a demonstration of American "sincerity."

This was an unmistakable challenge to President Johnson and national policy. The President had announced only two days earlier that he would not stop bombing North Vietnam and would not end the aggressive tactics of American troops, the so-called search-and-destroy missions. He said critics who objected to U.S. tactics should bring pressure to bear on Hanoi. Johnson said that U.S. troops would begin withdrawing not now, but six months after the war was over. Kennedy's proposal was a minority view still. The Democratic party endorsed a platform plank on Vietnam at its national convention one week after the Worcester speech that was much in line with the presidential view. Kennedy's August view was nearer to that in the Republican platform, adopted two weeks before his speech. That platform did not go into specifics the way Kennedy did in his speech, but it did say it looked forward to "a progressive de-Americanization of the war."

After Richard Nixon won the presidency, Kennedy tended to be a little less critical of Administration policy— for a while. Early in 1969, North Vietnam stepped up its attacks. Nixon's refusal to retaliate, Kennedy said in March of that year, showed restraint. Kennedy endorsed the speeches of Republican senators Hugh Scott of Pennsylvania and George Aiken of Vermont in early May in which they called for U.S. troop withdrawals. But the honeymoon ended later that month.

Two weeks later, on May 20, Kennedy rose in the Senate to denounce in the strongest terms an American attack on Apbia Mountain, which had been nicknamed "Hamburger Hill" for the bloody human results of the ferocity of the fighting launched against it. He called the attacks "senseless and irresponsible . . . madness," a sentencing to death of American soldiers who were ordered to win territory not related to ending the war, for no aim related to national policy. That Kennedy was regarded in the White House and the Republican party as a dangerous foe and shaper of American public opinion (this was two months before the incident at Chappaquiddick) was obvious from the reaction to the speech. The counterattack made the Senate look like Hamburger Hill. Hugh Scott immediately rebutted Kennedy, accusing him of second-guessing military commanders in the field. The next day a military spokesman in Saigon attacked the Kennedy interpretation of the battle. He said territory was not the goal, enemy troops were. The next day the general who commanded a division at Apbia, who was also a Kennedy constituent, attacked the senator. The next day it was White House Press Secretary Ronald Ziegler. The next day Kennedy attacked the battle and the war as "immoral and unjustified." The next day Defense Secretary Melvin Laird reminded the public that Nixon's policies regarding keeping military pressure on the enemy forces were consistent with that of the Democratic administration of President Johnson.

In June there was a short, standstill cease-fire between Kennedy and the White House. That month President Nixon announced that the United States would begin withdrawing troops unilaterally. A number of Democratic senators criticized the move as less than enough. George McGovern called the withdrawals only "token." Kennedy said he hoped that the strategy would reduce the level of violence. The antiwar forces simmered that first summer of Nixon's presidency, many of the activists and Senate doves feeling that Nixon was not really bringing the war to a close, but was bringing the antiwar movement in the United States to one, with his carefully managed campaign of withdrawing troops a few at a time. Kennedy remained quiet, too. That July the accident at Chappaquiddick occurred. It was not until mid-September 1969, two months later, in a speech in Boston, that Kennedy made another public speech. Just as he had ended his postassassination withdrawal from the public stage with an antiwar speech, so did he end his post-Chappaquiddick absence with one. He picked up the charge that the announced withdrawals were "token," and said the lowering of violence he had hoped for in the spring had not occurred. Kennedy saw the central issue as U.S. commitment to the continued rule of General Thieu. He wanted a coalition government—Thieu supporters and Communists. "It is time to say to the Saigon government, 'If you will not agree to a sensible compromise—even if it endangers your personal power—then it is your war and you must fight it alone.' " Such a statement to Thieu was not even contemplated by President Nixon in 1969—nor in 1970, 1971, 1972, 1973, or *1974*. Nixon had determined that he did not have to do that to survive politically—and that he could not do it and expect Thieu to survive. And, of course, Nixon was right.

A month after Kennedy's Boston speech, the antiwar movement turned out hundreds of thousands of peaceful protestors in major cities and on campuses all across the country. The Vietnam Moratorium Committee sponsored the meetings—October 15 was called "Moratorium Day"— and a number of officeholders addressed the protestors. One of the largest demonstrations was in Boston, where a crowd of 100,000 jammed the Boston Common to hear Kennedy go further than before. He proposed that all U.S. troops be pulled out within a year and that all air and naval support be withdrawn by the end of *1972*. That would have accelerated the Nixon withdrawal rate by a factor of about two. The President had said withdrawals would be stepped up only if the Paris peace talks, or improvements in the South Vietnamese fighting capability, or a reducing of activity by Viet Cong and North Vietnam, justified it. Noting the last factor, Kennedy said, "It is no peace plan at all to say that what we do depends upon what Hanoi does."

In 1970 Kennedy had to run for reelection. One of his platform planks was the simple statement "End the war."

In 1971 Kennedy kept up what pressure he could bring to bear on the President. "Vietnamization" (as Nixon called his policy of gradual withdrawal of American fighting men), said Kennedy in January, "means war and more war." There was an element of despair in many of his speeches by now, the other side of the moral coin. "Can America ever wash its hands of the innocent Asian blood it has spilled?" Kennedy asked a meeting of Democratic state chairmen in the late winter of 1971.

The year 1972 was a presidential year and the high-water mark of the peace movement as a political force. Kennedy had ruled himself out of the race. Edmund Muskie was the front runner. He foundered, and the senator who had been most outspoken on the war issue, George McGovern, was nominated. At least, McGovern was perceived as the most outspoken. Kennedy, perhaps because he was speaking only as a senator from the most dovish state, was, in my view, delivering the strongest and most pointed anti-war speeches in that year.

In January 1972, the President went on national television to announce that he had proposed to the Communists through secret channels an eight-point program to end the war. That plan still did not go as far as the old Kennedy proposal of 1969. Nixon still foresaw withdrawals of all foreign troops six months after an accord was signed, but his plan did provide for elections in which all political elements in the south could participate and a standstill cease-fire, which meant the Viet Cong would, at least, be influential in the future government if the agreement had been honored by all. Some liberal Democrats approved, mildly. Senator Mansfield, for example, called the proposal a "long step forward," though he said he was still interested in setting a definite withdrawal date for U.S. forces, one not related to events in Vietnam. Kennedy said, "We do not need an eight-point plan to end the war. All we need is a one-point plan —a complete withdrawal of American ground, sea, and air forces by a date certain, in exchange for a return of our prisoners. . . . So long as we try to condition our withdrawal on things like free elections, a cease-fire, or any of the other trappings disclosed last night, reasonable as they may seem, we shall be pursuing the same blind alley in public negotiations that have followed with such futility in private."

U.S. bombing greatly increased in 1972, with the first B-52 raids deep into North Vietnam since 1967, and with the first raids ever directed at targets in the populous Hanoi-Haiphong area. The same small band of Democrats dominated the critical protests in the Senate at each upward movement of the escalator. Kennedy was one. When Ramsey Clark, the former attorney general, returned from a visit to North Vietnam, he testified in August 1972, before Kennedy's refugees subcommittee on the damage he had seen. He said North Vietnam's dike system had been a target. If it had been destroyed there would have been enormous flooding and uncountable civilian casualties. Kennedy, McGovern, and eight other senators introduced a resolution calling for an end to such bombing.

Nixon persevered, stuck to his plans, and, in the end, was able to end the war his way. Negotiations were concluded after the President ordered massive bombing raids over North Vietnamese cities during the Christmas season, 1972. Then and only then did Senate efforts to force a halt in the war dating back three years finally come to fruition. In 1968, Lyndon Johnson's last year in office, there was not a single significant roll-call vote in the Senate dealing with Vietnam, on either policy or funds to support policy. In 1969 Congress merely forbade the introduction of American ground troops into Laos and Thailand. In 1970 Congress voted to prevent expenditures in support of military operations in Cambodia (*after* the U.S. invasion). In 1971, after much maneuvering, Senate liberals won only enactment of an amendment stating that it was the policy of the United States to be out of Vietnam by a date to be announced—by the President. On signing this law, President Nixon said he did not consider it to be "binding" on him. The Senate had approved much more explicit, even binding language, but the House wouldn't take it. In 1972 the Senate went further still and approved legislation that would cut off all funds for the support of U.S. military activities in Indochina. But once more the House killed the Senate effort. These efforts were supported by Kennedy but not led by him.

Did Kennedy and the other peace Democrats in the Senate speed the end of the war by their speeches and legislative efforts to force the President's policy? Nixon seems to have gone into office with a timetable of withdrawal and settlement that coincided with his term—four years. He missed it by only a few months. Peace was "at hand" by election day, and the treaty itself was signed on January 27, 1973. Perhaps, but only perhaps, American involvement in the war would have lasted longer if there had not been Senate pressure on the President from the day he took office. The Senate was certainly the only focus for the peace movement in those four years. And Kennedy, while he did not always take the lead in trying to force the President to withdraw on a different schedule or take other actions he objected to, did do his part in keeping the peace movement's ideas alive and articulated. His speeches, written by Dale de Haan after David Burke left the staff in 1971, were circulated through the movement in the late sixties and early seventies not just via television, magazines, and newspapers (where he was probably quoted as much or more on the war as any other individual), but directly, via a "Vietnam mailing list" his office compiled. One hundred seventy academics, clerics, businessmen, journalists, and others active in the effort to end the war* received every Kennedy press release dealing with the war.

Kennedy was perceived outside the Senate as a leader of the movement, to a degree probably not justified by events in the Senate. Republican political strategists also so perceived him, as is seen by even a casual glance through *Monday*, the highly partisan magazine published by the party. For example, in the fall of 1971 Kennedy told a group of wives of servicemen being held prisoner or missing in Indochina that if he were president he would "crawl" into a peace-talks meeting room in Paris in order to get such men returned home. *Monday* ran a page and a half on that, with this headline: SENATOR EDWARD M. KENNEDY: ALL PROFILE, NO COURAGE. A cartoon showed him on his hands and knees entering a room labeled "Paris Peace Talks." A crier announced, "Ladies and gentlemen, the distinguished Senator from the state of Massachusetts." It was a real case of overkill.

North Vietnamese politicians also thought Kennedy was a leader in the peace movement and in the Senate. He was the first senator given lists of prisoners by Hanoi to be made public. Many liberal Democratic senators regarded Kennedy as the best spokesman for the peace movement— in 1970 Senator Harold Hughes of Iowa stated that publicly. And some supporters of the Nixon policy in the press believed Kennedy was the most influential antiwar senator. Joseph Alsop used his column in the Washington *Post* and other papers on May 13, 1970, to appeal to Kennedy to help turn the peace movement away from some of its goals. This was after the massive demonstrations in Washington and elsewhere and campus riots following President Nixon's sending of troops into Cambodia. "I address you," wrote Alsop, "because the events of the last weekend seemed to indicate the widespread prevalence of sheer political lunacy

*Including Daniel Ellsberg.

in this poor country of ours and because I suspect that you, almost alone, have it in your power to bring my people back to their senses." What he feared, Alsop said, was a nation so peaceful that it would let Russia become more powerful— and Israel be destroyed.

Kennedy's reply four days later, which probably was read by more people than anything else he ever wrote on the subject, made the following personal statement.

I must say, without qualification, that I fully and openly protest against what has now become the war in Indochina. I am sure you feel that in taking this position I have allied myself with the naïve, the idealistic and the young. I ally myself with no one, and I seek no one to join with me.

I simply protest the war and its consequences, as one person who has obligations of office, some sense of the responsibilities memory has placed upon me, and as a man who has not escaped the "harshness of the historic process."

"Political lunacy" it was that brought upon us the events of the past two weeks. Yet I would not place the charge against those who came to Washington but to those who caused them to come here. As a nation we have had enough of war, of death, and divisiveness.

What goal do we have in mind, what prize so enviable that this great nation must pursue Asians through endless jungles, across borders, in and out of their burning villages to give and take life?

Do we do these things in 1970 for trucks and rice, rifles and bunkers, some mythical Pentagon in the forests?* Or do some among our military or political leadership still suffer the illusion that a military victory can be won in Vietnam? Unfortunately, I must conclude, all public statements aside, that the motivation to move into Cambodia was the latter.

The continuation of these acts, if justifiable at all, could only be morally defended if the vital security interests and welfare of the people of the United States were at stake. I do not believe that they are. Nor do I believe that it was the very survival of our country that involved us in this tragedy in the first place. . . .

Perhaps we have now realized that what once was

---

*Nixon had justified the invasion of Cambodia by saying its goal was a huge Communist headquarters complex.

rationalized, in that atmosphere of a decade ago, as an attempt to maintain a balance in the game of world power politics has deteriorated into a monumental and historic catastrophe. Now we know it was an error.

Kennedy disputed Alsop's other points, saying American involvement in Vietnam emboldened the Soviet Union in the Middle East, and he called it "strange logic" to suggest "that every Asian child who dies becomes a messenger to Moscow, warning the marshals of the Soviet Union that they must go easy on the banks of the Suez."

If there were still a hint of justification for John Kennedy's Vietnam decisions in Ted Kennedy's mind at that late date, he seemed to be saying in that letter that he was no longer giving his dead brother the benefit of it, that the moral imperative of the peace movement demanded a complete break with the past. However, he salvaged this: "You are quite right in noting that President Kennedy did not hold the view that our country is immune to history's dangers. I would only add that while holding that view he also never doubted that the future could be different."

It is difficult to assess Kennedy's impact on the war in Vietnam. In speeches and statements such as the Alsop letter he did, to recall the State Department official, present to the public the moral obligations of foreign policy. His subcommittee's unsparing investigations of the refugee and civilian casualty problems created much public disgust with the effects of the war. As a *senator* Kennedy's influence on Nixon policy was probably no greater than that of the other antiwar members of the Senate, such as McGovern, McCarthy, Fulbright, Church, and the others. As an expert on refugee problems he did influence senators directly. As a much-quoted media hero he did influence public opinion, and thus, indirectly, senatorial behavior. As a potential presidential nominee he kept some pressure on President Nixon—at the very least made him try harder to make the November 1972 deadline for withdrawal of U.S. troops (until the summer of 1972, when McGovern won the party's nomination). Kennedy joined the antiwar effort early and stayed the course, but you cannot neatly quantify what he did in the Senate to hasten the end of the war, or even to ease its burdens on its victims.

Fittingly, Kennedy did get credit for two of the Senate actions that put the cap on the American involvement, direct and indirect, in South Vietnam. In January 1973, at the opening of Congress, he proposed to Senate Democrats that they state as policy that the war in Indochina should be ended, that no further funds be spent in behalf of the American war effort there, once American troops and prisoners were out. After a three-hour closed session on January 4, in which a number of emotional speeches were made in behalf of the proposition, the caucus approved the motion by a 36–12 vote, after only barely defeating a "compromise" proposal made by Senator Henry Jackson, inviting President Nixon to discuss the war situation with Congressional leaders. That vote was 24–23. The Kennedy proposal was embodied in legislation introduced by senators George McGovern and Mark Hatfield. Ultimately all that Congress was prepared to do was to forbid direct support of U.S. combat activities in the area after August 15, by which time a more or less "orderly" transfer of the burden of the fighting to South Vietnamese forces had been accomplished. In 1974, Kennedy was the author of the amendment that finally made the Senate a full partner in the making of policy in Vietnam. In 1973 the Administration had requested $1.6 billion in military aid for South Vietnam in fiscal 1974. Congress cut that to $1.1 billion. In past years the Administration had been able to recoup such cuts with supplemental requests. But when in 1974 it attempted to get authority to spend the disputed half billion dollars, first the House and then the Senate refused permission. In the Senate Kennedy put forward the amendment to forbid such a level of spending. The vote in the House came on April 4, and the antiwar representatives won by a slim margin, 177–154. The Nixon Administration believed that if it could overturn that in the Senate, it could get its way in conference and when the House was again asked to vote.

A close vote was expected in the Senate, the following month. Vice-president Ford presided, anticipating that there might even be a tie vote that he could break. Armed Services Committee Chairman John Stennis, highly respected and usually effective, made the principal effort in behalf of the increase in aid. Kennedy spoke for his amendment. The debate was held against the backdrop of that contretemps involving Ambassador Martin and Senator Kennedy. On the crucial test of sentiment, a Stennis move to table and thus kill Kennedy's amendment, Kennedy prevailed, 41–39. Then the amendment passed 43–38. It became law. In early 1975, President Ford made a new request for some half billion in fiscal 1975 funds. Congress made it clear almost immediately that it would not provide that much money. While the debate raged on how much, if any, money could be agreed on, South Vietnam collapsed (in part because of the debate, some charged) and the war abruptly ended, as did military assistance.

7. SENATOR
FOR THE YOUNG

One of the Harvard professors who sat across from Kennedy's Stryker frame in New England Baptist in the fall of 1964 was Samuel Huntington. One of his concerns was the draft. He didn't think it was fair. This was not an issue of intense interest in 1964. The draft was still a peacetime draft; few American youths were being called; and those who were weren't being shipped to Southeast Asia to die. In April of 1964 President Johnson had ordered the Department of Defense to study selective service, primarily to see if the military needed it still. (The report came back two years later, concluding that the draft would be needed another ten years.) But it was not till the growth of the war and the snowballing larger monthly draft calls that there was any general public concern about the equities of the way the system worked.

In early 1966 the House Armed Services Committee held hearings on the way the draft was administered, but the committee was obviously looking at things from the military's point of view, not the draftee's. What were the needs of the army? Not what was fair for the society. Ted Kennedy testified at those hearings, criticized the existing system, and proposed a complete overhaul. The central feature of his plan was a lottery system. The major cause of the unfairness in the draft was that many, many more young men turned draft age each month than were called by the army. So draft boards and the army had allowed a complicated system of deferments to grow. Student deferments, particularly, created an unfairness, in Kennedy's view. A draft-eligible young man who could afford college and had the intellectual capacity for it would win deferments adding up to six or seven years (and could marry and have children in that period, thus winning permanent deferment). Under a lottery, Kennedy told the committee, he would not allow any deferments for education, occupation, fatherhood, or dependence, except in cases of extreme hardship. All qualified would be equally vulnerable to having their number chosen in a lottery.

Lieutenant General Lewis B. Hershey, for a quarter of a century the director of the Selective Service System, opposed this as "substituting chance for judgment," and even such liberals as New York's Senator Jacob Javits were unwilling to take him on. Opposing the lottery, Javits said, "I believe we must defer to the wisdom and experience of General Hershey." Nothing came of the Kennedy proposal. The Senate Armed Services Committee held no hearings that year.

The following year, with the draft law due to expire, there were hearings in the Senate. Not only did the Armed Services Committee hold them, but so did a Labor and Public Welfare Committee subcommittee, of which Kennedy acted as chairman. He asked Chairman Richard Russell of Armed Services if he objected to subcommittee hearings limited to the economic and educational effects of the draft. Russell said No, go ahead. Kennedy leapt out at the starting gun and ran far ahead of the Russell hearings—and far beyond what Russell expected. On opening day Kennedy told the subcommittee, witnesses, and the audience that he wanted "broad reform" in the draft; this before any record had been developed on the draft's impact on educational institutions or the economy. Before the hearings even started he and Senator Joseph Clark had introduced a resolution that endorsed, among other things, a random selection—a lottery—of men as they became eligible; no more graduate-school deferments, uniform administration, youngest-first order of call. (Under the existing oldest-first order, youths who were not called remained in a state of uncertainty for years.) After the subcommittee hearings, Kennedy went before the Armed Services Committee to propose reform legislation embodying those principles. The Johnson Administration was proposing similar reforms, based on a study by a commission chaired by Burke Marshall, once Robert Kennedy's assistant attorney general for civil rights, now back in private life.

The committee sent the Administration proposal to the floor of the Senate that year (with minor changes). Under this bill graduate-school deferments would be eliminated, nineteen-year-olds would be drafted first, not last, and the president was given authority to institute a lottery. The only thing Kennedy wanted that was not in the bill was the institution of national criteria, so that local boards would not be so autocratic and unpredictable. On May 11, 1967, the Senate passed the bill a week after the committee finished it, as was usual then with Armed Services Committee bills. Russell, imperiously, vanquished every senator who proposed changes. The only real effort to change the law was made by Senator Mark Hatfield, who wanted to see an end to the draft and the beginning of a volunteer army. Russell mustered a 69–9 vote against him. The bill passed 70–2. The House passed a terrible bill two weeks later, and the conference meeting began to iron out disagreements. The Senate conferees were all members of Russell's committee. They eventually gave in to the House conferees on several significant points. The lottery was expressly forbidden. The test for conscientious objection, not even mentioned in the Senate, was made narrower, and the Justice Department was directed to give priority to draft-law violations, another subject not mentioned in the Senate bill. When Kennedy learned of all this, he exploded. He decided to do something foolish—or at least unpromising: challenge Russell on the floor.

In 1967 time was running out for the Russells of the Senate. Since that cloture vote in 1964, power had been flowing away from the conservatives. It was a persistent tide but a slow one. Aloof from it all, Russell still tried to run his committee as he had always run it. When the conference ended, House members made up a report on the outcome and submitted it to the full House. Russell disdained such a procedure. Senators who wanted to know what had occurred to their bill had to read the House conferees' statement. On June 12 Russell prepared to call the conference report up. The next day the Senate was scheduled to begin debating a resolution of censure of Senator Thomas Dodd of Connecticut. No one knew how long that might last. The draft law was scheduled to expire on June 30. So, said Russell, the Senate had to act on June 12 or risk expiration of the law. Kennedy believed a somewhat longer debate was needed on the conference report. He wanted to wait till the following week to begin it, interrupting the Dodd censure debate if necessary. No, said Russell.

Russell not only didn't see the need for a lengthy debate, he saw no need for *any* debate. The chairman of the Armed Services Committee was not accustomed to explaining, much less defending, his decisions. "Mr. President," he said to the presiding officer, "I move the adoption of the conference report." Kennedy asked if Russell planned to discuss the conference report. Russell said he had prepared some remarks, which he would make after the Senate voted. "I would like to discuss the conference report prior to the time that the Senate acts," Kennedy said.

So a smouldering Russell told the Senate at length what was in the conference report, and why he felt it should be approved. On item after item he said he preferred the Senate bill *"but"*—his true preference for the Senate version came through as almost nil. When Russell had finished, Kennedy arose and said, "Mr. President, the conference report . . . does not in my opinion reflect the careful judgment and concern for fairness that the Senate-passed bill did. I believe that acceptance of the conference report will constitute an abrogation of responsibility by the Senate, and I intend to vote against it. I urge my fellow senators to do similarly." Thus began a lively debate back and forth between Kennedy and Russell, with only a few senators supporting Kennedy. One who did was Oregon's Wayne Morse, who proposed a delay so that senators could study the report. Russell acidly remarked that Morse was opposed to the bill, to the draft, and to the war in Vietnam, implying that his request for a delay was made in bad faith. Another senator who supported Kennedy at that point was Vermont's George Aiken. A Republican, and no maverick like Morse, he did not draw Russell's acid, only his scorn. To Aiken's request for a compromise, Russell replied, "No. . . . I do not propose to gamble with the security of this country!"

But Russell reserved his most biting comments for Kennedy, charging him with doing nothing but reintroducing statements already considered and rejected. Kennedy gave as good as he got. Once he was interrupted in his reading by Russell saying he was reading from the House conferees' report. Kennedy: "The senator is correct. That is why I think it is so helpful for us to have a chance to consider and discuss the report on the floor. We do not have a written explanation of it by the Senate conferees."

Finally Majority Leader Mansfield got Russell to agree to wait two days before forcing a vote. Russell returned to his office burning and planning. Two days later he subjected Kennedy to a solid defeat. Kennedy proposed that the draft be extended for a year instead of four. In a year Congress could come up with a good bill, he said. Russell responded that that was not a possible parliamentary procedure, since both original House and Senate versions of the bill had been four-year extensions. Furthermore, said Russell, he would not serve as a conferee if the parliamentarian ruled against him. The full Senate knew that Russell was a master parliamentarian, and that it was folly to vote for a procedure that Russell would then challenge. You might end up making an enemy of Russell and still losing on the issue, even if you won a majority. So by 72–23, with most Democratic liberals falling in line behind Russell, the Senate approved the conference report.

Russell's reaction to this challenge was interesting. On the one hand, he was impressed by Kennedy's good staff preparation and mastery of the subject. On the other, he was outraged by the challenge to the way he conducted business. On the Monday that Kennedy won the two-day delay, Russell went back to his office in a book-throwing mood, determined to teach Kennedy a lesson. On Wednesday, after the final debate and vote, he met Kennedy in the cloakroom and praised him for his efforts on the floor, remarking that he knew they would be fighting over the draft for years to come. Kennedy agreed with that. Before the debate began he told Dun Gifford, the aide who had worked on the draft issue, that he thought it would take years of constant chipping away to get the reform accepted by the military establishment, as represented by Russell and Senator John Stennis and, more especially, by the senior members of the House Armed Services Committee. Kennedy also decided then that it was not an effort that could be left to the Russells and Stennises and the Armed Services Committee.

In 1968, Kennedy again introduced a bill calling for broad reform of the draft. Nothing came of it. In early 1969 he tried it again—new Congress and new president. President Nixon had campaigned for draft reform. His long-term goal was an all-volunteer army, which Kennedy opposed, but his short-term goal—i.e., for the duration of the Vietnamese war—was reform of the existing system. He favored the lottery, with youngest called first. His proposal for a change in the 1967 law to allow him to institute a lottery went to the Hill in 1969, for hearings before the House and the Senate Armed Services Committee. The former held three days of hearings, beginning on September 30. The latter held one day of hearings, on November 14. In between Senator Kennedy held seven days of hearings on the draft with his Judiciary Committee Subcommittee on Administrative Practice and Procedure. He had become chairman that year. Kennedy interpreted the mandate of the subcommittee broadly. His hearings were not concerned with the legislative proposal before Congress, but with whether or not mere changes in the Selective Service System's rules and regulations could not result in what he called a "more fair, more certain, less disruptive" draft. The House hearings brought forth only Defense Department officials, General Hershey, and members of the House to testify. The Senate Armed Services hearings heard even fewer witnesses. Kennedy called before his subcommittee not only Administration officials but critics of the draft from universities and other private citizens who made a good case for a reform much more substantial than the President was proposing.

Kennedy tried to force congressional action on his own broader proposal. The House passed the President's bill on October 30, and the Senate was prepared to—if those who wanted more were willing to go along. That was a big "if." Senator Kennedy, Majority Leader Mansfield, and many other senators who wanted the more sweeping reform thought of holding the lottery proposal hostage to the Kennedy reform package. Senator Stennis, who had succeeded Senator Russell as chairman of Armed Services (Russell having switched to Appropriations chairman), threatened to kill all reforms if he did not get assurances that only the lottery legislation would be considered on the floor. It looked like a game of Chicken. But Kennedy, at the request of Yale president Kingman Brewster, Jr., who had become a leading campus spokesman for draft reform, agreed not to make a floor fight of it at the time, *if* Stennis would agree to begin hearings early the following year on comprehensive reform. Stennis was willing to make a deal and got the full committee to approve such a trade-off. The Senate passed the bill on November 19. On December 1, for the first time since World War II, a lottery was held for draftees. Kennedy had achieved part of his 1966 goal.

As it turned out, the Senate Armed Services Committee took no action in 1970, at the request of President Nixon, but Kennedy and the reform-the-draft movement kept the pressure on both the Congress and the President. One more goal was achieved that year. On February 3 Kennedy's Administrative Practices Subcommittee, over the objection of its senior Republican, Strom Thurmond of South Carolina, the subcommittee issued a report, "The Selective Service System: Its Operations, Practices and Procedures." The report included a long list of recommendations "[to] serve as a blueprint for action by the Administration." Among these were an end to all deferments except hardship ones, abolishment of state and local quotas, changes in the representativeness and training of board members, and a number of technical changes to give registrants more rights before the board. On April 23, the President abolished occupational deferments by executive order, and asked Congress to give him the authority to end undergraduate deferments and to do away with local and state quotas. His request was put aside by Congress until the following year, when the basic draft law would have to be extended again.

That year there was a lengthy debate that was snarled and complicated by antiwar senators, who used the draft-extension act as a vehicle for a statement calling for an end of the war in Vietnam. Much of the Senate debate on the bill was thus concerned with foreign policy, not the Selective Service System itself. Nonetheless, the 1971 draft law that emerged called for wholesale reforms in the draft, including many of those Kennedy had been interested in since 1966. The new law gave the president discretionary authority over student deferments and eliminated local quotas, to name but two proposals on the AdPrac subcommittee list. Also, and this was very much a personal victory for Kennedy, the new law provided registrants with the right to appear personally before a quorum of a draft board, accompanied by a lawyer and witnesses, and to require a record of a board's adverse decision. These recommendations were also on the AdPrac list. Neither the House nor the Senate Armed Services Committee wrote such rights into the 1971 bill. Kennedy tried to add the section to the bill on the floor, failing the first time on a roll-call vote but succeeding the second. Senate conferees managed to keep the language in the final version of the act. A number of other Kennedy floor amendments were also accepted, most of them not controversial. Actually, as the final vote on the draft-law extension showed (298–108 in the House, 55–30 in the Senate), drastically reforming the Selective Service System was not that controversial anymore. In an interview in 1974 Kennedy looked back on the draft-reform fight as one he believed he had been instrumental in winning—or helping win—by keeping specific recommendations before the public and the Senate. In this case, as in so many others, it is difficult to assert with certainty whether the individual senator or the mass movement received the most nourishment from the other. Perhaps there would have been draft reform by 1971 with or without Ted Kennedy. It is safe to say, I believe, that if there had been no draft-reform advocate who was chairman of a subcommittee like AdPrac, and who was willing to use the subcommittee imaginatively (as he had used a Labor and Public Welfare subcommittee in the same cause before he became AdPrac chairman), the full record of draft-law inadequacies and draft-board failures and abuses would never have come before the Senate. No such record was developed by either of the Armed Services Committees, or even by the presidential commissions that studied the draft. *Someone* had to use the legislative tools at hand to force the issue, both in the arena of public opinion and congressional determination. If that someone had not seen the legislative possibilities and had not been outraged by the inequities he saw in the draft's impact—and if that same someone had not been willing to take on first Richard Russell and then John Stennis—and if that someone had not been viewed as a potential rival by President Nixon, then I suspect there might very well not have been any meaningful reform of the draft by 1971. The only "someone" around in the late 1960s who fit that description was Senator Edward Kennedy.

Just as he was criticized for attacking the war in Vietnam obliquely with his efforts in behalf of refugee problems, so Kennedy was accused of using his effort for draft reform as a way to undermine American support for the war aims. Dun Gifford, the legislative aide most involved with this particular effort, agrees in part that Kennedy was aware of what he was doing. "It was a chance to raise the issue of was the war, itself, equitable, in terms of its impact on America. What's wrong with that?" Kennedy made no attempt to duck the charge. In fact, he seemed to cultivate it. While the war in Vietnam was still raging, a number of military manpower reformers began to push for an end to the draft and the substitution of an all-volunteer army for the civilian-professional mix. Kennedy opposed this, saying in testimony before the Senate Armed Services Committee in 1971, "I frankly do not want to insulate middle- and upper-class Americans from the horrors of war. I have grave doubts whether the pressures for deescalation of the Indochina war would ever have built up to its current level if young men from every social background were not threatened with service in that war." He said the concept was aimed at getting "poor men's sons to fight rich men's wars." Whenever he spoke to youthful male audiences in that period, Kennedy repeated these arguments. Sometimes he went further. Once or twice he attacked an army proposal for a $3000 bonus for volunteers for combat duty as "a blood bonus . . . a bounty." He had a favorite device he used in such settings. He would ask how many in the audience believed in the all-volunteer concept. Almost every hand would go up. Then Kennedy would ask, "How many of you would join an all-volunteer army?" Almost every hand would go down.

Kennedy said, grudgingly, that he would support an all-volunteer army in peacetime; and when President Nixon reduced draft calls to zero in 1973 and let the 1971 draft-act extension die without a replacement, the senator turned his attention to another facet of the problem—what to do about those youths whose disapproval of the war effort had led them to avoid the draft by illegal means, or who had gone into the military service and then deserted.

Kennedy had been concerned about amnesty for such youths from the start of his involvement with the draft-reform issue. Gifford was a strong believer in amnesty. He, with the support of other young staff members, forcefully brought to Kennedy's attention their belief that he should be working toward that goal. This was at a time (1968) when almost no public figures were speaking to the question. Kennedy agreed to go along to the extent of leaving in an early draft-reform proposal a Gifford recommendation that the attorney general and the Department of Defense study the history of amnesty. That led to headlines in Boston and elsewhere: TED FOR AMNESTY. That in turn led to a great deal of mail criticizing Kennedy for his assumed stand. *That* led to Kennedy's becoming upset with Gifford. When he cooled down, he told Gifford, "This is a good lesson in public affairs. We did the right thing. I'm glad we did. But you have to understand that I knew this would happen to me at some point if I did what you kept proposing." To Gifford the "lesson" was "that speechwriters never have to speak to the VFW in Boston. He was really saying, 'Think beyond your research, your desks.' After that I did."

Early in 1972, Kennedy's Administrative Practice and Procedure Subcommittee held hearings on amnesty. The year before, amnesty legislation had been introduced by Senator Robert Taft, among others, but the Senate grandees weren't having any. Kennedy's hearings were not related to legislation, and ranking Republican Strom Thurmond of South Carolina made it clear at the outset that he would

object to any attempt by Kennedy to get into the Armed
Services Committee's jurisdiction. Kennedy and Thurmond
got off to a bad start. Kennedy referred to the amnesty
granted Southerners after the Civil War as compassion
toward people who had been guilty of treason. Thurmond,
sitting next to Kennedy, exploded at that characterization—
"My grandfather was no traitor!"—and vowed to follow
Kennedy throughout the South if he ever ran for president,
telling Southern audiences what Kennedy had said about
their forefathers.

David Harris, husband of folk singer and youth-cul-
ture heroine Joan Baez, appeared as an early witness. Harris
had been to jail for refusing to accept military service. He
expressed the prevailing antiwar view of the draft and the
Indochina war, to the hearty applause of the audience in the
hearing room. But that audience was predominantly young
and dovish. A more serious challenge to Kennedy followed,
one that was somewhat threatening to Kennedy politically.
The next witness was a Kennedy constituent, Martin Kelley
of Dorchester, whose son Daniel had been killed in Vietnam
in 1968, while serving with the First Cavalry. Kelley spoke
for what was still a majority of Americans when he bitterly
condemned Harris's views and the committee's purpose:
"Now the purpose of this committee . . . was to decide
whether or not we would grant blanket, total amnesty. I
would suggest . . . that this committee would be better engaged in suggesting and designing a memorial to the over
fifty thousand military men who died believing in this country's cause. Now in Vietnam men are being wounded; they
are being killed in Vietnam; and we sit here with stinking
empty platitudes."

And then the unkindest cut:

"When I hear the empty phrases of a Fulbright, or a
Mr. McGovern, with the turnabout of yourself, Mr. Chairman, when for three years John F. Kennedy stood in the
White House—John F. Kennedy who talked about bearing
any burden, paying any price, et cetera. These words led
men to join the Army, to accept the draft, and to fight for
their country. And now with a very casual statement, 'Well,
we were wrong; these draft dodgers are right.' . . . That is
all I have to say." It was a poignant and painful moment.

Kennedy, whose own mail in this period was running twenty to one against any granting of unconditional amnesty, could only thank Mr. Kelley for his statement and go on from there to provide a forum for others with different views. For whatever blame Kennedy assigned to the bear-any-burden-pay-any-price rhetoric of Camelot, he had come to a conclusion that saw the real unfairness from exactly the opposite perspective of that of Mr. Kelley. At the hearings, Kennedy put it this way: "For those of us who have condemned the war as an outrage, it is difficult to conceive of denying amnesty to those young men who saw the things we now see, but saw them sooner and who did the only thing they could. Faced with the dilemma of violating the Selective Service law or violating what to them were moral imperatives against participating in a war they saw as evil, they chose prison or exile."

Kennedy never proposed legislation himself, but he told questioners in this period that he favored blanket unconditional amnesty for all youths who refused to be drafted on grounds of antiwar conscience. He said he favored amnesty for deserters if, on a case-by-case basis, conscience was proved to be the determining factor in their desertion. The reason he gave for not introducing or working for amnesty legislation was that he knew it had no chance to become law in the early 1970's. He did contribute to creating the public opinion which eventually, in the fall of 1974, allowed President Ford to announce a clemency program. He did that beginning with the 1972 hearings. Those had been the first congressional hearings on amnesty. They gave Harris and other, more influential advocates of amnesty, such as historian Henry Steele Commager, their best forum to date for telling the American people why amnesty ought to be considered.

Nor was Ford's 1974 declaration the end of it.

After President Ford's announcement of a limited clemency plan, a number of antiwar groups and individual critics of the war, including Senator Kennedy, expressed numerous objections. Kennedy applauded the President for "courage and compassion," but urged him to be more lenient. Basically what Ford proposed was a program under which deserters and draft evaders could turn themselves in and serve "alternate service" as a means of "earned reentry" into American society. Kennedy had written Ford a private letter before the presidential decision, urging that wherever conscience was the motive for the young man's act, prompt amnesty should be granted, not earned clemency. However, even the President's program prompted outrage from conservative Republicans and many Democrats. Kennedy evidently decided that the political situation was such that the President had gone as far as he could go. So he set out to make sure the presidential program was as helpful as possible to the antiwar young. In December 1974, Kennedy held two days of hearings by his Administrative Practice and Procedure Subcommittee, opening them by saying, "Whether or not we are satisfied with the scope of the nature of the present 'earned reentry' program announced by President Ford on September 16, that program is in operation. For those who want to participate, the program should be publicized, the procedures made more equitable, the terms clearer, the results fairer." Then, even before the hearings began, he made what he termed "preliminary recommendations." One of those was for the compilation of a "final" list of individuals in jeopardy. Once that was done the literally tens of thousands of draft resisters who did not know whether or not they were sought by the Justice Department could find out and come home, either without fear of harrassment or to the certainty of a trial. A second recommendation was that the President extend the deadline for youths to apply for clemency. (The original deadline was January 31.) Kennedy pointed out that there had been a light response in the first three months, probably due to lack of publicity and uncertainty, and urged a postponement. The following month the President did postpone the deadline and the Justice Department did publish a final complete list of individuals either under indictment or investigation for Selective Service registration violations. Both actions, plus increased publicity, led to a greatly increased participation in the then faltering clemency program.

Edward Kennedy—like his two senatorial brothers before him—has always had a strong following among young citizens. Youthful Americans form a constituency of sorts for Kennedys. In Edward's case part of that is, of course, derived from the glamour and tragedy of his family and life. But more of it, probably, derives from his *service* to that special constituency. He has behaved at times as if he were senator from the state of the young. His long years invested in reforming the draft, an issue of direct special interest to young men, certainly won him points with them. So, too, did his stand on amnesty. There have been a number of minor, less well-known legislative maneuvers of this sort: Once he held up a conference report on an education bill because he felt the student-loan procedures were more in bankers' interest than students'. But the Kennedy effort in the Senate that outshines all others as a bow to youth was the winning of the law that allows eighteen-year-olds to vote. That law *created* the constituency of the young—and it might very well not have become law when it did—or at all—if it had not been for Kennedy's initiative.

In January 1970, Kennedy listened to a proposal by a new legislative aide, Carey Parker. Parker came to Kennedy from the Justice Department and a clerkship to Supreme Court Justice Potter Stewart. His idea was to lower the voting age for federal elections from twenty-one years to eighteen—and to do it by statute. Most legal opinion was to the effect that such a goal would have to be reached by constitutional amendment. There was at that time a resolution before the Senate Judiciary Committee to lower the voting age in federal elections. Hearings were scheduled on the resolution beginning in February. The idea of lowering the voting age appealed to Kennedy, and he was interested in doing it the fast way, by statute. He might have lost his bid in 1965 to ban the poll tax by statute, but he had not lost faith in the idea. He remembered that while he was losing in 1965, Robert Kennedy and Jacob Javits had fastened to the same civil-rights bill an amendment that forbade denying the right to vote to citizens who could not speak English but who met the state's literacy requirements in another language. He also remembered that in 1966 the Supreme Court had upheld the voting-rights act and had sustained the suit against the poll tax that Kennedy had forced the government to file.

Kennedy asked Parker to put together a memorandum to serve as a basis for his own testimony on the constitutional amendment. Parker hit pay dirt with his early research. First, Paul Freund of Harvard Law School, a respected and nonradical scholar, told him he not only agreed with the proposal, but had said so in a speech sometime before. That was important, in that it showed that Freund was not merely endorsing the plan at Kennedy's request. Also, Harvard's Archibald Cox, who had been solicitor general under John F. Kennedy, provided an article he had written in support of lowering the voting age by statute —three years before the Kennedy request came. Armed with this and Parker's list of Supreme Court decisions from 1965 and 1969, Kennedy circulated a seven-page letter outlining the precedents and his arguments to his fellow senators. That was on February 23, 1970. The letter was leaked to *The New York Times* and created a heated public debate out of what up to then had been a low-key private one.

The principal reason for this heat was that Kennedy had decided that the best way to get his statute enacted was to attach it as a floor amendment to the 1970 act then before the Senate that would extend for five more years the 1965 voting-rights act. The immediate reaction was (1) yes, the arguments in favor of lowering the voting age by statute are impressively and imaginatively marshaled, but (2) you're jeopardizing the extension of the 1965 act. It was 1965 all over again. Kennedy found himself up against some of the same liberal, procivil-rights allies he had fought in the poll-tax-ban battle. The Leadership Conference on Civil Rights implored him to drop it. In late February, after listening to a specific appeal from Clarence Mitchell, Jr., the NAACP lobbyist, Senator Philip Hart, the principal co-sponsor with Senator Hugh Scott of the bill, and others, Kennedy said publicly that he might agree to hold back on his plan to add the eighteen-year-old amendment. There was a filibuster going in the Senate, and in the House, which had already passed an extension of the 1965 act, Judiciary Chairman Emanuel Celler was expressing strong objections to the Kennedy proposal. With his course of action still in doubt, even in his own mind, Kennedy flew to Europe for a meeting of North Atlantic Treaty Organization parliamentarians and to deliver a lecture in Ireland. Then a funny thing happened. On February 28 Senate Majority Leader Mike Mansfield and Senator Warren Magnuson of Washington were driving home from the Senate together. Both had long been interested in seeing eighteen-year-olds voting. Magnuson had tried unsuccessfully to get his state to lower its voting age when he served in the legislature nearly forty years before. He had been impressed by the Kennedy memo. "Mike, you know Kennedy has a pretty good idea," he was later quoted as saying. "Why don't you and I get together and introduce it as an amendment to Scott-Hart? Ted's in Ireland, but what do you think?"

"I'll think it over," Mansfield is supposed to have replied. The next day he said to Magnuson, "I think your idea's a good one. I'll introduce it in all three names." Mansfield instructed one of his aides to call Kennedy's office to make sure he wanted his name on the bill. He had, after all, been quoted as saying he might hold back out of deference to Senator Hart and the civil-rights lobby. Parker complained to Mansfield's aide, Charles Ferris, that this was Kennedy's project to begin with, and that if Mansfield now wanted to join him, the proper way to go about it was for him to wait until Kennedy returned, then the two of them could talk it over. With Mansfield and Magnuson behind the amendment, the proponents stood a good chance of overwhelming the opposition. Parker naturally wanted it to be the Kennedy-Mansfield-Magnuson amendment, not the Mansfield-Magnuson-Kennedy amendment. But Ferris said Mansfield couldn't wait. The amendment was going to be offered that day. "We're going. Yes or no?" is the way Parker remembers Ferris's words. Parker said "Yes," and put his boss's name on the amendment. The amendment slipped quickly and easily through the Senate; few senators wanted to be on record as opposing eighteen-year-old voters if there were going to be any.

The obstacles in the House melted away. If the eighteen-year-old provision was unconstitutional, the Supreme Court would get rid of it, Representative Celler told the House. Since the law would not go into effect until after the 1970 election, House members found that assurance acceptable. Kennedy played a role in the successful lobbying effort, lending his office staff and his direct lines to Harvard scholars, and, most important of all, helping to convince that non-Harvard Bostonian, John McCormack, to endorse the proposal. "Nothing would make John McCormack happier," the aged retiring Speaker eventually told the House, "than to see this resolution adopted." It was adopted. Nixon, who had opposed it, signed it, saying that it would surely be thrown out in court. Ted Kennedy then went one extra mile with the effort to enfranchise this new constituency. Rebuffed by the Senate when he proposed that the body hire Paul Freund to represent it in defending the law in court (Nixon's Justice Department did not seem eager to make the best case), Kennedy accepted an appeal from a youth group to present an *amicus curia* argument in the District of Columbia District Court.

That court upheld the Kennedy view. So did the Supreme Court, in a curiously split decision. Four justices concluded that Congress had the right to lower the voting age by statute in federal, state, and local elections. Four others (including Parker's former boss, Potter Stewart) ruled that Congress could *not* lower the voting age by statute, even for federal elections. And Hugo Black ruled that Congress could lower the voting age for federal elections only. Thus, by a 5–4 ruling, part of the law was upheld. The states quickly fell in line (in order not to have to maintain two voting lists), and by June of 1971 a constitutional amendment had been adopted lowering the voting age to eighteen for all elections. The Supreme Court ruling was a justification of sorts for Kennedy's original view. At the start he had favored limiting the statute to federal elections. This probably was based less on legal and constitutional philosophy than on family loyalty. John Kennedy had been a states'-righter on local election laws.

So the eighteen-year-olds got the vote. It was a near thing. If eighty-two-year-old Hugo Black had not voted the way he did, that part of the 1970 Voting Rights Act would have been thrown out. Or if Congress had waited a year before passing the statute, there would have been no Black on the court; he resigned before the next term of the court started. If Congress had waited, there is some doubt that it would have passed a law later. There is even some doubt that a constitutional amendment would have been ratified. Public opinion was not pro-youth in 1970. The year before the Congress voted, three states had turned down proposals to lower the voting age. In 1970's fall elections there were referenda to lower the voting age in fifteen states—and in ten the voters turned the proposition down.

It is not too much to say that if Kennedy had not written and circulated that letter and legal memorandum, and if senators Magnuson and Mansfield had not been spurred to act by it, and if Kennedy had not lobbied in the House and Senate for the bill, eighteen-year-olds would not be voting yet.

8. SENATOR FOR THE UNDERDOG

There is no more visible senator than Edward Kennedy.
Almost everything he gets involved in leads to headlines.
Yet what he does in a substantive way often remains invisible in the shadow of his personality or his behavior.

A famous case history in this regard is the 1969 expedition to Alaska. Robert Kennedy developed an interest in Indian affairs when he was in the Senate. In 1967 he became chairman of a special subcommittee on Indian education. His primary interest was the Bureau of Indian Affairs schools, though only about 30 percent of Indian children attended such schools. He planned a subcommittee visit to Alaska, where Indian poverty was widespread, in the spring of 1968. This was canceled because of the assassination of Martin Luther King, Jr. When Robert Kennedy was slain, Senator Wayne Morse was made chairman of the subcommittee, which was scheduled to expire in March of 1969 anyway. But in February the Senate extended the subcommittee's life until the following November. Edward Kennedy was named chairman, and in April he led a delegation of senators to Alaska for a firsthand look at Eskimo schools and other facilities the federal government provided. A subcommittee staff memorandum proposing that the trip be used as sort of a media event, dramatizing the poverty of the Eskimos, was leaked to the press. Because it was a Kennedy event, too, a lot of reporters flew out to Alaska with the senators. All but one of the Republican senators on the trip quickly dropped out of the tour, charging that it was an effort to publicize Kennedy, then still a presumptive presidential candidate, not Eskimo poverty problems.

There was plenty of publicity, but it wasn't all good. What emerged in the press reports of that first really national *senatorial* activity since he had become the heir apparent was a very unsenatorial, very un-Kennedyish character. Kennedy was portrayed in some journalistic accounts as a heavy-drinking, sophomoric junketeer, alternately jocular and morose, chanting "Eskimo Power." But he came back to Washington and began working for legislation and bureaucratic change that would improve the lives of the Indians in Alaska and elsewhere. In the next five years he was responsible for as much federal government activity on behalf of Indians as any but perhaps half-a-dozen senators, all of them Westerners with large Indian constituencies. The special subcommittee expired at the end of 1969 and was not extended again, but he simply transferred the responsibility for working in behalf of Indian interests to his Administrative Practice and Procedure Subcommittee. Today only the Interior Committee and its subcommittees are as much involved in Indian matters as that subcommittee.

The expiring Indian-education subcommittee made a long list of legislative recommendations in 1969, many of which were eventually carried out. Meanwhile there were other successes. In 1969 Kennedy led the fight on the Senate floor to restore funds for Indian education that had been in the budget but were cut out in the Appropriations Committee. The largest amount was for kindergartens in public schools serving Indians. The Senate accepted this Kennedy amendment, and most of the money was left in the final version of the bill approved in the conference between House and Senate. A more direct result of the Alaska trip was a bill Kennedy and Senator Ted Stevens of Alaska introduced shortly after they returned from Alaska. (Stevens was the only Republican senator who stuck it out the whole three-day trip.) The bill called for the construction of three water-treatment plants in Alaskan Indian villages. Use of polluted water was blamed for a high incidence of inner-ear diseases among Eskimo children. The bill became law the following year, and eventually two of the plants were built.

Kennedy's Administrative Practice Subcommittee held hearings related to Indian affairs in 1970, 1971, 1972, 1973, and 1974. Most of these were concerned with the various government agencies' handling of Indian rights in the area of natural resources. Kennedy aides give the hearings credit for changes in personnel at the top level of the Land Division at the Interior Department, for creation of a new Indian Water Rights office there, for a good, strong message and program on behalf of Indians by President Nixon, for the decision by the Justice Department to go to court in behalf of the Paiutes, who were involved in a dispute over resources, and for the decision by the Administration to cede to the Yakima Indians 21,000 acres in Washington state the government originally disputed their claim to. (I asked a non-Kennedy-staff expert on Indian affairs on Capitol Hill to comment on a longer list of accomplishments claimed for Kennedy. He checked each off with such comments as "Doubt if they can take full claim for that"; "They helped but Jackson led the fight"; "The Native American Rights Fund is more responsible for getting that lobbied through"; and on down the list. At the end, he said, "But Kennedy has done more for Indians than almost any other member of Congress, certainly more than any other Easterner. He is known by the Indians, too, to be a champion of the poor and downtrodden. They are part of his constituency, and they know it."

They seem to. When armed Indians took over the reservation at Wounded Knee, South Dakota, they first called for senators Kennedy and William Fulbright, chairman of the Foreign Relations Committee, to come there and discuss treaty rights. Later they got senators McGovern and Abourezk of South Dakota—and Tom Susman, Kennedy's chief counsel at Administrative Practice. Kennedy has been made an honorary Paiute, has been awarded an eagle shield by the Yakimas, and was asked (and agreed) to let the "Red Raiders," who are young members of the National Indian Youth Council, use his office while conducting their investigation into "if America and its government really give a damn about American Indians." They knew Kennedy gave a damn.

Giving a damn, being a symbolic champion and articulator of tribal desires, being a goad to bureaucrats and presidents, are not the only tests of a senator's commitment and effectiveness. Legislation is another. Kennedy has been able to push through to law a number of bills and amendments important to Indians. In 1970 Kennedy fought for an amendment to the federal manpower-training and public-service-employment bill to have set aside 10 percent of the authorized funds—that is 10 percent of $9.5 billion for three years—for aiding Indians, who had a chronic high-unemployment rate. The bill as finally passed earmarked somewhat less money, based on Indian population as a proportion of the total low-income population, but President Nixon vetoed the bill anyway, and the Senate upheld him. In 1971 Kennedy sought and obtained a law making Indian tribes eligible sponsors of public-service employment. In 1972 Kennedy's aid-to-Indian-education bill became law—the culmination of the hearings that had begun under Robert Kennedy on the old special subcommittee. Over the objections of the Administration, Kennedy steered through to passage a bill that greatly increased federal aid to Indian children in public schools. Robert had been criticized for focusing his attention on the 30 percent in Bureau of Indian Affairs schools. His critics said he didn't want to offend powerful political figures in Western states who might be embarrassed by a spotlight on the poor records of state education programs. Edward shifted the emphasis to the other 70 percent, but at the same time called for improving BIA schools. His 1972 bill, which passed the Senate in 1971 but was sidetracked for a year, finally landing on the statute books as a separate title in an omnibus aid-to-education bill, was the first aid-to-education bill for Indians in over thirty years.

The bill authorized federal aid to meet special needs of Indian children in "impacted school districts" (those whose student population is increased by the presence of federal employees or wards); authorized grants for programs to improve educational opportunity for Indians; authorized grants for pilot and demonstration projects for adult-education programs for Indians; and created an Office for Indian Education and a National Advisory Council on Indian Education. Legislatively that achievement was undoubtedly Kennedy's most impressive in behalf of Indians. There was no House Indian-education bill in 1971 or 1972. After the Senate passed it in 1971 a procedural complication forced a second Senate vote in 1972. What had been a separate piece of legislation became an amendment to an omnibus bill. That bill went to conference, where Kennedy and Senator Walter Mondale prevailed on House conferees to accept the totally new (to their bill) title. So Kennedy, picking up another family fallen standard, really walked the bill through Congress from beginning to end, using committee resources and personal aggressiveness in an imaginative way to win enactment of legislation that very probably would not now be law if it had not been for his personal commitment.

Naturally all of this activity has ruffled some feathers. The Interior committees of House and Senate were not accustomed to having such aggressive "outsiders" dealing with Indian matters, traditionally their own concern. Members and particularly staff of those committees have often found themselves in a relationship with Kennedy and his staff that was characterized by tension. At least once Kennedy pressured Senator Henry Jackson to take an Indian-related bill back to Interior after he thought he was through with it to consider changes Kennedy was willing to make a public complaint over. (That was the Indian Self-Determination and Educational Reform Act of 1973.) At least once Kennedy won changes in language in a Jackson bill in the Interior Committee, by proposing those changes in a detailed letter to all members of the committee the day the hearings opened, following that up with a floor speech, then making sure that Indian lobbying organizations were aware of his proposals (many of which had been urged on him by Indian groups). That was the Indian Health Care Improvement Act of 1974.

A second minority group that Kennedy has been associated with is the Chicanos, Mexican Americans, led by Cesar Chavez. Kennedy has lent them his visibility and encouragement, his sympathy and his energy, his political clout, rather than his talents as a drafter of legislation. Most Chicanos are agricultural workers in the Southwest and California. Kennedy immortalized his affection for and relationship to the Chicanos in his speech to the 1972 Democratic National Convention, which he began, "Fellow lettuce boycotters. . . ." That boycott had become the test of one's commitment to the party's left wing's alliance with the farm workers.

Robert Kennedy was the most outspoken and ardent supporter of the Chicanos and their charismatic leader Chavez in 1968. Edward Kennedy's truly close association is often dated from the spring of 1969, when he went to Calexico, California, at the invitation of Chavez, who was on a fast. The invitation was something of a problem for Kennedy. He was on his own then, for the first time, and the doubts and questions he had had upon Robert's assassination the year before were beginning to fade away. He had been elected Senate whip (next chapter), and was considered the almost certain choice of his party three years later for the presidential nomination. On his own and his own man. Many of his friends and staff advised him not to go to Calexico. "It will look like you're trading on Bobby's memory," one said. "You *will* be trading on Bobby's memory," said another. (In fact, Kennedy had helped the United Farm Workers out two years before, answering a plea for help from organizers in Texas who were having trouble with the police. Kennedy and other members of the Labor and Public Welfare Committee responded to pleas for hearings in the area. So in 1969 it was not just trading on Bobby's name.) The deadline for Kennedy's leaving Washington to do what Chavez wanted was 5 P.M. on a Sunday. On Friday most members of the staff thought it had been decided that there would be no visit. Ted and some friends, including Dun Gifford, were playing touch football at Hickory Hill that Sunday afternoon. In a huddle, Kennedy suddenly said to Gifford, "Dun, I'm going to California. You better go inside and find out about the planes and all." And he went.

Since then Kennedy has been to other Chavez rallies in California, has designated staff to assist UFW lobbyists in Washington in drafting legislation, has lobbied with Democratic leaders in Western states against local and state legislation aimed at slowing down the UFW or otherwise inimical to the Chicanos' interests. He has also lobbied in the AFL-CIO in behalf of the UFW and against their organizing foe, the Teamsters. Kennedy went to the first UFW national convention in 1973 to deliver the keynote speech. ("The question is not whether the union will be victorious. The only question is, when the victory will come.") He has raised money for the farm workers, notably by appearing in a money-raising film about the tough fight for union recognition and better life for the farm workers.

"He has always been a friend," says Gilbert Padilla, a UFW representative in Washington. Dun Gifford explains this in terms of Kennedy's "incredible thing for the underdog." That and the family "thing" probably explain it. There may be political mileage in it—but there may not be. It can cut both ways, as is evident in the fact that California's two liberal Democratic senators, John Tunney and Alan Cranston, alike in thought and feeling on so many issues, often disagree on the farm workers.

"It is eerie, Kennedy's appeal in the black community," says Clarence Mitchell, Jr., the chief Washington lobbyist of the National Association for the Advancement of Colored People. "When he speaks to a black audience, people stand on chairs, the help comes out of the kitchen to listen, everybody wants to be in his presence, to touch him. It isn't due to his work. They don't know about that. It is a mystique." It is a family mystique. Black audiences who hear Kennedy almost always hear an introduction by a black political or cultural leader in which the trinity of Martin Luther King, Jr., Robert Kennedy, and John F. Kennedy is invoked. So, as in so many areas of activity, Edward Kennedy is the beneficiary of the family legend. Yet in this case (as in others) Edward's record is probably better than his brothers', his contribution probably greater. Both John and Robert were authentic champions of civil rights for blacks in the early and mid-1960s, but both were also very much aware of their need to go only moderately fast toward their goals. In the summer and fall of 1963, even as conservative Southern senators led by Richard Russell slowly brought government toward a halt, Martin Luther King and other black activists pushed the Kennedy government more and more toward intervention on their behalf.

Edward, in fact, was the only Kennedy who planned to go to the Lincoln Memorial in August 1963 to speak to the assembled black and white members of the March on Washington. He had a speech prepared, but the President, nervous, vetoed his appearance. The following year, in his first major Senate speech not dealing with a Massachusetts issue, Kennedy called for enactment of the omnibus civil-rights bill. His voice broke when he referred to his slain brother's introduction of the bill. The following year was the year he forced the Justice Department to attack the poll tax in court.

Kennedy has had a moderately successful career in the Senate in getting his own bills related to civil rights or black causes passed, and in helping other liberal senators get their bills passed. Clarence Mitchell says that those audiences that react to the Kennedy mystique could just as well applaud him for his legislative work. "There are other senators who do more," Mitchell says, "Phil Hart and Hugh Scott. But Kennedy is one of the very best. He works at it. He gives his time. He will attend strategy meetings and lobby senators personally, once he sees the importance and feasibility of what we are after." Kennedy has a legislative assistant who devotes most of his time to the problems of blacks. He is Robert Bates, a black native of the District of Columbia, who handles black politics as well as social legislation of interest to blacks. He points to two Kennedy successes as typical of the kind of unsung work the Massachusetts senator has been doing. One is the 1971 bill co-sponsored by Senator Tunney that provides federal grants to educate blacks about sickle cell anemia, a disease peculiar to the race. Tunney had pushed for a bill for the District of Columbia alone. He and Kennedy joined in seeking a bill of national application. A Kennedy subcommittee held hearings and a law eventually resulted. The year before, Kennedy and Representative William Fitts-Ryan of New York had introduced and led the effort for a bill providing grants for a program of testing slum children, usually black, for lead-based-paint poisoning.

Bates admits that Kennedy has had his failures. He

has tried unsuccessfully to get Congress to approve a constitutional amendment giving the District of Columbia's three-quarters of a million residents, most of whom are black, two senators and two representatives in Congress. That is not such a far-out proposal as some conservatives in Congress claim it is. President Nixon supported the amendment in 1970. Kennedy was a great deal more active than the President and most senators, however. Conservatives torpedoed the 1970 effort, allowing only a mild bill that gave the District a nonvoting delegate in Congress and home rule, something it had not had in nearly a century. The bill passed the House and was assured of Senate passage, until Kennedy put a "hold" on it. He threatened to kill that bill, since he knew that its passage would make it more difficult to get the constitutional amendment he wanted. But at the pleading of District officials, who wanted home rule as soon as possible, Kennedy relented. The same year he also thought of attaching his amendment to the equal-rights-for-women constitutional amendment scheduled for Senate action early in 1971, an idea that did him no good with the women's movement when rumors of it appeared in the press. In 1971 he lost by a lopsided margin when he sought to add the amendment to the constitutional amendment lowering the voting age in state and local elections to eighteen years. He continued to lead the fight, and in 1975 he, Maryland's Representative Gilbert Gude (from the District's well-to-do western suburbs), and the District's delegate in the House, Walter Fauntroy, united to make another try, expecting the heavily Democratic 94th Congress to support them.

But it is not so much legislation that Kennedy has provided his national black constituency, or even his vote, or even his staff.*

_____

*He provided his staff most notably in the two successful Senate vetoes of President Nixon's nominations of semisegregationist justices to the Supreme Court: Clement Haynsworth and G. Harrold Carswell. Senator Birch Bayh led the fight in Judiciary Committee and on the Senate floor and did the lion's share of the behind-the-scenes work in those efforts, but with substantial help from James Flug, who had just moved from Kennedy's Senate Office staff to become chief of staff at the Administrative Practice and Procedure Subcommittee, but was still a Kennedy man. Kennedy voted against Haynsworth, Carswell—and against William

The principal Kennedy benefice to black Americans has been his voice. Nowhere has his voice been more noticeable or consistent, despite changing currents of public opinion, than in the bitter national debate over busing. Kennedy, at times one of a small handful even among liberals, has stuck to his guns in defending the practice of desegregating schools by busing, even—in fact especially—after this became an issue of incandescent heat in his home town.

Busing as a tool to end desegregation was principally used in the South, beginning in the late 1960s as the full force of the 1964 Civil Rights Act finally came into play. For years Southern school officials had made black children ride buses for hours, in some cases, to reach second-rate schools miles beyond nearer, better schools reserved for whites. When federal bureaucrats and judges began requiring similarly long rides in some cases in order to end finally the old dual school systems in the South, white Dixie politicians let out a howl. But it was not until similar busing schemes began to be ordered in a few non-Southern cities that non-Southern politicians began to oppose the plan. To many, including long-time leaders of the fight for civil-rights laws, a court order in Michigan or California, though representing only a few thousand children, looked suspiciously like the handwriting on the wall. Southerners thought they were going to turn things around, as they began to find new and unexpected allies.

Edward Kennedy, though a consistent supporter of efforts aimed at desegregation, had come out *against* busing very early in his Senate career. He said in a letter to a Massachusetts resident in early 1965, "I do feel as a general rule that compulsory busing of children over long distances away from the schools in their neighborhoods is a poor ap-

Rehnquist, who was confirmed 68–16 despite strong opposition from the NAACP and other civil-rights-battles veterans. Thus Kennedy was three and three when it came to voting on Nixon appointees to the Supreme Court. (Kennedy's first open challenge to Nixon, by the way, came in early 1969, when he led his Administrative Practice Subcommittee into an investigation of the Defense and Transportation departments' policies relating to racial bias. The probe embarrassed Nixon by bringing out evidence that suggested that policies were changed in order to appease industrialists and contractors in the South.)

proach to the problem." By then it was becoming pretty evident that in many cases in the larger cities of the North and West balance could only be achieved in the short run by transportation. Boston, certainly, was such a city. Its blacks were concentrated for the most part in the Roxbury section, where school populations were almost 100 percent black. Neighboring Dorchester and South Boston were working-class white neighborhoods whose schools were almost all white in composition. The whites of Dorchester and South Boston wanted no part of busing of their children into Roxbury schools, or black children out of them.

Yet in 1965 Kennedy submerged the private opposition to busing he had manifested in the letter quoted above, and came out publicly and strongly for an end to "imbalance." That spring, on the day before the Massachusetts legislature was to take up a civil-rights bill, Kennedy came to Boston to call on the state government to withhold funds from schools in districts where segregation was allowed to continue. This led to a stinging attack on him by the emerging heroine of the antidesegregation forces, Louise Day Hicks of the Boston School Committee. In 1966 Kennedy endorsed the state's racial-imbalance law again, and during a hearing of the Senate Constitutional Rights Subcommittee he suddenly announced that he would favor withholding federal aid from schools that were, like Boston's, segregated in fact if not by law. The U.S. Commissioner of Education, Francis Keppel, tried to cut off aid to Chicago's schools because of de facto segregation, but he was promptly overruled by President Johnson responding to an outraged Mayor Richard Daley. Shortly thereafter Kennedy went to a civil-rights organization meeting in Jackson, Mississippi, to call for spending $2 billion a month, the then cost of the Vietnam War, to eliminate black slums in Chicago and Boston. President Johnson took this as an attack on *his* record in the field of civil rights and poverty. It upset him. He was getting used to sniping from Bobby by then, but not from Teddy.

In 1967 Kennedy urged several Bostonians who thought as he did to run for seats on the Boston School Committee. He also put his prestige on the line in opposing Mrs. Hicks, who was running for mayor against incumbent

Kevin White. Her campaign was based almost solely on the school issue. Kennedy attacked her indirectly during the primary, urging a vote "for candidates who deal with problems on the basis of experience and understanding, not from emotion and intolerance." It was a strong statement—and dismayed White. This was unusual interference in a primary election by an "outsider." It solidified Mrs. Hicks's support, and she and White ended up in the runoff. Kennedy, who has been criticized for his lack of involvement in Democratic party politics in Massachusetts before and since, met with White thereafter, helped him with staff and fund-raising, and White won.

That busing and desegregation were becoming national rather than regional issues was no longer in doubt by the beginning of the 1970s. President Nixon's own appointee as chief justice had ruled in a Charlotte, North Carolina, case that busing could be used to bring about desegregation— and there were cases pending in many non-Southern cities, including Boston. There the issue was double-edged. The Department of Health, Education and Welfare was moving toward cutting off federal aid to Boston schools unless there was further desegregation, and a federal judge, a John Kennedy appointee, was moving toward ruling that, federal aid or not, there had to be busing between Roxbury and its white neighbors. In the Senate Southerners and conservatives, with the understanding and sometimes support of moderates and liberals in both parties, began pushing for a national law restricting busing orders. In 1971 the House added stringent language to a bill providing funds for postsecondary education. The Senate didn't get the bill till 1972. Though some $20 billion in programs was involved, practically all of the Senate debate was devoted to the busing issue. Kennedy was not a leader in the floor fight, but he made his views clear. He opposed any language aimed at banning busing. The two party leaders, Mansfield and Scott, got the Senate to accept somewhat milder language than the House had approved, after the Senate had gone tentatively on record as supporting a tough approach. Kennedy voted for the Mansfield-Scott language, contained in a series of amendments, then voted for the bill. Kennedy was a conferee. The conference was a long and occasionally bitter one. One session lasted all night. The full House twice voted to order its conferees to insist on their tough antibusing language. Eventually, the Senate conferees agreed, or a majority of the conference did. Kennedy opposed the bill because of its provision postponing all federal court orders for busing until all appeals or the time for them had expired. The provision itself would expire on January 1, 1974. Kennedy and only fourteen other senators voted against the conference report when it came back to the Senate floor.

When the 1974–75 school year came around in Boston, the court-forced plan requiring busing was in effect. After over a decade of dragging its feet, Boston had to integrate. It did so with something less than grace. Despite appeals for calm acceptance by the mayor, the governor, several candidates for governor (1974 was a state election year), Kennedy, and Senator Edward Brooke, despite the massive use of city policemen and state troopers, there was so much antiblack violence by fearful white parents and resentful white students that South Boston looked, as one national magazine's put it, "like Little Rock in the bad old days." Kennedy sent his black aide, Bob Bates, to Boston to work with local officials and civil-rights leaders, in efforts to keep the schools open and peaceful. Kennedy's outspoken support for the busing plan seemed to anger the Irish whites of South Boston more than other official pronouncements. When he came to an outdoor meeting of parents protesting the busing plan, he was shoved, heckled, and made the target of such abusive statements as, "Why don't you let them shoot you like they shot your two brothers!" and "Why don't you put your one-legged son on a bus to Roxbury!" He was forced to flee the scene, City Hall Plaza, to his office in the nearby John F. Kennedy Federal Building. Later in Quincy a police phalanx was called in to rescue him from antibusers.

Kennedy's vote against the 1972 education bill had been a symbolic one, and indeed, he had become a symbol to those angry whites of Southie. This was despite the fact that he had made two other symbolic gestures that were intended to demonstrate to "Southies" everywhere that Edward Kennedy was on their side, too, or at least sympathetic to their point of view and responsive to their needs.

The first gesture came in 1973. Billy Joe Camp, press secretary to Governor George Wallace of Alabama, telephoned Kennedy's appointments secretary, Chris Capito, to invite Kennedy to attend a Fourth of July rally with Wallace in Alabama. She went to Paul Kirk, the senator's political aide, who treated it as a joke at first. When he learned it wasn't, he sent a memo to Kennedy with the details of the invitation. Kennedy called in senior staff to discuss it. No one thought he ought to make the trip. "Too cynical" was a view expressed over and over. Bates, the black, thought other blacks would be disheartened by the visit. But Kennedy showed interest. He showed, too, that he felt sympathy for the crippled Wallace. He had visited Wallace before at the Silver Spring, Maryland, hospital after Wallace was wounded in April 1972, and again at the Governor's Mansion in Montgomery during the fall presidential election campaign. So why not again? Why not make a move to try to close the still wide division between the working-class whites Wallace championed and the blacks, youths, and other minorities Kennedy spoke for so often? Kennedy sought advice from black leaders Jesse Jackson, Vernon Jordan, and Andrew Young, and perhaps others. They recommended he go, for political reasons. It would attract voters to him. For whatever reasons, he went. He appeared on the same platform with Wallace (the first liberal Democrat to do so) and told the Southern audience of 10,000 that they perhaps could teach the North how to bring about white-black accommodation.

The visit got a mixed press. The Boston *Globe*, the *Christian Science Monitor*, the Detroit *Free Press*, and the Chicago *Daily Defender* (a black paper) praised Kennedy. The Washington *Post* and the Norfolk *Ledger-Star*, among others, were strongly critical. Most of the criticism was along the lines that Kennedy (and Wallace) were being cynical, that their differences were so great that they sullied the name of politics to speak from the same podium and commend each other.*

*The aftermath of the event was that a number of Democratic politicians with national ambitions began to commend Wallace. Some went so far as to say flatly that they would support a national party ticket with Wallace on it—run with him, in fact. In 1974 Kennedy told an Alabama newspaper reporter that *he* would not even vote for a ticket with Wallace on it. This

The second symbolic gesture Kennedy made to the working-class whites of South Boston and their counterparts everywhere was to reverse himself in 1974 and vote for an education bill that had antibusing language in it. The bill was one extending the 1965 Elementary and Secondary Education Act, which has become the basic federal aid to education law. The House passed its version of the bill in March, with a prohibition against busing for desegregation purposes beyond the "next closest" school, a prohibition that would have made busing meaningless and desegregation impossible in many jurisdictions where there were large concentrations of blacks. The Nixon Administration supported this prohibition. The House vote on it was 293–117. The House bill would also allow parents or communities to get previous court orders changed to conform to the new law. It was the toughest and most solidly supported antibusing, antidesegregation legislation yet to emerge. The bill came to the Senate floor in May, where liberals found themselves hanging on for dear life. The House antibusing language was defeated by one vote, 47–46. Just before the vote Kennedy summed up his views on the subject in a speech that the NAACP's Clarence Mitchell later called one of the finest he had ever heard on the subject of school desegregation and busing, but which was also an appeal for fairness to the urban working-class whites, presumed by many to be the group most opposed to desegregation.

Kennedy made these points, among others: that desegregation was working, that blacks did better when they attended integrated schools because those schools got more money for equipment and facilities than did all-black schools, that Americans of different races ought to be living and learning together, and that the next-nearest-school provision insured that what desegregation there was would be accomplished with whites from poor urban neighborhoods adjacent to black ghettos. And that the law was sure to be declared unconstitutional anyway.

Several times in that speech Kennedy complained

***

was an echo of 1972. In April of that year Kennedy told Theodore White that the *only* circumstance that would make him a candidate for the Democratic presidential nomination would be the impending nomination of Wallace.

that the busing arguments were "an appeal to emotion," and that what the Senate should be doing was concentrating its attention on improving education for the poor blacks and whites whose education the legislation was supposed to help. (His one substantive contribution to the legislation on the floor was an amendment that made sure urban areas would not lose funds for slum schools to rural and Southern districts, where the relatively lower cost of living meant less money was needed.) Kennedy felt that the antibusing argument was hypocritical and worse. "In every possible way, the President has sought to use the issue of busing for political purposes. And the effect of his actions, which serve as the genesis for the [antibusing legislation] before us today, has been to appeal to the fears and emotions of the nation," Kennedy said. He criticized fellow senators, though not as directly: "All we have to do is look back over the history of public education in this country, and we find that there was no real concern for busing when white children were being bused to white schools and black children were being bused to black schools. It is also interesting that in some states where this issue is the most emotional, where the feelings run the highest, there is actually less busing going on today to promote desegregation than there was at the time of the Brown decision or even after later decisions to promote segregation. I think that all of us in this body recognize that, or should recognize it, in spite of the speeches that many of us make."

The Senate's version of antibusing legislation was mild compared to the House version. It banned busing beyond the next nearest school unless courts determined such to be necessary to protect constitutional rights, an important concession to advocates of busing. The Senate also voted down the reopener provision in the House bill. Kennedy and other liberals supported this antibusing language. The two versions of the bill then went to conference (Kennedy again a conferee), where a heated dispute over the busing amendments held up action for a month. Three times during this period the House went on record as instructing its conferees to stick to their tough bill. But the conferees finally gave in and accepted a compromise nearer to the Senate bill. The Senate provision on next nearest schools was left in the bill, and a milder reopener provision than the House had originally proposed was added.

Some blacks told Kennedy he ought to vote against even this compromise. They saw a momentum building up that could turn the nation around in its drive to end all segregation. Some senators, also, presumably feeling pressure from some black groups and constituents, thought about casting a symbolic vote against the conference report. "About eight or ten came to me and asked me how I was going to vote," Kennedy recalled later. "They were concerned about the provisions relating to busing. They knew that I participated in the conference. I would tell them about the various kinds of considerations that I felt were important. I told them quite frankly that I had difficulty in balancing the values, but, you know, '$18.5 billion for poor kids' education, you've got a very interesting vocational program, a very interesting program for handicapped children, an expanded program for bilingual education. . . .' " In fact it was not Kennedy's assessment of the details of the program that those senators were interested in. They wanted to know if he was going to cast that symbolic antibusing vote. Whatever he did would be symbolic, because of who he was and his standing with blacks. He later admitted himself that a number of liberals look to him as a shield on civil-rights legislation, the way they look to Senators Javits and Ribicoff as a shield on Israeli-related legislation. If Kennedy votes for a questionable bill, another senator can do the same and defend himself to blacks by pointing out Kennedy's vote.

So the first Senate approval of antibusing legislation was a liberal victory, of sorts, after all. Both chambers accepted the compromise. President Nixon had been staunchly for the original House version, but by the summer of 1974, he was too preoccupied with his own fate to be a factor in the contest over busing. The Senate approved the report on July 24, two weeks before Nixon resigned, six weeks before schools opened in Boston.

The trouble in Boston cooled down somewhat after a crisis-ridden start in the fall of 1974, but for the most opposed residents of the white South Boston neighborhoods, Kennedy remained an enemy. When he brought his Administrative Practice and Procedure Subcommittee to Boston in February to hold hearings on Civil Aeronautics Board regulations regarding airline fares and schedules, he was delayed for over an hour and a half when antibusing demonstrators from a group calling itself Restore Our Alienated Rights (ROAR) began heckling him, with references to Chappaquiddick and the private-school education his children were receiving. The following month representatives of another group, Massachusetts Citizens Against Forced Busing, went to Washington to lobby for a constitutional amendment forbidding busing. House Majority Leader Thomas P. O'Neill of Boston told the group he would help get a full House vote on such an amendment, and congressional support for such an amendment did seem to be building, even in the liberal 94th Congress. But Kennedy told the group, "The constitutional amendment is not the answer." What the group should be working for was "quality education," he said. As for busing, he pointed out, he could not be for it in Alabama and against in Massachusetts.

9. THE WHIP

Robert's death was a crushing blow, causing Edward Kennedy to withdraw almost totally from public view and from public affairs for most of the rest of the year. When he told his audience in his "fallen standards" speech in Worcester in 1969 that he had been at sea, he meant it literally. He all but cut himself off from the continent, sailing up and down the Maine coast, growing a beard, only half-heartedly going through the motions of responding to political appeals from Democrats convened in Chicago (though Stephen Smith and others were investigating the possibilities of a presidential candidacy for him). Once he rowed in to shore to take a call from Mayor Richard Daley. Daley wanted Kennedy on the ticket, but Kennedy refused. Kennedy made a speech in Washington in August. In September he endorsed the Humphrey-Muskie ticket, in a speech in Chicopee, Massachusetts. He urged his chief political aide in Massachusetts, Lester Hyman, to work for the Muskie campaign. Otherwise, Kennedy and his family kept to themselves through the end of summer, through the fall, and into the beginning of winter. Some friends thought the surviving brother was at sea figuratively, too. He did not show signs of recovering interest in his career. There were rumors, sad rather than ugly, that he was drinking heavily.

Just before Christmas, Kennedy paid a holiday visit

to his father in Palm Beach, Florida. Then he flew to Sun Valley for a skiing vacation. En route he learned from a newspaper article that a planned liberal overthrow of the Senate assistant majority leader, Russell Long, had been abandoned.

With a Republican taking over the White House, several Democratic liberals had decided that the party's congressional leadership ought to reflect the progressive views of the party's majority. Majority Leader Mike Mansfield was a bona fide liberal, but from a sparsely populated Western state. Long, a Louisianian, was a liberal on some matters, but almost reactionary on such issues as civil rights. But the important thing about Long from the point of view of the liberals was not that he was illiberal, but that he was vulnerable. He had become whip, as the assistant leader is called, in 1965, and proceeded to embarrass the party with his erratic and arbitrary behavior. He seemed to be drinking heavily in that period, and showed up on the floor at least a couple of times in what some observers in the galleries took to be a state of intoxication. He often went his own way on legislation on which most Democratic senators felt the party leadership should have been united.

Long became chairman of a major standing committee, Finance, late in 1965, leaving him less time to devote to his whip's duties. Yet he declined to give up the job. One of the principal responsibilities of the whip is to schedule routine business in a manner that allows the rest of the Democrats to spend as little time on the floor as possible. This means keeping senators informed of precisely when votes may occur on bills or amendments they feel strongly about. At least once Long handled floor time in a way in which liberal senators were defeated without getting a chance to speak or vote.

Senator Mansfield soon had enough, and set up a system in which four nonelected "assistant whips" were given the responsibilities Long was shouldering so poorly. Not long after that, in 1967, Senator Robert Byrd of West Virginia was elected secretary, the third ranking post in the Democratic leadership, and he began to do what Mansfield wanted and needed. Long was getting tired of the game, anyway. He told Byrd he was thinking of retiring in 1968 and would support him for the job. But when he heard that Senator Philip Hart of Michigan and other liberals were planning to try to replace him with Senator Edmund Muskie of Maine, Long promptly began asking colleagues for their votes, saying he was a candidate again for the job. That was late in November and early in December. Muskie had emerged from the 1968 presidential campaign, in which he was Hubert Humphrey's running mate, as a new national liberal Democratic hero. He wasn't sure the contest was worth taking on. While he mulled it over, Hamlet-like, Long got—or thought he got—forty promises of support, far more than he needed to win reelection in the fifty-seven-member Democratic caucus. In mid-December Muskie decided he would not take Long on. Kennedy read a story to that effect on the plane from Florida to Sun Valley.

When his flight reached Chicago, Kennedy called his administrative assistant, David Burke, and asked him what he thought about taking Long on. Burke, who thought the job was nothing and told Kennedy so, was nevertheless "delighted . . . flabbergasted and delighted. After Bob's death, he had been a different person. There was a lot of wind out of him. He was very slow in coming back. It ended when he ran for whip. That fight was a delight not because of the whip's job but because the other period was ending. He was spunky and wanted to do something—even if it wasn't a good thing to do. It wasn't a good thing to do because he wasn't built for that job, hustling around and taking care of everybody's little problems, or sitting on the floor endlessly minding the store. But it was still worth doing, because of what it was bringing back."

Another theory is that Kennedy's decision to seek the whip's job, with its routine, almost menial requirements, was based on a desire to slip into the anonymity (if a Kennedy ever could be anonymous) the position could provide. He was, of course, under extreme pressure to lead a liberal movement foretold by John and Robert, to carry forward that "fallen standard," to speak everywhere every night. Bound to the Senate, he could beg off most applications for his leadership.

A third theory is different still: Kennedy saw the need to establish himself as *party* leader early in the jostling for the 1972 presidential nomination. What better way to demonstrate his availability and relatively greater talents as a party standard-bearer than to win a fight the cautious Muskie could not have won?

Of the three theories, Burke's always sounded the most believable to me. But when I asked Kennedy, in late 1974, if the fight for the whip's job and the job itself had indeed been therapy or a sign that he no longer needed therapy, that he was no longer disabled by his brother's murder, he gave an answer that doesn't really conform to any of the theories. "I didn't look at it that [Burke's] way," he said. "I just thought it an opportunity to learn more about the range of issues that was coming up, to become more of a generalist rather than a specialist." To become a more modern senator.

Burke discussed the situation with a number of Kennedy confidants. He informed his boss that in general the advice was, "Don't do it." But Kennedy's mind was already made up. On December 26 he began calling Democratic senators at home, first just sounding them out, very shortly asking for their votes and their help. Most of the liberal and moderate members of his party said they would support him. Some of the conservative Southerners, particularly those who ran the so-called Inner Club, gave Kennedy encouragement even as they told him they could not vote for him. Long's erratic behavior reflected on the Senate, in their view. Richard Russell was one of those. An aide to the senator who was with him in his Winder, Georgia, home when Kennedy called said later that Russell emphasized to Kennedy so strongly and repeatedly that he would not "raise a hand against you," that Kennedy had to interpret the conversation as an endorsement of his candidacy.

Meanwhile, Kennedy supporters in labor, business, the universities, and other professions across the country were being importuned to ask their own senators to support the challenge. This sort of campaigning is rare in the Senate. It happens, but as a rule senators don't like to have their constituents lobbied by their colleagues. That is particularly true when the issue is a matter of national policy and the vote on it will reflect on a senator's philosophy and politics.

But a party fight is a little different. For one thing, the vote is by secret ballot.

Soon Russell Long's forty votes began dwindling. Many senators who had told him in early December they would support him when the opponent was Muskie felt they were not obligated to stick with that in a Kennedy-Long fight. (Though some did, including some liberals.)

On December 30, Kennedy formally announced his intention to run, citing Mansfield's need for a more devoted and energetic aide when a Republican took over the White House. He pointed out that he had no committee chairmanship to distract him. He and Long both were in Washington then, campaigning in person with the few senators who had begun to return to the capital. On January 2, the day before the vote, each senator privately believed he had enough votes to win. Kennedy counted thirty sure. Long counted twenty-nine. As it turned out, Long had been misled—or had misled himself. The morning of the third, Muskie nominated Kennedy, Allen Ellender of Louisiana nominated Long, and the secret ballots were cast. Freshmen tallied the slips and found that Kennedy had received thirty-one votes and Long twenty-six. Kennedy had pulled off the first successful challenge to an incumbent floor leader since the leader-whip arrangement had developed around the time of World War I. Long said he thought he would have easily defeated any other senator but Kennedy, and that may be true. "I had him out-gunned in the Senate, but he had me out-gunned in the country," Long added. That may be true; but the vote took place in the Senate. Kennedy's campaign reduced Long to his natural constituency of Southerners, Westerners, conservatives, elders, and those younger liberals who committed themselves unequivocally to Long before the Kennedy blitz began. This judgment is based on Long's own list of how senators voted.* The list is partly

*For Kennedy—Bayh of Indiana, Burdick of North Dakota, Church of Idaho, Cranston of California, Eagleton of Missouri, Fulbright of Arkansas, Gore of Tennessee, Harris of Oklahoma, Hart of Michigan, Hughes of Iowa, Inouye of Hawaii, Jackson of Washington, Magnuson of Washington, Mansfield of Montana, McGovern of South Dakota, McIntyre of New Hampshire, Metcalf of Montana, Mondale of Minnesota, Moss of Utah, Muskie of Maine, Pastore of Rhode Island, Pell of Rhode Island, Proxmire

guesswork, of course, since some senators keep their secret votes secret, but both Long's and Kennedy's political aides believed it was pretty accurate. Gaylord Nelson of Wisconsin, Eugene McCarthy of Minnesota, and Vance Hartke of Indiana were the only industrial-state liberals to support Long. Hartke and McCarthy were both members of Long's Finance Committee and probably intimidated by that. Nelson, who that month proposed the creation of a liberal-senators group, which he said had to be led by Kennedy "if the group hopes to succeed," supported Long because he had helped a large Wisconsin manufacturer with a tax legislation problem. Kennedy picked up only three Southerners —mavericks William Fulbright of Arkansas, Albert Gore of Tennessee, Ralph Yarborough of Texas, plus the freshman from Virginia, William Spong.

Kennedy's victory statement stressed the legislative portent rather than the personal. "The winds of change, so evident this year, have expressed themselves. . . . I think [my election] means a positive, constructive legislative program in this session."

What had he won? The job itself was not that important. Historically the assistant party leader in the Senate had been almost a neuter. "We had to shanghai whips," Richard Russell recalled. In the thirties and forties that was certainly true. Republicans did not even name a whip from 1935 to 1944; Democrat Lister Hill quit the job in 1947. But when Lyndon Johnson arrived in the Senate in the fifties things began to change. Johnson got himself shanghaied into the job, and promptly provided himself with a staff and chores. He went on to become majority leader, as did his whip, Mike

---

of Wisconsin, Ribicoff of Connecticut, Spong of Virginia, Symington of Missouri, Tydings of Maryland, Williams of New Jersey, Yarborough of Texas, Young of Ohio, and, of course, Kennedy. For Long—Allen of Alabama, Anderson of New Mexico, Bible of Nevada, Byrd of Virginia, Byrd of West Virginia, Cannon of Nevada, Dodd of Connecticut, Eastland of Mississippi, Ellender of Louisiana, Ervin of North Carolina, Gravel of Alaska, Hartke of Indiana, Holland of Florida, Hollings of South Carolina, Jordan of North Carolina, McCarthy of Minnesota, McClellan of Arkansas, McGee of Wyoming, Montoya of New Mexico, Nelson of Wisconsin, Randolph of West Virginia, Russell of Georgia, Sparkman of Alabama, Stennis of Mississippi, Talmadge of Georgia, and Long.

Mansfield (*his* whip, Hubert Humphrey, became vice-president and may yet become majority leader). By 1969 there was a new tradition of whip-as-springboard. Also, Mansfield had changed the nature of party leadership so that the whip had a say in party affairs. Johnson never held caucuses, and did not consider the Policy Committee, of which the whip was automatically a member, a consultative body at all. Mansfield responded to the full Democratic membership, and while he was the first-among-equals on the Policy Committee and set the agenda, still he allowed that body to chart the party's course in the Senate. The Policy Committee was beginning to take on a less conservative hue in the sixties. Two-thirds of its members were in the liberal mainstream of the party in 1969. Kennedy was the first New Englander in the job in twenty years. He was also the first liberal to win an actual contest for whip or leader or secretary since 1947. In all other contests the more conservative candidate for the job had won.

Because he was a liberal, because he was a Kennedy, because he was a potential presidential nominee, because Mansfield was widely believed to be a reluctant leader, it was assumed in many quarters that Kennedy would be the party's true Senate leader in the next four years. Mansfield was warned to that effect. Russell Long went further. In commenting on his defeat, Long warned Richard Nixon to watch out; which Nixon did. Bryce Harlow, his chief adviser on relations with Congress, a veteran lobbyist for business and the White House, reportedly told Nixon that Kennedy was running the Policy Committee. That does not seem to be true at all. However, Kennedy did forcefully argue his position on strategy in committee meetings, and was instrumental in setting policy on some occasions. For instance, he convinced Mansfield to hold up floor consideration of the Nixon tax bill until specific reforms were added. On another occasion he was able to pressure the Administration to provide aid to Biafra.

Kennedy began the job of whip with customary energy and imagination. First he hired an assistant, Wayne Owens, a young Utah lawyer who worked for Senator Frank Moss in Utah and had run Robert Kennedy's 1968 presidential campaign in several Western states. Kennedy not only wanted a non-New Englander in the job, but specifically a Westerner. He was impressed by the fact that nearly half of the Senate Democrats were from the West. Kennedy told Owens that he felt the job the whip could do—and had not done—was to "educate and communicate to" senators what was going on in that body of individualists. Kennedy and Owens worked out seminars for the staffs of freshmen, and soon instituted a "whip notice," a newsletter somewhat like the one whips in the House of Representatives used to communicate with a party membership over four times as large. They also improved the telephone recording system, which allowed senators to follow floor activity from elsewhere.

Kennedy, Burke, and Owens talked at length about the way the office should function. All three agreed that not for them was the traditional role of glorified flunky acceptable. Kennedy wanted the whip to influence legislation and Senate business substantively. They did not see the whip's responsibility as making it easier for each senator to be a senator, but rather as making the Senate a more influential institution. Kennedy has always had a great belief in outside experts. He arranged for such experts to come in and speak to the Democratic Policy Committee, creating a sort of free bureaucracy or advisory group to supplement the existing Senate resources. There were many late-afternoon meetings in the whip office suite with small groups of Democratic senators to plan and, occasionally, plot on issues and directions. These were convivial meetings, with Owens serving as bartender. Some Kennedy friends thought that that was the part of the job Kennedy liked best. Not the drinking—he seldom had a drink, according to Owens—but the relaxation and the privacy.* Kennedy still had not come to terms with the political pressures he was being subjected to as the last Kennedy. Outside of that office almost all the attention he received was related to his advancing that famous fallen standard *as president*. Someone even scratched "Mr. President" on his Senate desk. In the whip office on late afternoons, some of that could be forgotten. It was a refuge.

---

*The hottest story on the rumor circuit in Washington in 1969, however, was that the senator and his wife were turning to alcohol much more often than in the past as the pressures on both of them increased.

Maybe that is all it was. The job itself soon palled. No amount of energy and imagination could make the assistant leader the leader. Kennedy chafed under the restrictions. He hated staying on the floor during pro forma debates. Most of the Senate sessions are not dramatic or even mildly disputatious, as puzzled tourists learn every day. Most sessions do not bring more than a handful of senators to the floor at any one time. There are many sessions where there is only one senator making a speech, one senator presiding, and one Republican and one Democrat "minding the store." Often—too often for Kennedy—that one Democrat was him. He complained that he could not leave town when he wanted to (though on some occasions he simply left, whip duties be hanged), and, he told Owens, he was finding that he had to take his identity as Mansfield's deputy into account when he spoke on issues, a new and uncomfortable restriction.

He was also uncomfortable with the third man in the leadership team, Senator Robert Byrd. The West Virginian was performing many of the duties of the whip, and making sure that his Democratic colleagues were aware of it. Byrd was spending more time on the floor than Kennedy. He was arranging for senators to miss a vote without missing an opportunity to make their stands known. He was putting articles and speeches in the *Congressional Record* as a favor to absent or late-arriving senators. Kennedy may have felt that even though he did not find the job all that rewarding, he had to keep it simply because he resented the challenge of Byrd (as Long had resented the challenge of Muskie).

If Kennedy's performance was less than splendid in the first six months on the job, it was even worse later. On July 18, 1969, Kennedy was involved in the tragic automobile accident on Chappaquiddick Island. As the whole world knows, a young woman, Mary Jo Kopechne, was drowned, and Kennedy apparently tried to cover up his involvement in the episode. At the very least he seems to have considered doing so for a few hours. The adverse publicity that came crashing in on him was so destructive that Kennedy thought seriously of withdrawing from public life. He went on television and made what even many of his admirers thought was a tasteless appeal to the voters of Massachusetts to instruct him in whether he should continue his career. "Only Senator Edward M. Kennedy can answer whether he should or should not resign from the United States Senate," said the Boston *Globe*. "It is not a matter for a plebescite. . . . It is a bit like the umpire turning about in Fenway Park to ask the audience whether Carl Yastrzemski is safe at the plate."

It seemed that Kennedy was still as popular as Yastrzemski in his state, whatever public opinion across the nation might have become. A Becker Research poll conducted on July 26 and July 27 (the Kennedy speech was on July 25) showed that 84 percent of the respondents approved of Kennedy's performance and 78 percent opposed his resignation. On July 30 Kennedy announced that he would seek reelection. That may not have translated into spendable political currency, however. House Speaker David M. Bartley filed a resolution urging Kennedy to stay in office, but several Democrats told him they had nothing to gain and something to lose by voting on such a resolution. So he dropped the idea. In Washington a number of senators seemed to feel the same way. Some told colleagues and friends they thought the Chappaquiddick incident demonstrated a moral weakness in Kennedy that should not be tolerated in a leader once it was revealed. Others seemed to feel compassion, even empathy, for Kennedy's plight personally, but felt that the politics of the situation compelled (or allowed) them to move away from and even against him.

Also, in his statement to Massachusetts voters announcing that he was a candidate for reelection, Kennedy had pledged not to seek the presidential nomination in 1972 (the accident itself probably precluded a successful attempt for that prize); Kennedy's political influence in Washington was further diluted. In addition to which, David Burke later said, "when he came back to Washington, he wasn't in any mood to go roaring after issues." So much for the idea of a substantive whip. When he came back it was to slights and snubs. That pet piece of legislation of his, the statute allowing eighteen-year-olds to vote, was converted into a Mansfield-Magnuson project despite the protests of the Kennedy staff. And when President Nixon invited congressional leaders to the White House to a dinner for the astronauts (whose success story was launched by John Kennedy), one leader was not invited, the Democratic Senate Whip.

In November, Joseph Kennedy died. Another blow, and another compelling reason to leave Washington—and to leave it to Wayne Owens and to Robert Byrd to do those things senators expected of the whip. At the end of the session Kennedy's record of attendance was slightly below the average: He voted on 83 percent of the roll calls, and the average for Democratic senators was 84 percent. The following year, Kennedy performed even less well. He was ill with pneumonia early in the year. Later he felt the need to spend a great deal of time in Massachusetts campaigning for a big reelection margin. That summer and fall he would often budget four days a week campaigning. His voting percentage fell off to 70 percent—and that percentage was increased by a lengthy postelection session. He voted on fewer than two out of three pre-election roll calls.

Meanwhile, some senators were grumbling not only about his absences but also about his refusal or failure to perform the routine favors they expected of the whip. Senator Byrd was beginning to think of challenging Kennedy for the job at the end of 1970. As secretary of the conference, Byrd was continuing to pick up the slack Kennedy's performance caused. He was asked by a few senators from time to time in 1970 if he would not consider seeking Kennedy's job in the next Congress. He always indicated that he was interested, but he never made a campaign out of it. Byrd had resented Kennedy's election to the office from the start. He felt he should have been the next whip after Long. He told one interviewer that he viewed the secretary's job as a rung on the leadership ladder. The next rung was whip. (The next rung is majority or minority leader. However, Byrd said in 1974 he might be interested in the presidential or vice-presidential nomination.) He had not sought the job, because he supported Long. But he did not support Kennedy. Nor did he agree with him and the predominant liberal faction of the party on the central issue of civil rights. Byrd, from a poor family in North Carolina and West Virginia, was a former Ku Klux Klan member. What was particularly objectionable about his anti–civil-rights history and record (he had filibustered all night long against the 1964 civil-rights act) was that he generally supported the party's majority on most other matters. This led some of his critics to conclude that his opposition to civil-rights legislation was not based on conservatism (à la Senator Sam Ervin, say), but on racism.

But despite his anti–civil-rights record—in fact, because of it—Byrd knew that he could count on a large base of conservative Democrats if he should choose to run. He also knew he could count on the votes of some moderates who objected to Kennedy's conception of the whip's job. And he thought that at least a small number of liberals might support him in the hope of further damaging Kennedy's presidential aspirations. The Senate at the beginning of 1971 was an incubator of presidential hopefuls, serious and semiserious—Muskie, McGovern, Humphrey, Jackson, Harris, and Bayh. Kennedy had suffered a net loss of one vote from 1969: four senators who voted for him were not coming back, and only three who voted for Long were not coming back. Byrd also had something else Long had not had—the enthusiastic support of the Southern Inner Club of the old Senate. Russell believed that Byrd loved the institution of the Senate as much as he did, and would be its servant. He also had come to disapprove of Kennedy. Kennedy had crossed him on a number of issues involving military affairs, something he was not used to in junior members. Russell's support would turn out to be the key to the fight that year for the whip's job.

As the postelection session wound to a close in 1970, Byrd was still not committed to making a challenge. He was quietly campaigning for the job, planning to become a candidate formally and openly only if he was sure he had the votes in hand. He made a quiet campaign, he said later, because he remembered Russell Long's explanation of his own loss. Byrd didn't want to scare Kennedy into activating the national network of Kennedy friends and supporters.* Kennedy, meanwhile, played right into Byrd's hands. He didn't campaign all out because he felt that would seem a sign of weakness. And he did not fear Byrd. By year's end, Kennedy had made personal requests of his colleagues and received, he thought, a firm thirty-one promises of votes. There would only be fifty-five Democratic senators in the

---

*When Kennedy asked Byrd if he was going to challenge him, Byrd refused to give him a yes or no answer, to Kennedy's irritation.

91st Congress. Kennedy and his staff aides believed that several other senators were probably going to vote for him. If there was a challenge, that is. At year's end that was not certain, or even likely in the Kennedy camp's view. Byrd had not announced. Byrd's own private calculating showed at best twenty-eight votes, the bare majority, and that twenty-eight included Russell, who was dying in Walter Reed Hospital. On the weekend before the vote was to be taken, Byrd arranged to get a written proxy from Russell, with the understanding that he would check on Russell's condition at the last minute before the vote. Russell's death was that imminent. An aide to Russell, Charles Campbell, took a typed proxy statement to the dying man, who could barely scrawl his signature on it. Concerned, Campbell insisted that physicians there approve the signature—that is, tell him they were willing to stand up and say that Russell was in full control of his faculties when he signed the letter.

Byrd got another proxy, one that spelled trouble for Kennedy. It was Warren Magnuson's. Magnuson and Jackson both had expressed anger at Kennedy's opposing them on the issue of federal financing of a supersonic transport plane, a project dear to their Washington state constituents' hearts, since the Boeing Airplane Company is located there. Both senators had supported Kennedy against Long; now they were switching. Jackson made that clear to Kennedy in a face-to-face meeting in Jackson's office.

On his vote-count lists, Kennedy had put Jackson and Magnuson under the "probable" category, anyway. So when he went into the party caucus on January 21, 1971, he still expected to win comfortably. Senator Inouye nominated him. Byrd, making a last check with Walter Reed, decided to go, and Jennings Randolph of West Virginia nominated him. The votes were cast and counted and Byrd was announced the winner, 31 to 24. Seven senators who had told Kennedy they would vote for him hadn't. Even if Kennedy misunderstood the nature of the commitments, apparently somebody still lied. Newspaper efforts to reconstruct the vote after the fact turned up twenty-six senators who said they voted for Kennedy. There has been a lot of speculation to the effect that *who* lied was the important question to Kennedy immediately after the vote. Columnists Frank

Mankiewicz and Thomas Braden reported that Kennedy was sure he got McGovern's vote, thinks he got Muskie's and Bayh's, wasn't sure of Humphrey's and Hughes's. Actually he never got a pledge from Humphrey.*

At any rate, the fact that *some*body misled him was probably more important to Kennedy than *who* it was. He told David Burke, "I'm not concerned with who had said they were for me and weren't. It's over. Let's go on." He said some other things that Burke interpreted to mean that that 1971 loss marked "the end of the clubby period." At that point he finally shed the skin of the conventional "good senator" and became the modern one. That is, he used the power his seniority and aggressiveness had brought him to be both a specialist and a generalist. Thereafter he became less concerned with his colleagues' sensitivities so far as jurisdictions were concerned. The "clubby period" was pretty much over for the whole Senate as the 1970s began. Mansfield had successfully diffused much power to the caucus, the Policy Committee, and the Steering Committee. Much power remained in the hands of the chairmen of the standing committees and their subcommittees—and these were increasingly liberal non-Southerners elected in the early six-

---

*Political scientist Robert L. Peabody of Johns Hopkins University constructed a tentative breakdown of the vote, which Kennedy aides say is as close as anyone is likely to get to the truth: For Kennedy—Bayh of Indiana, Burdick of North Dakota, Church of Idaho, Cranston of California, Eagleton of Missouri, Harris of Oklahoma, Hart of Michigan, Hughes of Iowa, Humphrey of Minnesota, Inouye of Hawaii, McGovern of South Dakota, Metcalf of Montana, Mondale of Minnesota, Moss of Utah, Muskie of Maine, Nelson of Wisconsin, Pell of Rhode Island, Proxmire of Wisconsin, Ribicoff of Connecticut, Stevenson of Illinois, Tunney of California, and Kennedy. For Byrd—Allen of Alabama, Anderson of New Mexico, Bentsen of Texas, Bible of Nevada, Byrd of Virginia, Cannon of Nevada, Chiles of Florida, Eastland of Mississippi, Ellender of Louisiana, Ervin of North Carolina, Fulbright of Arkansas, Gravel of Alaska, Hartke of Indiana, Hollings of South Carolina, Jackson of Washington, Jordan of North Carolina, Long of Louisiana, McClellan of Arkansas, Magnuson of Washington, Montoya of New Mexico, Randolph of West Virginia, Russell of Georgia, Sparkman of Alabama, Spong of Virginia, Stennis of Mississippi, Talmadge of Georgia, Williams of New Jersey, and Byrd. That leaves Mansfield of Montana, McIntyre of New Hampshire, McGee of Wyoming, Pastore of Rhode Island, and Symington of Missouri unknowns.

ties or that landslide year of 1958. In 1971 Kennedy, who turned thirty-nine that year, was chairman of three important subcommittees. He probably would have been a worse whip in the 91st Congress than he had been in the 90th. Having the job would probably have made him less effective a chairman and "substantive" senator.

If the clubby period of the Senate did die on January 21, 1971, future historians and political scientists will probably find a more dramatic and appropriate event to symbolize it than Ted Kennedy's loss to Robert Byrd. Early that afternoon Richard Russell died. He had been a senator for thirty-eight years. He helped develop and then epitomized the Inner Club system of rule that characterized the institution in the forties, fifties, and early sixties. He may not have been conscious at the hour his vote was cast, but it was a valid vote when he cast it and he was alive when it was counted.

Byrd framed the proxy and hung it on the wall of his outer office.

10. CAMPAIGN
FINANCE REFORM

The less you speak and the narrower your range of interest and activity, wrote Professor Donald Matthews in a study of the ideal senator of the 1950s, the greater your effectiveness. That changed somewhat in the 1960s. By the 1970s, a number of senators had the inclination and desire and ability to affect legislation and policy substantially in a variety of areas. To a degree not yet fully realized a number of historical developments came together at the beginning of this decade, and resulted in something close to senatorial government. These were the election of a Republican president who was neither particularly activist nor particularly concerned with the details of domestic legislation; the reelection in 1970 for the second time of that group of liberal Democratic senators of the class of 1958; plus that of other, slightly younger liberals, plus the return of Hubert Humphrey. These men were for the most part liberal Democrats with seniority—and presidential ambitions. The fact that for the first time since the 1950s they were opposing a conservative Republican in the White House—and one preoccupied with foreign affairs at that—meant that there was an opportunity for the Congress to originate a great deal of legislation. For the presidential hopefuls in the Senate this opportunity was a godsend, and none was shy about acting in a broader range of interest and activity than the traditionalists in the Senate preferred. As Carey Parker, the chief of Senator Kennedy's legislative staff, once concisely explained it, "You cannot be a national leader and not have a program." Parker's equivalents on the staffs of senators Muskie, Humphrey, Jackson, Bayh, and a few others would put the same thought in similar words. All of those men do involve themselves with a variety of issues, a variety of abuses.

Kennedy probably spreads himself thinner than any of them. Majority Leader Mansfield, who more than anyone created the Senate environment in which these liberals have been able to grow to power and influence, once mildly reproved Kennedy in an interview with a journalist for "covering the waterfront," as he put it. Parker winces at that description and the one about :"spreading himself thin." He prefers to compare Kennedy to the fox in Isaiah Berlin's essay on the two types of modern men—the hedgehog, who takes a narrow view and knows one thing very well, and the fox, who surveys the world and knows many things pretty well. Or, as Parker put it on another occasion, "he [Kennedy] likes to keep three or four balls in the air at all times." Senator as juggler.

One of Kennedy's most dramatic personal successes in a field in no way related to his various subcommittee specialties dealt with campaign-finance reform legislation. As the 1970s began reform-minded members of Congress had been working toward improving the nation's archaic and loophole-ridden campaign-practices laws for as long as anyone could remember. But the only success had been a bill Senator Long pushed through in 1966 to allow taxpayers to designate $1 of their federal income tax for a presidential campaign fund. That law was promptly suspended.* Ted Kennedy's own interest in some sort of public subsidy for candidates, in stronger requirements for limiting contributions from special interests, in limiting total spending, and in making contributions and expenditures public was a longstanding one. John Kennedy had recommended reform in

*Robert Kennedy helped to get it suspended, fearing that it would allow President Johnson to control the party even more closely than otherwise.

1962. (Edward had apparently seriously underreported his own spending in 1962, though that never became an issue in that or later campaigns.) By the middle 1960s Ted Kennedy was working with academics and politicians in Massachusetts trying to get comprehensive campaign finance reform at the state level. In 1970 Congress passed a bill limiting some, but not nearly all, campaign expenditures. President Nixon vetoed it. The veto was upheld partly because Senate Minority Leader Hugh Scott promised he would work for a better bill in the following Congress. He did, and that bill passed Congress in 1972 and the President signed it. The new law limited media spending, improved reporting requirements, and limited spending by a candidate's family. Left untouched was the total amount a candidate could raise and spend and the total amount special interests could give through individual donors. The ideas that taxpayers should pay for campaigns and that private contributions should be barred were not seriously considered. Kennedy introduced his own bills in 1969 and in 1971. He supported the effort to pass the 1970 and 1972 bills, but was not a leading player in the drama.

By 1973 Kennedy had become quite interested in the idea of public financing, however. One reason was that he had become involved in a series of fights with that most powerful of special interests, the medical-pharmaceutical professional axis. Kennedy had become chairman of the Health Subcommittee and a leading advocate of liberal reforms dealing with medical services and the drug industry. On a number of occasions he felt that his efforts to win votes for legislation were thwarted not because a member of Congress disagreed with his views, but because that member was obligated to the American Medical Association or some related lobby which had a great deal of money to pass out as campaign contributions. Also in 1971, Carey Parker joined his staff. Parker was an expert in the field, having worked on drafts of reform legislation while serving in the Justice Department in the 1960s. But also, in 1973 Kennedy probably expected to be a presidential candidate in 1976. That factor made him a reluctant leader in the effort to take reform further than the 1972 act had taken it. He didn't want to appear to be seeking personal advantage, since to do so would hurt his own reputation and the chances of the legislation.

In 1973 Senator Phil Hart, another long-time advocate of public financing and other campaign reform, decided to make a major effort to get a new bill. His approach to Kennedy to join him was turned away. This was before the Watergate investigations revealed so much sordid campaign-financing activity that campaign reform suddenly became a highly visible and highly popular cause. Then Kennedy decided to make a major commitment to the cause. Some of his colleagues have criticized him for that, accusing him of opportunism. Undoubtedly he did seize an opportunity to identify himself as leader in a popular cause, but that, of course, is what politics is all about. And he also accepted the responsibility to spend a lot of time and energy in behalf of the cause. And he made the key political accommodation that made enactment likely, if not a certainty. He enlisted Hugh Scott in the fight.

Scott was his party's elected leader in the Senate in 1973. He was also a member of the Rules Committee, which writes all campaign legislation. Scott and Kennedy testified before the committee in favor of reform legislation early in 1973. Kennedy was for a much more advanced bill than Scott was. Scott was not in favor of public financing. But he remarked in almost an aside during the committee hearings that he liked the *idea* of taxpayers earmarking public funds for presidential campaigns. Kennedy's ears perked up at that. Later in the day he asked Scott if there might not be some congressional candidates campaign-finance legislation in behalf of which the two of them could join forces. Scott, to the surprise of some members of both men's staffs, said yes.

They worked out a bill that was both a delight and a disaster to the long-time workers in this vineyard. It was a delight because the joining together of these two influential senators from the different parties meant that the day was no longer far off when public campaign subsidies would become law. Everybody could see that. But many people also thought they saw that day a little farther off than 1973. Many of the early advocates of subsidies to congressional candidates had unexpectedly and abruptly developed cold feet. Their fear was that trying to get public financing would jeopardize the excellent opportunity that Watergate had created to greatly tighten up contribution and expenditure laws. Kennedy and Scott wanted to tie the reform effort up in one big package. The liberal-oriented people's lobby, Common Cause, which strongly supported public financing in principle, opposed Kennedy on this at that time. California's Alan Cranston, one of the leaders of the fight for reform in the Senate, opposed Kennedy. So even did Phil Hart. These liberals argued that there probably wasn't a majority in the Senate behind such a drastic new departure, and that if the liberals took a big defeat on campaign subsidies, that might so strengthen the enemies of all reforms that the package of reforms dealing with reporting and spending and contributing limitations might also be defeated. Kennedy argued that the Watergate opportunity was too good to pass up, that the Senate had to act now or never again have the luxury of a public opinion in favor of far-reaching reforms and new departures. Kennedy's staff, led by Carey Parker, and Scott's aide, Kenneth Davis, got what they considered a "hard" count of thirty senators in favor of their bill. That, they felt, undercut the argument that they were jeopardizing the entire bill. Losing with thirty or more votes on subsidies would not lead to a rout on the other elements of reform.

The bill before the Senate in 1973, S. 372, did the following things when it came to the Senate floor—limited all spending by candidates for federal offices (fifteen cents per eligible constituent in a primary, twenty cents per in a general election); limited the amount an individual could give to a single candidate ($10,000 to a congressional candidate, $30,000 to a presidential candidate); limited cash contributions to $100; repealed the equal-time provision of the communications act; established a Federal Elections Commission to enforce campaign laws; and required candidates to have only one campaign committee responsible for all reporting of expenditures and contributions. Nothing about subsidies to congressional candidates. (Presidential candidates in 1976 and after, of course, would be eligible for subsidies in the general election under the old check-off law.)

This bill came to the Senate floor on July 25. Some fifty changes would be considered and voted on before the Senate passed the bill on July 30 by the overwhelming vote of 82–8. The two major changes involved reducing the expenditure limit from fifteen and twenty cents to ten fifteen, and reducing the contributions limit from $5,000 and $15,000 to a flat $6,000. The most heated debate came on July 26, when the Kennedy-Scott proposal was brought up. Kennedy explained that the basic idea was to pay for congressional campaigns directly from the Treasury, with candidates getting in general elections the amount of money they were limited to spending in S. 372. Only nominees of the major parties would get such subsidies. Minor party candidates would receive somewhat less. The definition of "major" and "minor" was related to the number of votes received by the candidate of the party in question in the last previous election. Candidates running without party status or nominated by a party that had not fielded a candidate before would get no advance payments, but would be recompensed after the election in accordance with how many votes they received.

In addition to the basic objection that Senator Cranston made on the floor—that the reform was too far-reaching and new to be written into law on the floor without full-scale investigation by committee—there were a number of specific objections. Some were political: in some states, Republicans or Democrats would not qualify for subsidies. Some were philosophical: Senator Robert Packwood of Oregon objected that what was needed to cleanse politics was greater public participation, which would not come about if federal funds were used to pay for campaigns. Kennedy led the rebuttal to these charges. "Kennedy was tremendous," said Common Cause lobbyist Frederick Wertheimer. "He was on the floor every day and for long hours. He *knew* his stuff. Other senators may have known more, I don't know, but he knew what was in the bill and he certainly knew what was in his amendment. His staff had prepared him well. He handled the arguments against his amendment quite well. He was an extremely effective legislator. Carey was terrific. But Kennedy's greatest contribution may have been bringing Hugh Scott along. We knew it had to be a bipartisan effort. We had enlisted Mathias and Schweiker, but they aren't Hugh Scott." Wertheimer didn't say so, but I suspect that if Common Cause had known that Scott would endorse public financing, the organization would have made an all-out push for the original Hart bill, rather than deciding to go for limited reform that summer.

Kennedy called up the amendment, but after a few hours of lively debate, Senator Cannon, chairman of the Rules Committee, moved to table and thus kill it, without, technically, a vote being taken on the merits of the legislation. Cannon's tabling motion prevailed, but only by 53–38. (Kennedy and Parker, Scott and Davis had counted well. They had their thirty hard votes—and eight more. The total of thirty-eight included ten Republicans. It also included a majority of the Senate Democrats voting that day, twenty-eight of fifty-two.) As a guide to the Senate sentiment on the idea of campaign subsidies for candidates for Congress, the vote was really shocking. Since a number of members of the Senate who voted to table announced to the public in one way or another that they favored what Kennedy-Scott would do, clearly nearly a majority of the Senate favored public financing *now*, without hearings, without prolonged debate.

In the face of this evidence, Common Cause and other advocates of reform decided that summer to make the effort they had originally feared was premature. In September, the Senate Rules Committee began four days of hearings on six separate major public-finance proposals, including the tabled Kennedy-Scott amendment, now reintroduced as a separate bill. On the eve of those hearings thirty-one senators, plus spokesmen for Common Cause, the AFL-CIO, and the United Auto Workers, endorsed a statement of support for eight basic principles of public financing, the key one being the core of Kennedy-Scott—full funding for major party candidates, some funding for others.

Kennedy-Scott proposed the "purest" system of financing. Major party candidates could not accept private donations. Senators Walter Mondale of Minnesota and Richard Schweicker of Pennsylvania, authors of one of the six major bills before the committee, preferred federal matching contributions for small private contributions. Proposals sponsored by senators Cranston, Hart, Stevenson, and Mathias all allowed some private contributions.

Most of the major bills would, like Kennedy-Scott, fund presidential* and congressional candidates. Most also were limited to general elections, though some advocates of reform believed that if special interests were ruled out of general elections but left free to influence decisions in primaries, nothing would have been accomplished. Kennedy recognized this, but said he did not believe that incumbent members of Congress were willing to subsidize challenges in their own party. The debate before the Rules Committee was almost all positive. The Watergate hearings in the Senate, with all their sordid revelations, had concluded, and practically no one in Washington was willing to defend politics as usual. Not in public. That fact was by no means an assurance that the Kennedy-Scott proposal or any of its competitors was likely to become law that year, or even in that Congress. The reform bill the Senate had passed in July was not even a cinch, for it was opposed by the chairman of the relevant committee in the House, and he was holding things up there.

Common Cause by now was involved not only in pushing some public-finance law through, but in melding the various proposals of a growing number of senators into one legislative package, then getting it before the full Senate (no problem) and the House (seemingly impossible). Also, Common Cause was by now interested in damping down any fires of ambition that might burn up the carefully constructed legislation. All the senators involved wanted credit for the bill. It had become a daily front-page story. But only one could introduce it and give it his name. The two most serious candidates for that were Kennedy and Mondale. Common Cause had told Kennedy it wanted him to lead the effort in behalf of the bill. Lobbyists from Common Cause and other reformers began a "shuttle diplomacy" (as one called it, saying, "I sympathize with Henry Kissinger now") between the Kennedy and Mondale offices, both on

---

*The old check-off provided funds for presidential campaigns but did not spell out how much each could get.

the fourth floor of the Russell Senate Office Building. Agreement was quickly reached on substantive issues, and Kennedy was accepted by all as floor manager and chief sponsor. The bill was basically a merging of Kennedy-Scott and Mondale-Schweiker, with a little of Cranston, Hart, Stevenson, and Senator Robert Stafford of Vermont thrown in. That all occurred late in October and early in November, 1973. In the House there was still delay on the first bill. Senators, senatorial aides, and reformer lobbyists seized on the idea, which seems to have originated with Kennedy and his staff and been endorsed by Hugh Scott, to press the advantage public opinion was creating and try to pass the new bill in the Senate immediately, without waiting for the House to act on the old and without waiting for a lull in a Senate busy with end-of-the-year rush of legislative activity. The Kennedy idea was to attach the bill as an amendment to some nongermane but vital piece of legislation. A bill that *had* to be enacted could not be quietly killed in committee. In this case the routine extension of the debt ceiling was chosen.

The permanent debt ceiling was set by law at $400 billion. A temporary ceiling law had been passed allowing the Treasury to borrow more than that, which it had, but that temporary law expired on December 1. So the House routinely voted to extend a temporary limit through the following June. Without such a law, the Treasury would be prevented from paying bills after a small cash reserve was used up, probably in a week. It was a perfect detour-proof locomotive to attach the campaign finance car to. So on November 27 Kennedy stood up on the floor and announced that he was calling up the campaign finance amalgam as a four-part amendment to the debt ceiling.

"This is legislation by blackmail," complained Utah's conservative Republican, Wallace Bennett; as, of course, it was. It was the sort of manipulating of Senate rules that conservatives had refined to an art over the years. Senator Russell, for example, was a power in the Senate primarily because of his grasp of how the place operated. A number of liberal Democrats had in recent years begun to do what Kennedy was now doing—using the rules as a weapon. As it turned out in this case a Southern conservative would have the last word, but Kennedy still won something.

In rapid-fire order on the 27th, Kennedy called up the separate parts of the amendment—federal financing in House and Senate general elections and limits on contributions and expenditures, which passed 52–40; matching federal payments for contributions of $100 or less for presidential primary campaigns, which passed 54–38; doubling the amount taxpayers could direct the Treasury to pay into the campaign fund and doubling the size of contributions to candidates taxpayers could claim as deductions or credits, which passed 63–28. Solid majorities down the line on legislation that only four months before had been considered opposed by a two-to-one majority in the Senate. Liberals were elated. Some more than others—not unexpectedly, Kennedy's emergence as the star of the show rankled some. As the staff member of one of the senators involved in all this later put it, "No one likes to be upstaged. No one likes to miss out on the kind of coverage you get for floor leadership in a fight like this. We were in on the ground floor on this. It hurt to see Kennedy come in later and get the credit." Actually, Kennedy was in on the ground floor—or at least the second—and then and later he devoted as much time and thought to the issue as anyone.

As it turned out, no campaign-financing law resulted in 1973, despite Kennedy's strategy and the solid bloc of liberal votes. The amended debt-ceiling bill was sent back to the House, which now had to repass it before December 1. Opposition there was fierce, especially to the section dealing with congressional campaigns. On November 29 the House voted 347–54 to send the debt-ceiling bill back to the Senate, after the Rules Committee had stripped it of its campaign-finance amendments, seemingly a defeat for Kennedy, Common Cause, and the liberals. However, before the vote House leaders and the Kennedy forces worked out an agreement to this effect: If the Senate would take the bill back and delete the portions dealing with congressional campaigns, then the House would vote on the debt-ceiling bill with the presidential-campaign features attached.

The next day, a Friday, one day before the temporary debt ceiling was to expire, debate began, and Senator James Allen of Alabama, who had become the chief Southern strategist since the death of Dick Russell, and who had tried and failed to kill the Kennedy amendments on the 27th, announced that he would filibuster, and thus hold up action on the bill till beyond December 1, unless the Senate agreed to drop all campaign finance amendments. With time so short, all niceties were put aside. Mansfield immediately filed a cloture petition to take Allen off his feet. Under the rules the petition could not be voted on for two legislative days, so Mansfield scheduled a Sunday session. Allen was no lone conservative; he had the White House solidly behind him. Over that weekend the usually ghostly Capitol was crawling with lobbyists from the White House and from Common Cause, the Center for Public Financing, and the big unions. What it was not crawling with was enough liberal senators. On Sunday the cloture vote was 47 to shut Allen up and vote on the bill and 33 to let the filibuster go on. That was seven votes short of the required two-thirds. Among those missing were five or six senators who favored campaign financing.

On Monday, the first day of business since the debt limit reverted to $400 billion and borrowing from the cash reserve began, a second cloture try failed. This time the vote was 49–39, with seven supporters of cloture and another two or three supporters of campaign financing not present. Mansfield and Scott then decided time had run out. "We are at a stalemate," Scott said. Allen had won. One parliamentary trick had been foiled by another. Kennedy, Mondale, and the other liberals reluctantly agreed to give up the fight, after Rules Committee Chairman Howard Cannon promised to draft a bill and report it to the floor within a month after Congress came back to work in January.

Cannon was as good as his word. The Kennedy-Scott bill was referred to a Rules and Administration subcommittee headed by Senator Claiborne Pell of Rhode Island. On February 21 the full committee reported out the Kennedy-Scott-Pell bill, basically unchanged from the year before. The vote was 8 to 1, with only Senator Allen opposed. There was almost no question now that the Senate would pass a comprehensive bill. The big hurdle was still the House and particularly Representative Wayne Hays, chairman of the House Administration Committee, which had bottled up the first Senate reform measure of 1973, the version with no public-financing provisions. Hays opposed public financing and, indeed, most campaign reform. He introduced his bill late in March. It did not provide public financing for candidates for the House. It authorized only about one-third as much public assistance to Senate candidates as the Kennedy bill did. It authorized $20 million to each major party candidate in primary and general elections, compared to $22 million authorized in the Kennedy bill. It also did not establish a Federal Elections Commission. There were other bills, including one favored by the Administration that set no spending limits and provided no public financing.*

Hays had unveiled his bill the day after Senate debate started on the Rules Committee's version. Senator Pell spoke for those who saw the Senate bill as an answer to the abuse of power such as the then unfolding Watergate drama highlighted. A number of reformers seemed to feel that Watergate abuses were the target of the effort. But as Walter Pincus of the *New Republic* and other journalists kept arguing, this reform was much more basic than that, transferring power from that small segment of the population (1 percent) which made large contributions to the taxpaying public as a whole. Kennedy acknowledged this. In his March 26 speech in the Senate, for example, he said that the proposed new law should "end the corrosive and corrupting influence of private money in public life. . . . Public decisions will be taken in the future by persons beholden only to the public as a whole." (Kennedy did not acknowledge another criticism Pincus and a number of other followers of the political show made of the new proposal. That was that it was such a new departure, and its results therefore so unpredictable, that it should be tested at the presidential level in 1976, then applied to other elections if that test worked out as reformers were anticipating.)

With Howard Cannon now managing the bill on the floor (a chairman's prerogative), the Senate promptly found itself in a filibuster, led by Senator Allen, maintained by other Southern Democrats and some conservative Republicans. The parliamentary situation, unlike that end-of-the-year fight before, favored the reformers. They had time to

---

*Nixon, his presidency in shreds that spring, threatened that he would veto any other bill, but was not heeded.

let the filibuster run on. On April 4 the first cloture was tried and failed, despite intensive lobbying by Kennedy, Scott, and Cranston. They continued their senator-to-senator campaigning in the cloakrooms and offices. On April 9 the Senate voted 64–30 to end debate. Two days later the bill passed, 53–32, pretty much exactly as it had been introduced, despite some thirty separate attempts on the floor to weaken it. The only significant change was reducing the amount of subsidy authorized from thirty cents (total primary and general elections) per voting-age member of the candidate's constituency to twenty cents.

The House did not act for nearly four months, but on August 8, by a lopsided vote, that body approved a bill weaker than the Senate had passed but stronger than Hays had proposed.

The House-passed version would have established a weak supervisory board, controlled by House and Senate leaders and the president, to administer the law instead of the Senate's independent commission. Reform elements were split on this. Most preferred the independent commission, feeling that it would be above politics. Some, however, preferred a part-time or supervisory or advisory group somewhat like the House version's. The House bill also did not provide for any congressional campaign subsidies, only presidential. Furthermore, where the Senate bill allowed candidates for congressional offices to spend about $180,000 total in primary and general elections, the House version would allow only $120,000. Reformers were almost unanimous in their belief that the higher level was necessary to give challengers a good chance against incumbents. Wayne Hays, who chose and lead the conferees for the House, announced that unless the Senate agreed to accept the House version on spending limits and on the nature of the group to oversee and administer the law, there would be *no* law. Most followers of the long campaign-finance fight probably assumed at that point that Hays could realistically expect to get what he wanted. Certainly no one in Washington believed there was any likelihood of the conference trying to force campaign subsidies on the House. The House had voted on only a partial subsidy plan, one in which federal payments matching private payments would be made, up to one-third of the total spending limits. Even that lost by over forty votes, with a majority in both parties opposing it. *Congressional Quarterly* quoted an aide to a member of Congress who spoke the prevailing wisdom: "The Senate will accept the supervisory board in the House bill with some modifications. You'll probably get House-set spending limits for House races and Senate-set limits for Senate races. Congressional campaign financing will be out, as will be most of the [Senate's] extraneous amendments." The House had voted for a limit on honoraria for federal officials. *CQ*'s source said that was only put in as a bargaining chip, and would be dropped.

Hays was viewed as a single-minded and strong-willed individual who did not like the idea of campaign-finance reform. He would be opposing conferees from the Senate Rules Committee who were not particularly devoted to their own cause. Indeed, committee chairman Cannon and subcommittee chairman Pell had only taken on nominal leadership of the fight after Kennedy, Mondale, Cranston, Mathias, Scott, and Hart had forced the subsidy bill to stage center and kept it there. Four of the nine members of the Rules Committee, from which Senate conferees would normally come, had voted against final passage of the bill back in March. Hays could choose who from the House would sit in on the conference. But at that point, Carey Parker found a single precedent in the previous thirty years for the naming of a conferee who was not a member of the committee which originated a piece of legislation. Kennedy went to Mansfield and asked to be named to the conference.* With Cannon's approval, he was so named. Mansfield then named three other senators not on the Rules Committee: Russell Long, John Pastore, and Dick Clark. Scott named Bennett, Mathias, and Ted Stevens. So suddenly Hays was faced with a formidable opposing force. He complained, but could do nothing more.

That is, he could do nothing more about the composition of the Senate conference committee. He saw to it that

---

*An aide to Mansfield says the initiative was Mansfield's. I believe it was to name others not on Rules to the conference, but that this initiative followed Kennedy's request.

the twelve House members were on his side of the major questions. The conference meetings began in an out-of-the-way committee office under the Capitol dome and were held on and off for over a month. It promptly became obvious that Hays and the House conferees were going to vote as a twelve-member bloc—at Hays's command—on every issue. The three most important issues in dispute stayed in dispute the whole month. Kennedy and Clark were the hard-noses on the Senate side. They attended every conference meeting and they did their homework. One participant in the conference said those two were able to stave off several defeats by pointing out intricacies in the two legislative proposals on the table that other members of the conference were not aware of. In some cases this knowledge stiffened up senators who were ready to concede a point to Hays.

On September 23 Kennedy called a press conference in Boston to announce that he was not going to be a candidate for the presidential nomination in 1976. That may have affected his relationship with other conferees, as has been speculated. I suspect not. Most members of Congress probably do not take such announcements as irrevocable. By late September the presidential sections of the bill were not the source of deadlock: It was the limits on congressional spending, with the House wanting less allowable than the Senate, the nature of the Federal Elections Commission, with the House wanting a less-than-full-time supervisory group serving at the pleasure of officeholders, and subsidies for candidates for Congress, with the House opposing any. Seven times in the last two weeks in September the conference met. On September 25, late in the afternoon, Kennedy called on Hays privately, and something like a bargain was apparently struck. The following Monday, Kennedy, Clark, and chairman Cannon worked out a final Senate position. Campaign subsidies for House and Senate candidates were thrown out. A compromise was reached on the FEC. House and Senate leaders would get to select some commission members, instead of just the president, as the Senate bill proposed, but the job would be full time and the commissioners thus ostensibly free of political control. The limits on congressional spending were a compromise between the House and Senate versions: $140,000 for the House, twenty cents a voter or $250,000, whichever was greater, for each election for Senators. However, the conferees eliminated some campaign expenditures from the total, thus making the conference compromise more like the Senate version. The true limit on House races became $168,000.

So Kennedy's tough stand paid off. Had he and Clark not insisted on congressional campaign financing until the very end, it is likely that the compromise would have come earlier and been more in line with the House version. That became the bargaining chip. One surprise in the final compromise was that the limit on honoraria, which the House thought was the bargaining chip, was kept in at Kennedy's insistence. Most students of campaign reform called the bill (which was passed by House on October 10 and Senate on October 8) a landmark. Neal Gregory, co-director of the Center for Public Financing of Elections, called it "a major breakthrough." President Ford, clearly unhappy, signed the bill anyway. Congressional leaders knew he would if they got it to him before the congressional elections; to have vetoed it would have added a final burdensome straw on the Republican elephant's back. Corruption in government and campaign reform had become linked in the public's mind.

Amid the songs of praise, there were a few harsh notes. Senator Allen was predictably outraged when the Senate passed the bill for the final time. So were some other members of the Senate—including Senator Edward Kennedy. The day the Senate voted, he said in a lengthy statement:

It is with mixed feelings that I support the conference report on S. 3044. . . . There are many worthwhile provisions in this bill . . . but there is also a glaring deficiency . . . its failure to adopt for Senate and House races the same important and basic reform it adopts for presidential races—public financing of elections. Abuses of campaign spending and private campaign financing do not stop at the other end of Pennsylvania Avenue. They dominate congressional elections as well. If the abuses are the same for the presidency and Congress, the reform should also be the same. If public financing is good enough for presidential elections, it should also be good enough for Senate and House elections, too.

The people understand the simple logic of that lesson,

but the conference bill ignores it. . . . In plain view of the nation, Congress is now adopting a blatant "holier than Watergate" attitude on election reform, in spite of the common knowledge that the need for public financing is probably greater for congressional elections than it is for presidential elections. . . . Most, and probably all, of the things that are wrong with Congress have their roots in the way we finance campaigns for the Senate and the House. We get what we pay for. As a result, as Mark Twain liked to say, we have the best Congress that money can buy. . . .

For years, going back in some cases over many decades, on issue after issue of absolutely vital importance to the country, national policy by Congress has been made under the shadow of the mammoth dollar sign—a sign that is the symbol of the enormous private campaign contributions that are flooding federal elections and corrupting American politics.

Who really owns America? Who owns Congress? Is it the people or is it a little group of big campaign contributors and private interest groups? Take six examples that are obviously current today:

Does anyone doubt the connection between America's energy crisis and the campaign contributions of the oil industry?

Does anyone doubt the connection between America's reluctance to enforce effective price restraints and the campaign contributions of the nation's richest corporations?

Does anyone doubt the connection between America's failure to enact decent tax reform and the campaign contributions by private interest groups who benefit from the endless loopholes in present law?

Does anyone doubt the connection between America's health crisis and the campaign contributions of the American Medical Association and the private health insurance industry?

Does anyone doubt the connection between the transportation crisis and the campaign contributions of the highway lobby?

Does anyone doubt the connection between the demoralization of the foreign service and the sale of ambassadorships for private campaign contributions?

. . . These areas are only the beginning of the list. . . . I would venture that for at least a generation, few major pieces of legislation have moved through the House or Senate that do not bear the brand of large campaign contributions with an interest in the outcome.

I quote at length because this speech seems to me to summarize so well Kennedy's legislative mind. But in context it was a strange victory speech. For Kennedy had won a substantive and personal victory. He had forced the general campaign-reform issue precisely by making congressional campaign financing a real possibility. Had there never been that threat to Hays and those who think like him, a much milder reform law would have been enacted. Kennedy enlisted Hugh Scott, forced a revealing vote "when the iron was hot," mastered the subject, put in the long hours on the floor, kept the issue alive and urgent with the debt-ceiling tactic, dominated the conference. What political scientists call "senatorial time" is precious, and Kennedy invested a lot, probably more than any other senator.

Susan King, co-director of the Center for Public Financing of Elections, believes that a great tide was running for campaign reform in 1973 and 1974, and that with or without Kennedy there would still have been significant legislation in 1974. Others agree, and some say Kennedy got more out of the issue than he put into it. All that may be so, but he did put a lot into it, and the shape of the legislation would have been different despite the tide if he had not been involved. His gravity influenced the tide's current more than a little. Another lobbyist who worked on this issue almost daily during this period gives this assessment: "Kennedy's one hell of a legislator. I had never worked with him before. He's prepared. He's committed. He's a fighter. He understands what Jim Allen understands, and what too many liberals don't, that you have to do battle to win." Speaking just of the conference, another lobbyist said, "If it had not been for Kennedy and Clark, the Senate conferees would have given in every point the first day. They kept it going. Hays had all of the House members plus Bennett, who was opposed to the law in any form. They could have voted right down the line at least thirteen to eleven one right after the other and that would have been it." So the tide could have run out. Thanks in large part to Kennedy, it didn't.

The October 8, 1974, speech was a clear sign that Kennedy would keep pushing for campaign reform. Some participants in the 1974 struggle believed that Kennedy and the other liberals made at least an implicit promise not to seek congressional campaign financing in the 94th Congress, to wait until the 1976 presidential campaign had displayed the new system in action. This promise was part of the deal, in this view. Parker and Kennedy say absolutely not. And in February the four men who fought the hardest in conference for congressional financing, Kennedy, Scott, Clark, and Mathias, reintroduced those sections of the 1974 bill which had passed the Senate but had been lost in conference. The Democratic landslide had created a much more liberal and reform-oriented House than that of the 93rd. Whether it was liberal enough and reform-minded enough to go against Wayne Hays on the issue was another question. Hays fended off a challenge to his chairmanship at the organizational meetings early in 1975. And as this is written the prospects for the 94th Congress enacting the Kennedy-Scott-Clark-Mathias bill are considered doubtful.

11. ON THE
WATERFRONT

Not every adventure along the waterfront worked out so successfully for Kennedy in the postclubby 1970s. One reason was that there were just so many adventures. He spread himself thinner and thinner after 1971. He kept tossing more and more balls in the air. "Sometimes it is goddamned impossible to get him to sit down and *listen* to you," said a confidant with some specific ideas about what Kennedy should be doing in the Senate.* A good measure of his ever-widening interest is the card file his office keeps on bills and amendments to bills sponsored or co-sponsored by Kennedy. In the file box in mid-1974 I counted 401 three-by-five cards. There were 134 for bills and amendments Kennedy had introduced, and 267 for those of which he was a co-sponsor, joining forty-nine of his colleagues.

There are a lot of reasons why senators co-sponsor each other's bills. A liberal Democrat might benefit politically by saying to his constituents that his pet project was co-sponsored by Ted Kennedy. A conservative Republican might be able to defuse political opposition by announcing

*His daily schedule gets more and more crowded. It is presented to him every morning on three-by-five cards. Once it took five cards to list all his appointments. In exasperation he tore the cards in half and flung them back to be winnowed down.

that he had been joined by the senior senator from Massachusetts. For Kennedy the advantages are similar. There are arcane, internal, institutional reasons that only senators know for playing the co-sponsorship game. Favor trading, tactical maneuvering, posturing. Kennedy may not even have known what was in some of those 267 bills. He may not even have known what was in some of the 134 bills he introduced as his own. And, of course, some were minor items, some even of a purely technical nature, the "amendment to the amendment" type of thing that to Bob Kennedy epitomized the legislative rut. But still Kennedy, both as sponsor and co-sponsor, gets himself involved with a *lot* of bills, serious bills that become laws. In the 93rd Congress (1973–74), some thirty more or less "major" bills sponsored or co-sponsored by him were enacted into law; another half-dozen passed the Senate but didn't become law. Thirty substantive amendments to legislation were enacted into law. There was a moderately wide range of subject matter. In the postclubby period, expertise was only part of the armor a crusading senator wore. "Just being an expert is not enough," says Kennedy. "I think the way one senator influences another is being extremely well prepared. And the idea itself on its own must have appeal. There are some people here who have the reputation of being experts on subjects who still don't have much influence, because they have the reputation of being on the fringe edges of programs. You have to build a reputation around here so that when someone mentions your name [in connection with a legislative proposal], senators know that that's going to be a responsible type of amendment." Kennedy and a number of other senators take it as an article of faith that a man's reputation for "responsibility" does him as much good in Senate debate as a reputation for expertness. They all cover the waterfront (some range wider than others), and they are the senators who will probably set the tone and the direction of the Senate in the immediate future and beyond. I have in mind Alan Cranston, Frank Church, Adlai Stevenson, Birch Bayh, Charles Mathias, Walter Mondale, and among the more senior senators, Edmund Muskie and, perhaps, Hubert Humphrey and Henry Jackson.

Kennedy's range is wider than any of these, for

good or bad. There are several reasons for this. One is that he sees himself as a national leader, a man who may be president someday, and therefore a man who must be concerned with *all* the nation's problems, even more so than the average modern senator. A second reason Kennedy is effective in a number of areas is that the sweep of the mandate for his Administrative Practice and Procedure Subcommittee is the broadest of that of any legislative unit. AdPrac's responsibility is, according to the resolution that created it:

> to make a full and complete study and investigation of ad-ministrative practices and procedures within the depart-ments and agencies of the United States in the exercise of their rule making, licensing, investigatory, law enforcement, and adjudicary functions, including a study of the Adminis-trative Conference of the United States, with a view to deter-mining whether additional legislation is required to provide for the fair, impartial, and effective performance of such functions.

With a license like that a senator can go hunting anywhere. A third reason Kennedy ranges so far and wide is that there are so many "Kennedy issues." Fallen standards to be picked up. In some cases the surviving brother has really devoted more time and intensity to these issues, held the standards higher, than John and Robert. A lot of Ted Kennedy's inheri-tance, to mix the metaphor, he has carefully reinvested, till that part of his estate is much greater than it was when he received it. Once he was, but now he isn't, living solely off the interest on their capital.

As a national leader, Kennedy has long felt he *had* to be involved in tax policies and legislation. Very high pri-ority, even though until 1975 he had no committee assign-ment in the field. Beginning back in 1969 he showed increas-ing interest, not only introducing tax bills and amendments to bills, but actually investing a good deal of senatorial time in them. Usually his investment has not paid off, at least not directly. In January 1969 the retiring Secretary of the Treasury Joseph Barr warned Congress of a taxpayers' revolt as criticism of the unfairness of the income tax laws mounted. The Democratic Congress responded by initiating and enacting the most comprehensive tax reform in history and the largest tax cut since 1964. Kennedy tried and failed to close some loopholes for wealthy taxpayers (or nontaxpayers). The great reform turned out to be less effective than advertised. Taxpayers still saw the system as inequitable, so liberals in Congress began again to press for reforms. In September 1972, Kennedy tried to force President Nixon to submit a tax-reform proposal. That lost by a 52–24 vote in the Senate. The following year Kennedy proposed that the Secretary of the Treasury be required to submit proposals for comprehensive reform of the Internal Revenue Code within 120 days after enactment of his proposal. The Senate accepted that by voice vote on March 27 as an amendment to another bill. The House Ways and Means Committee, which originates most tax legislation, had begun hearings on tax reform the previous month, but the Administration remained silent on the issue. Members of Congress, special-interest representatives, and economists paraded before the Committee to offer suggestions. Kennedy testified on April 17, presenting twenty specific proposed reforms. Included were a tightening of the minimum tax law aimed at wealthy individuals with sheltered income, a $150 tax credit instead of the existing $750 personal exemption, a reduction of the oil depletion allowance from 22 percent to 15 percent, an increase in the capital gains tax. It was a comprehensive, liberal reform program, summarized philosophically in this exchange with committee Representative James Burke:

> *Mr. Burke.* Senator, with this rising cost of living and the escalation in food prices, housing, rentals, clothing, everything that is taking place, don't you believe that something should be done to transfer the burden of taxation from the low-wage earner and middle-income person?
>
> *Kennedy.* Congressman Burke, I would certainly agree, and as I understand it, that is a major purpose of these hearings. I think that there are a num-

ber of steps, just a few of which I outlined here this morning, which would very definitely provide the kind of relief suggested in your question.

Especially in the area of credits rather than exemptions and deductions, as I indicated in my statement, Congress has the opportunity to provide a considerable amount of tax relief not only for the low-income wage earner, but also for the middle-income person.

Meanwhile, Kennedy's amendment compelling the Treasury secretary to submit a proposal had been dropped in conference because Secretary George P. Shultz had announced that he would testify before the Ways and Means Committee. He did on April 30. All he proposed was the closing of some loopholes. "It doesn't go far enough," Chairman Wilbur Mills told him. It appeared that Congress might repeat the 1969 scenario, when it wrote its own tax-reform legislation and forced it on the Administration. Had it done so, Kennedy might have played something of a central role, for he was determined to become involved in tax-policy-making if he could. Carey Parker was proficient at working on legislative proposals in this field, and Kennedy was able to draw outside assistance from such liberal economists as Walter Heller of the University of Minnesota, who had been chairman of John Kennedy's Council of Economic Advisers, Joseph Pechman and Arthur Okun of the Brookings Institution, and others. But Congress did not act on a comprehensive reform bill. Wilbur Mills was ill and unable to attend to committee business, so the House decided to postpone the matter until 1974.

Another tax "reform" was in the works. The House approved a minor measure easing tax burdens on former prisoners of war. In November the Senate Finance Committee, which is notorious for its responsiveness to special interests, added on to that amendments giving special tax treatment to a large number of private groups. Such Finance Committee handiwork usually comes at the end of a session, when it is relatively easy to slip or force such legislation through a weary Senate. The timing and the nature of the legislation have produced the name "Christmas tree tax bill." This one didn't quite make it for Christmas. But on January 23 Finance chairman Russell Long brought the bill on the floor. Senator William Proxmire tried and failed to kill the various amendments. Then Kennedy dove in from another direction. He, Parker, Okun, and Pechman met at Kennedy's home the night after Proxmire failed in his attempt to smash the Christmas tree ornaments. They decided to use the Christmas tree strategy for another purpose. The next day Kennedy proposed an amendment raising the personal income tax exemption from $750 to $850, retroactive to 1973. This was not a reform measure but an attempt to pump spending money back into an ailing economy. Kennedy and a number of other liberals had begun to fear that the country was sinking into a bad recession. Kennedy's measure would, he estimated, put $3.5 billion into circulation. Harry Byrd and other conservatives argued that this would increase the deficit and add to inflation, but the Senate went along with Kennedy 53–27. Then Kennedy made a gesture at reform, while he had the Senate's attention. He brought up his old amendment to tighten the minimum tax on the investment income of the wealthy. That would offset an estimated $860 million of the deficit, he said. Conservatives on the Finance Committee objected that rewriting basic tax law on the floor, without hearings first, was the wrong way to legislate, as it probably is. But the Senate again went with Kennedy, 47–32. Chairman Russell Long then arose and said it was obvious the Senate wanted to pass a tax bill, so he proposed that the Finance Committee start all over. The whole bill was sent back to committee by a vote of 48–27.

It is not all that unusual for a liberal Democrat not on the Finance Committee to lead the fight on the floor for liberal tax laws. There are liberals on the committee, but not a majority. Russell Long's power as chairman is awesome. His willingness to use it is legendary. And he is not always sympathetic to liberalizing tax proposals. So usually such liberal Finance members as Minnesota's Walter Mondale, Wisconsin's Gaylord Nelson, and (since 1975) Maine's William Hathaway and Colorado's Floyd Haskell cannot be as assertive and challenging on the floor as noncommittee liberals. Since 1975 the situation has begun to change. The liberals on the committee are a large enough minority to constitute a near balance to Long and the conservatives.

This does not mean that those liberals do not ever make a fight for legislation they consider important. Senator Mondale had a tax bill of his own in 1974. Its centerpiece was the substitution of a $200 tax credit for the personal exemption. A credit is a more progressive way of cutting taxes than an exemption increase. It is worth exactly as much to a low-bracket taxpayer as to a high-bracket one. A deduction is worth more the higher your bracket. Mondale announced his intentions on January 28. The following month, Kennedy's Parker and Mondale's James Verdiere began working together on a "blending" of the Mondale bill and a Kennedy proposal. Kennedy had begun to feel some liberal backlash over his priorities: cut first, reform later. He agreed that a bill should have both the cut and reform features. The staff-level conferences were expanded to include representatives of other liberal senators who had pet tax measures. These included Nelson, Birch Bayh, Dick Clark, Alan Cranston, Phil Hart, Hubert Humphrey, and Edmund Muskie. While these negotiations were going on, a compromise version of the Kennedy and Mondale bills was introduced. A taxpayer could opt for a $190 credit or an $825 exemption. From Mondale's aides' perspective, the bill was "ninety percent Mondale," but Kennedy insisted that it be introduced with his name on it first as principal sponsor. As noted above, there are complex reasons for co-sponsorship, but there is a very simple rule at work when two or more senators work out something together. The one with the most "muscle" gets to put his name first. Parker says that in this case Kennedy *deserved* to introduce the bill in his name ("By Mr. Kennedy and . . ."), since he was first to propose a credit for reform (to Ways and Means in 1973) and first to propose a cut for stimulus (on the floor the previous January). Actually it is almost impossible to establish who was for what first over long careers, but Parker had a point.

As it turned out, neither senator got to introduce the principal liberal reform bill of 1974. The conferences involving the seven senators named above plus Kennedy and Mondale produced in May a four-part reform-cut bill to be blended with the Kennedy-Mondale bill, then substituted for it. The principals now were just Kennedy, Mondale, Bayh, Clark, Hart, Humphrey, and Muskie. And civil war broke out over who would put his name on *this* bill. The usual arguments were advanced: one would work hardest, one would provide most staff, one had done the most work so far—one needed the publicity. Everybody had muscle, so on the last count the decision was made (after a suggestion that the senators draw straws was turned down): Birch Bayh was up for reelection, faced a tough challenge. Bayh introduced the bill. However, his campaign was so demanding that he was not available to invest the senatorial time necessary. So it became Humphrey's bill. (More tax men on his staff, more senatorial time promised.) Personal income taxes were cut by $6.5 billion, with about $4 billion of that made up by increasing business taxes, notably on oil companies, by reducing the percentage depletion allowance. So Kennedy's stimulus to the economy would not be as inflationary as conservatives feared. But they still opposed it.

Long wouldn't act in committee on the package, but agreed to floor efforts to attach the tax measures to a routine increase in the debt ceiling in late June. This was the strategy that had been followed unsuccessfully the previous year in the campaign-finance battle. Once again the crafty James Allen was the principal adversary. After four days of futile voting on procedural motions, the liberals had to give up. Kennedy called the week's events "a tragic circus." He blamed Allen's maneuvering for their defeat. It is doubtful, however, that the liberals had the votes for their program. Many senators did not believe that fiscal and economic policy could and should be set in the heated give-and-take of floor debates. Others believed that the recession Kennedy, Mondale, Humphrey, and the others were talking about was not as much of a problem as inflation was. Indeed, shortly after Gerald Ford became president later that year, he and his economic advisers proposed an immediate income tax *increase*. Events following that proved the liberals right, and the next Congress passed and the President signed a bill cutting 1973 and 1974 taxes by $22.8 billion. Kennedy said then that if his tax-cut bill of the previous January had been enacted, the worst of the recession might have been headed off at much less cost.

That 1975 tax-cut bill achieved one thing that liberals in Congress had been fighting for for years: a repeal of the percentage depletion allowance for major oil companies. It allowed companies to pay no taxes on a large part of their income. The House, lopsidedly Democratic after the 1974 elections, ended depletion for all oil producers on February 27, then passed the bill. The Finance Committee killed that provision on March 4. On March 7 Kennedy and South Carolina's Ernest Hollings announced that they would make the fight for repeal of percentage depletion on the Senate floor. Common Cause was the most active lobby in behalf of repeal. Fred Wertheimer, the chief lobbyist, wanted Kennedy to lead the fight. "We were so impressed with him on the campaign-finance legislation," said Wertheimer. "We had to have somebody who would work at it, put in senator-to-senator time, learn the issue. We knew he would." But at first he wouldn't. He told Common Cause he had his hands full. Senator Hollings volunteered, to the surprise and de-light of the organization and the liberals. Hollings is a courtly, moderately conservative Southerner. He knew the subject from his Oceans and Atmosphere Subcommittee's work on off-shore drilling. He was willing to work. With at least half the responsibility and work load thus removed, Kennedy agreed to co-sponsor the repealer. Aristotle Onas-sis's death and funeral took him away from the Senate the first two days of the three-day fight on repeal. Hollings led the successful effort alone, with his and Kennedy's staff working together.

Tax cutting and tax reforming are fairly exciting stuff in headlines, but it is tedious and time-consuming and bor-ing legislation to master in the prevote stage. That Kennedy, the most glamorous member of Senator Mansfield's gray flannel organization, as he terms it, should have become a respected worker in the tax field is surprising to me, as it was to Wertheimer, and as it was to a member of another liberal senator's staff who specializes in tax matters. Referring to the June 1974 effort to cut taxes $6.5 billion, he told me, "Let me give Kennedy an unsolicited endorsement—I was im-pressed with Kennedy. I had heard he was flighty. But of all the liberals only he and Humphrey were on the floor every day, and he was probably there more hours than Humphrey.

He knew the legislation, too. He obviously had done his homework." Referring to that same period, Kennedy once said to me, "I was on the floor every day. I stayed with it. *That's* why I get so much attention in the press." That's not the whole reason, by a long shot, but it is an overlooked part of it.

When in January 1975 Kennedy submitted his budget request for the Administrative Practice and Procedure Subcommittee, he needed nearly ten single-spaced typed pages to give "a brief review of some of the Subcommittee's activities [in 1974] and future plans." Here is a brief review of the brief review: oversight of the Civil Aeronautics Board, oversight of the Federal Energy Administration, oversight of the Food and Drug Administration, proposals for revision of the Administrative Procedure Act, drafting and getting enacted major Freedom of Information Act amendments, drafting but not yet getting passed legislation dealing with warrantless wiretapping and surveillance, administrative recommendations on fiscal and education accountability in special federal Indian education programs, administrative recommendations for the Clemency Board, rough-draft legislation to make it easier for citizens to intervene in administrative proceedings, an analysis of wage-price controls and a design of an administrative framework for a controls program, inquiry into Internal Revenue Service disclosure practices.

Previous budget letters were almost as full of accomplishments and desired results. The 1975 letter may have been a little unusual, in that it discussed and proposed legislation somewhat more than previous letters had. In its early years under Kennedy the subcommittee had been less a law-writing instrument and more a "bully pulpit," as Peter H. Schuck and Michael Massing of the Ralph Nader Congress Project concluded. Bully pulpit for the chairman, of course. Jim Flug, the former chief counsel for the subcommittee, called it "the fire brigade for liberal causes." To which Schuck and Massing responded, the subcommittee will inevitably be "rushing feverishly from one conflagration to another, leaving the rebuilding and analysis of source and solution to others. Perhaps that is as it should be. If Chief Kennedy's brigade is seen racing toward the Federal Power

Commission today, neither the Department of Labor nor the congressional committees that are supposed to oversee it may rest easy. [The subcommittee's] sirens may be shrieking at them tomorrow, with Walter Cronkite and Company close behind." That is a perceptive comment on the way the subcommittee (and the networks) behaved in the past, but beginning in 1974 the emphasis changed. True oversight and the writing of legislation began to occupy more of the subcommittee's and the chairman's time.

The Freedom of Information amendments package was the first significant piece of legislation produced by the subcommittee under Kennedy. This was an area of interest to Kennedy, but it was not a Kennedy bill when it began to move through Congress. To a significant degree it was a Kennedy bill when it became law.

The Freedom of Information Act, which provided for easy public access to government documents, had become law in 1966. Representative John E. Moss of California had been the leading congressional advocate of more open information policies. Within a few years after the law went into effect, Moss and other liberals in Congress concluded that it wasn't strong enough. Bureaucrats and policy-makers were getting around it, principally by claiming national security as an excuse for keeping records closed. So proposals for a tightening-up of the law began to make their way through the legislative mills. The House acted first, passing a new bill proposed by Representative William S. Moorehead of Pennsylvania, in March. The vote was 383–8. In the Senate two Judiciary subcommittees, Administrative Practice, Constitutional Rights, and the Intergovernmental Relations Subcommittee of Government Operations, held joint hearings on the Freedom of Information bill as introduced by Senator Edmund Muskie, and two somewhat related bills. Muskie's bill was similar to but tougher than the Moorehead bill. The Maine senator wanted judges to have more freedom in deciding whether to honor a government official's claim of national security in withholding information. Conservatives strenuously objected to that. After the joint hearings, the Muskie Freedom of Information bill was redrafted in Kennedy's name at Administrative Practice. The Muskie language on judges was deleted. Kennedy believed he could

not get the bill through the full Judiciary Committee otherwise. Kennedy did add one strengthening section to the bill.
It provided for sanctions—suspension up to sixty days—
against a federal employee who withheld documents "without a reasonable basis in law."

With the bill out of the then still conservative Judiciary Committee, Kennedy, who was floor manager for the
bill, lent his support to Muskie on the floor, and the Muskie
amendment regarding judges was voted back in the bill.
Kennedy also successfully supported an amendment offered
by Phil Hart of Michigan that would make it more difficult
for federal law-enforcement agencies to withhold information in investigatory files. Senator Roman Hruska of
Nebraska, senior Republican member of the Judiciary Committee, led the fight against these amendments. When they
were both adopted, Hruska said that he had planned to vote
for the bill, but couldn't now. He said he would urge President Nixon to veto it. The Senate passed the bill 64–17.

Kennedy was chief manager of the Senate contingent
to the conference. The differing versions of the bill were
worked out more or less in the direction of the Senate version. The only real conflict came over Kennedy's sanctions
section, but he held firm and it stayed in. The climate of
public opinion that summer of impeachment hearings was
clearly in favor of anything procitizen and openness and
antigovernment and secrecy. The conferees were just ready
to seal their work on August 21 when President Ford, in
office only two weeks, sent a personal appeal for a watering
down of the three key sections: judicial review, investigatory files, sanctions. The conferees, in a spirit of mild con-
ciliation with the new president, made some minor changes.
In October the Senate passed the bill by voice vote and the
House by 349–2. And Ford vetoed it.

That was not as much of a Kamikazi veto as it might
appear. The House was going to override, that was obvious
from the two lopsided votes in support of the bill there. But
Ford might be able to get his one-third-plus-one vote in the
Senate by making an appeal to Republicans to rally behind
their new president in a trying time. It wouldn't be like
rallying behind Nixon in behalf of secrecy, which had become impossible before he left. The votes on override were

scheduled after the election recess. As expected, the House vote was not even close, 371–31. Kennedy and Muskie, who had been hard at work rounding up votes, made the principal speeches in favor of the override, and prevailed, but only by a three-vote margin, 65–27, as Minority Leader Hugh Scott, who had voted for the bill the first time, now switched and took most Republicans along with him.

Because he likes to be in the thick of things legislatively, and because he uses the Administrative Practice and Procedure Subcommittee to educate himself on a variety of topics, Kennedy often gets out in front on an important issue before those of his Senate colleagues who have prime responsibility in an issue area realize there *is* an issue. A good example of this occurred in the winter of 1974–75. Congress passed and President Ford signed a new foreign trade act. One section of it required a president to hold hearings (except when "inappropriate") before imposing import limits for "national security" purposes. The authority of presidents to do that had long been a sore point with Kennedy. In 1970, not long after Kennedy became chairman of the subcommittee, he held hearings on a Nixon order imposing mandatory quotas on Canadian oil imports. (New England is keenly interested in the politics of imported oil, since so much of the energy for its long, cold winters is produced by imported oil. However, that comes from the Middle East. Canadian oil is used by Middle Westerners. Kennedy often uses his subcommittees to serve parochial interests, but in the case of the 1970 hearings, he was representing his national constituency, not his state or regional one.) The point Kennedy made over and over again during his interrogation of Administration witnesses was that invoking the phrase "national security" in order to impose quotas, which the President had done, could not go unquestioned, that it had to be proved. But it didn't then.

In late December 1974, there were press reports that President Ford was planning to impose a new $3-a-barrel tarriff on imported oil. In December Kennedy wrote Ford and asked him to hold hearings first. On January 13, Kennedy wrote him and "strongly urged" him to hold hearings. He told Ford in both letters that he believed action without hearings was illegal under the new trade law. On the night of January 13 the President previewed his policies in a televised speech, then went into more detail two days later in his State of the Union address: $1 a barrel on February 1, another $1 a barrel on March 1, another $1 on April 1. Kennedy promptly introduced a legislative resolution that would permanently prevent the President from taking such action. It was pigeonholed and ignored. Kennedy had discussed the situation with Senator Henry Jackson, chairman of the Interior Committee and a leading Senate authority on energy matters. Jackson wasn't interested in co-sponsoring the permanent resolution, but he agreed when Kennedy asked him to join in sponsoring a joint resolution that would delay the imposition of oil import fees for sixty days, after which increases could only be imposed if approved by Congress within thirty days. The Kennedy-Jackson resolution was introduced, with fifty-two co-sponsors, on January 23. Majority Leader Thomas P. (Tip) O'Neill, Jr., from John Kennedy's old congressional district, introduced both the permanent and temporary ban in the House. But the newly liberal Ways and Means Committee pushed through legislation that would have the same effect as the resolution delaying the fees for ninety days. This passed the House handily, and then the Senate by a 66–28 vote. President Ford vetoed the bill. Democrats did not force a veto override try and Ford agreed to a compromise: $1 in new fees, but nothing else for ninety days while the Congress worked on its own energy proposals. Congress got nothing done in the ninety days, so Ford added a second $1.

Kennedy got a fair amount of positive publicity during the period the Kennedy-Jackson resolution was being debated in the Senate, before the House bill came over. As did Jackson. Jackson formally announced his candidacy for the presidency on February 6, the day after the House acted on the import-fee bill. The fact that this announcement was coming was discussed by Kennedy and his advisers when they considered asking Jackson to co-sponsor the resolution. Would the alliance with Kennedy and the publicity that resulted seem to other Democratic hopefuls a Kennedy assist to Jackson? Would it help Jackson in his presidential quest? Participants in the meeting insist that *Kennedy's* political interests vis-à-vis Jackson were never discussed. The thought occurred to a few people there, though. But it was probably a secondary consideration, even politically. What Kennedy gained most, politically, in this episode was the opportunity to be a principal in a debate on an issue of great national import. Energy was as hot a topic as taxes in 1975. A senator who aspired to national leadership in the seventies could not afford to leave energy issues to the Senate specialists, any more than he could afford to leave taxes to them.

When Kennedy held hearings on the Canadian oil quotas in 1970, he justified them by saying that procedures of the Office of Emergency Preparedness were upsetting to him. OEP is responsible under the law for determining when changes are needed in quotas and similar arrangements. "No hearings were held concerning this," Kennedy said at the time. ". . . The Administrative Procedure Act was ignored." And so on. Since Kennedy used the forum of the hearings to berate the Administration, a number of commentators concluded that Kennedy was exercising not so much a legislative oversight function as a partisan political one. Yet oversight, a neglected congressional responsibility, has been a Kennedy interest. The reason Congress does not always do its duty in maintaining oversight of government agencies was once succinctly explained by Alan L. Otten in the *Wall Street Journal*.

> Trying to determine whether a government program is working well, or is working as Congress intended, is tedious labor. Frequently, the committee charged with oversight is stacked with lawmakers who have close ties to the people administering the program or benefitting from it. Unless it hits scandal or other publicity-rich paydirt, tough oversight gains an ambitious legislator far fewer friends than most other things he could be doing.
>
> All the more surprising then that Mr. Kennedy should invest substantial amounts of time and energy in this sort of activity.

What had caught Otten's eye was AdPrac's oversight hearings involving the Civil Aeronautics Board. In the sum-

mer of 1974, Kennedy was trying to hire professor Stephen
Breyer of the Harvard Law School for the subcommittee
staff. Breyer was a specialist in administrative law. Though
he would not accept a full-time job with Kennedy, he agreed
to devote part of his just beginning sabbatical to one project.
He told Kennedy he thought the subcommittee ought to
start focusing its attention on the whole question of government economic regulations. AdPrac's new chief counsel,
Thomas M. Susman, was similarly interested in the subcommittee's developing a single "theme" such as economic
regulation. Liberal Democrats like Kennedy had assumed as
an article of faith that this regulation kept large industrial
organizations from harming and gouging consumers. But
had it? Was that the way things had worked? Breyer argued
that in fact that may not have been what had happened.
Why not spend a year or two investigating some of the
government agencies that regulated economic activity? for
starters, the CAB. Kennedy liked the idea, because, as he
said later, his years of trying to get the CAB to improve
service or lower fares in New England had led him to won-
der if that might be easier for the carriers to do if there were
less or no regulation.

There was a catch in Breyer's idea. AdPrac had no
funds for such a study. In order to get extra funds Kennedy
would have to make a special request first to the Judiciary
Committee, which was no problem, then to the Rules Committee, which was very much a problem. The chairman of
that committee was Howard Cannon of Nevada. He was also
chairman of the Aviation Subcommittee of the Commerce
Committee, which was supposed to be exercising oversight
of the CAB. That subcommittee's coziness with the airlines
industry and the CAB bureaucracy was the sort of relationship Otten had in mind when he wrote his column.

On September 17 Kennedy and Strom Thurmond,
the ranking Republican on the AdPrac Subcommittee, won
Judiciary Committee approval to seek $56,100 in supple-
mental funds for the CAB hearings. Before the Rules Committee met to consider the request, Kennedy scheduled
hearings beginning October 7. Letters over his signature
began to go to airlines and government officials, requesting
data and/or their appearance to testify. While the prepara-

Kennedy, H. Stuart Hughes, and George Cabot Lodge prepare for a debate in the 1962 Massachusetts Senate race.

Joan Kennedy did the campaigning in 1964, as Edward recuperated from injuries received in a plane crash.

Kennedy greets his Republican opponent Josiah Spaulding in a 1970 campaign event. (BOSTON GLOBE PHOTOS)

A year after his plane crash Kennedy still used a cane. He is shown with administrative assistant Dave Burke. (UPI)

Kennedy and Judiciary Committee Chairman James Eastland, who boosted Kennedy's career despite their differences. (UPI)

President Kennedy and Senator Kennedy, at a party fund-raising dinner in Boston in 1963. (UPI)

Two Senators Kennedy marching in a Saint Patrick's Day parade in Dorchester in 1968. (BOSTON GLOBE PHOTO)

Senator Kennedy and Massachusetts State Auditor Thaddeus Buczko on a 1969 tour of an ABM site on the North Shore. (BOSTON GLOBE PHOTO)

Kennedy in a televised address after the tragedy at Chappaquiddick asked Massachusetts voters if he should stay in the Senate. (WIDE WORLD PHOTO)

Kennedy addressing the World Affairs Council in Boston in 1970.

Senators listen as often as they speak. Kennedy at a committee hearing on noise pollution at Logan Airport. (BOSTON GLOBE PHOTOS)

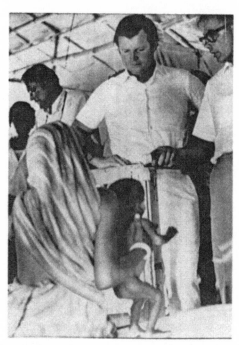

Kennedy visits a hospital in India in 1971 where refugees from the war in East Pakistan fled seeking help.

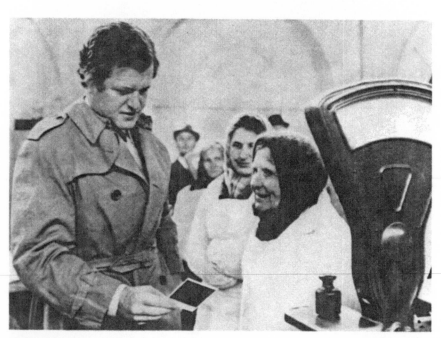

Kennedy at the central market in Moscow during a 1974 tour of world capitals.
(WIDE WORLD PHOTOS)

Senator Kennedy and Representative Wilbur Mills testify in favor of national health insurance before the 1972 Democratic party platform committee.

Kennedy, Senator Henry Jackson, and Senator Ernest Hollings outline the Democratic energy program at a 1975 press conference. (WIDE WORLD PHOTOS)

Boston opponents of busing of school children objected to Kennedy's support of the desegregation effort. Here he meets a picket en route to a Boston speech.

Meeting voters in a snowstorm in western Massachusetts in 1974, his mind then undecided about his 1976 plans. (WIDE WORLD PHOTOS)

tions for the hearings were being made, an article appeared in the Washington papers saying that the Department of Transportation had invited officials of both the trunk and supplemental airlines to a meeting on September 27, to agree on a minimum charge for charter flights. (The trunks are the major scheduled airlines, and often complain that they lose business to the supplementals, which charge lower fares for the same trips on a charter basis.) Breyer went to the DOT meeting. He later reported that the whole thing was "unbelievable." The CAB and Transportation officials were not just inviting but coercing the carriers to fix prices, he told Kennedy. The meeting was just the latest episode in that effort, which had begun in 1973. Kennedy decided to use the already scheduled hearings to pressure the government officials to retreat. The word got out. On October 4 Senator Cannon and Senator Warren Magnuson, chairman of the full Commerce committee and a long-time friend of the aviation industry (Boeing's home is in his state of Washington), wrote Kennedy, "We must strongly urge that these hearings be cancelled, or, at the very least postponed." Pan American Airways, said the two senators, was facing bankruptcy, and if the bankers who handled the firm's line of credit were led to believe Pan Am couldn't get the government to assist it against the supplementals, that could be the last straw. Pan Am was one of only two trunk airlines that was also in the charter business. The letter also made the point that "the issues which have been raised by your staff are properly within the jurisdiction of the Committee on Commerce." DOT officials had been making the same protestations regarding Pan Am's precarious state to Breyer. One high-ranking official gave Breyer Pan Am's latest financial statement and "shouted" at him, Breyer says, that it would be Kennedy's fault if the huge firm went bankrupt.

Kennedy quizzed Breyer about the threats coming from DOT and Magnuson and Cannon. Would the hearings hurt Pan Am? "There's no good answer." Is Pan Am likely to declare bankruptcy? "It might. But if it fails it won't be because of the hearings." Then why *not* have the hearings? "Because if you have the hearings and Pan Am does fail, you'll be blamed." Kennedy told Breyer to go ahead, and sent a letter to Magnuson and Cannon first insisting that his subcommittee did have jurisdiction over the issues involved, and second agreeing to a postponement of the hearings for three or four weeks. Cannon complained again at the Rules Committee hearing the following week, but on October 10 Kennedy got $31,100 for his investigation. He rescheduled the hearings for November 7 and 8. It was a fortuitous postponement. On October 18 CAB issued a "policy statement" that would in effect require charter flights to raise their minimum rates. On October 30 CAB announced that it was going to change its rules on so-called affinity groups that would curtail charter activity by supplementals. So Kennedy was able to come on strong at the hearings. He went at CAB, DOT, and State Department officials for working with airlines' officials to raise rates and for doing it out of sight of the public. The various contacts, agreements, and rules may even have been illegal, he said. Illegal or not, they were improper. And it was not just the charter-flight business that disturbed him, he told the witnesses in November and the full Senate in a speech in December. Some testimony and other evidence gathered by the subcommittee staff, plus criticisms of the industry from other sources, suggested that:

> There may be something fundamentally wrong with the manner in which the CAB carries out its statutory responsibility to regulate air carriers "in the public interest." Are its practices and procedures adequate to bring about the basic objective of airline regulation: adequate service at reasonable prices?
> The Senate Judiciary Subcommittee on Administrative Practice and Procedure, which I chair, intends to conduct a comprehensive inquiry into this basic question. . . . To be more specific, the hearings will . . . examine the Board's ratemaking practices and procedures. . . . The subcommittee will consider the Board's procedures for deciding route award cases. . . . The subcommittee will inquire whether the Board's regulatory practices and procedures are adequate to protect and further the legitimate interests of the nonbusiness, discretionary traveler.

Since he knew the answers to those questions to begin with, or thought he did, there was something of a verdict

first, trial afterwards aspect to the speech. That is not un-
common in legislative bodies. The role Kennedy and the
subcommittee were now going to play was that of a catalyst
rather than a fact-finder. There were a number of other
people in Congress, in the airlines industry, and in the executive branch who had concluded on the basis of old evidence that economic regulation did not work. The subcommittee was reviving some of them, spurring others,
embarrassing others, and forcing still others to compete
with it—and Kennedy—for the favor of a public that, it was
anticipated, would favor political officials who brought them
cheaper air transportation. The hearings began on February
6, with a blue-ribbon group of witnesses, Robert Binder,
assistant secretary of Transportation for Policy, Plans and
International Affairs, Thomas E. Kauper, assistant attorney
general (Antitrust—the one part of the bureaucracy that had
consistently if unavailingly opposed the rate-making and
route-awarding practices of the airlines and policies of the
CAB), several economists who specialized in transportation
matters, and a vice-president and the general counsel of the
Air Transport Association, the airlines industry trade organization and lobbying arm. These would be followed in five
more hearings that month by airline officials, travel and
consumer-group spokesmen, Ralph Nader, and a number of
government officials. The hearings made some headlines,
partly because it was Kennedy holding them, but mostly
because legitimate news was being made; including the
tragic suicide of William Gingery, head of the CAB's Bureau
of Enforcement, who had been scheduled to be a witness. In
a suicide note addressed to the subcommittee staff, Gingery
charged that airlines made illegal payments to government
and political leaders in order to get favorable treatment.
The staff turned the note over to the Special Prosecutor's
office. By March 3, the day before the final hearings,
Kennedy could announce to a conference on the CAB and
the consumer the concrete results of his investigation and
hearings, though he did not put it so directly. The way he
put it was, "Even without new laws or a restructured
agency, the flexible open-minded attitude of the present
CAB members is already bringing about a change in the
regulatory climate." He enumerated the victories: The CAB
had withdrawn its minimum floor for charter flights; a route

moratorium, which protected carriers from new competition, had been ended; and the board was planning hearings on new applications for routes. CAB staff recommendations for a more restrictive route-award policy had been killed by the chairman. The CAB had established a study group of outsiders to recommend reforms. Airlines were reducing fares through such devices as the National-inspired no-frills service.

The airlines were not particularly happy with all this. Kennedy had asked industry officials what would happen if there were deregulation to the point that each airline could set its own fares and decide for itself what cities it would serve. The Air Transport Association replied with a lengthy analysis, which concluded that of 994 carrier routes studied, 372 might be canceled and "nearly all" of the rest might have to curtail services. And 826 subsidized local service carrier routes might be eliminated. The ATA sent copies of the analysis and conclusions to every member of the Senate the same day it gave Kennedy and the subcommittee their copies. The threat of losing service is usually a quick way to get a member of Congress on an airline's side. Kennedy fired off copies of the study to the Council of Economic Advisers and the Council on Wage and Price Stability, asking them to criticize it. President Ford had recently announced that he liked the idea of deregulation. By May 1 Kennedy had replies from the two White House units. Economists at both debunked the ATA study. Kennedy also sought other rebuttal to the ATA, and kept his fellow senators informed in a counterlobbying effort consisting of "Dear Colleague" letters.

The final result for Kennedy and the subcommittee was a series of legislative changes recommended in late summer to the Aviation Subcommittee, which retained legislative authority, of course, and Kennedy's subcommittee turned its attention to the Federal Energy Administration.

Kennedy relished that year's effort almost as much as any of his Senate endeavors, according to confidants. "It was perfect," one put it. "He saw a big industry not doing its job, getting away with it because the government wasn't doing its job. The board wasn't doing what it was supposed to do to the airlines, and the Congress wasn't doing what it was supposed to do to the board. So he moved in. And as a result everything started happening. The withdrawal of the minimum rate for charters, the no-frills fares, the end of the moratorium, the President coming out for deregulation. He won't say so, but I think he got a big kick out of the fact that two senior senators didn't want him sticking his nose into what they regarded as their business, but they couldn't stop him."

Why did Kennedy do it? I asked Steve Breyer that once. I said it hardly seemed to me to be the sort of issue that fit his image of a man always fighting in behalf of the poor and the disadvantaged. Middle-class people use the airlines. "You're wrong about that," he replied. "Kennedy always thought that if fares could be brought down, then the working man could afford to take his family places he couldn't afford to otherwise." I looked back through the speeches and records of hearings and that thread did emerge. To use a much-abused word, I would say Kennedy was engaged in a modern *populist* crusade. The airlines of the 1970s became for him the railroads of the 1880s. It wasn't simple nineteenth-century concentration of economic power that he feared so much as it was the union of the economic power of the airlines and the governing power of the regulators. That concentration was costly to the consumer of air travel, and priced many would-be consumers out of the air. Time and again Kennedy complained in behalf of the working-man, who could afford $15 to fly from Boston to New York, but not $28, and so on. Another facet of this "populism" was expressed succinctly in his comments on the charter minimum rate. It may be important to subsidize Pan Am for reasons of national pride or national defense, he said, in which case the benefit would flow to all Americans. But there is no reason why passengers of charter airlines alone should do the subsidizing. "Indeed, since passengers of charter airlines are often poorer than passengers on scheduled airlines, raising charter rates to help Pan American is a classic example of government action that subsidizes the rich by taxing the poor."

In another sense, the subcommittee's effort and the payoff were politically and ideologically neutral. It was an institutional success. Next to Kennedy the senator who invested the most time and energy to the CAB project was Strom Thurmond, the conservative Republican (former Democrat, former Dixiecrat). Reflecting on that one day, Kennedy said, "You know, Strom was just great. He and I came at this from exactly opposite sides. I wanted lower fares so more people could afford to fly, so people who did fly would not have to spend so much. Strom just philosophically wants airlines, everybody, to be as free of government regulation as possible. But we came to the same conclusion, worked together, and got the desired results."

There is a uniquely "Kennedy issue" that is not exactly a fallen standard. Ted Kennedy has been deeply and, until now, futilely involved in fighting for legislation in connection with this issue, though he has no direct committee mandate to deal with it. The full Judiciary Committee writes the law in this field, but the work is done by a subcommittee chaired by Birch Bayh of Indiana. The issue is gun control. As a senator John Kennedy pushed for legislation banning the importation of cheap foreign guns, and as president he coerced Bayh's predecessor, Thomas Dodd, to come up with some sort of antigun bill after the June 1963 assassination of Mississippi civil-rights leader Medgar Evers. Robert Kennedy co-sponsored a bill with the same aim after he came to the Senate. But Ted Kennedy's commitment to the issue derived not from his brothers' earlier efforts, but from the fact that both were assassinated by gunmen.

Ted Kennedy's campaign for gun control can be said to have begun at a number of points in his career post-November 22, 1963. As good as any is the spring of 1967, when Kennedy went to the annual meeting of the National Rifle Association, most of whose members author Robert Sherrill characterizes as being "energized by mild-to-extreme paranoia on the question of gun controls."* Kennedy requested the invitation. He was allowed to ap-

---

*"If one wants to indulge in easy symbolism," Sherrill wrote in 1973, "it can be said that the fight over gun controls during the past decade has been between the three Kennedy brothers—through their active advocacy or because they have stood as the paramount lesson of why more controls were needed—and the National Rifle Association."

pear before the Executive Committee, but not the full membership. In his remarks, he criticized the NRA for blindly opposing legislation like that then before the Congress, a bill to ban the interstate shipment of weapons (John Kennedy had been killed with a mail-order rifle). He charged the NRA with having inspired a "flood" of abusive mail and telephone calls to members of Congress supporting the bill. He challenged the members to be citizens first and riflemen and pistol shooters second. "If your fellow citizens ask you to make . . . minor concessions, *can you really refuse?*" (His emphasis.) Could they ever! The NRA stuck to its opposition and the bill got nowhere. Kennedy tried to add an anti–mail-order rifle and shotgun sales amendment to the Administration's omnibus crime-control bill a year later, but lost 29–53. That bill just banned handgun sales through the mails. Kennedy's one success to that point had been a ricochet shot against the NRA. The summer of 1967 he wrote the Secretary of Defense complaining about the department's subsidies of civilian marksmanship programs conducted by the NRA. The annual matches were the NRA's major event. The government gave them an army camp's ranges (Camp Perry, Ohio), weapons, ammunition, and lodging. McNamara did not halt the 1967 matches, as Kennedy and Representative Richard McCarthy of New York demanded. And Congress refused to accept Kennedy-McCarthy antimatch amendments to the defense spending bills that year. But in the fall, Army Secretary Stanley Resor announced he was canceling the 1968 army participation. Since then the National Rifle Matches have been unsubsidized.

Less than three weeks after Ted Kennedy tried and failed to outlaw mail shipments of long guns, Robert Kennedy was killed in Los Angeles. Though his assassin used a handgun, the public reaction was strong enough to lead to a congressional reconsideration of the question of gun control. Through a hectic summer, Congress wrestled with the bill. Ted Kennedy withdrew from public life after the assassination. He did not attend Judiciary Committee meetings on the bill. He was not on the floor from May 23 till September 18, the fifth and last day of debate on the gun-control bill. He came in as the debate neared its end, sat in his rear row seat, and cupped his chin in his hands. He voted but took no part in the debate. The bill passed the Senate with ease. (It had passed the House earlier.) Conferees soon agreed and the act became law. Its basic provision was the Kennedy amendment of the previous May, a ban on interstate shipments of long guns to individuals.

One of the amendments the Senate turned down on September 18 would have required the registration of all guns and the licensing of all owners. Senator Joseph Tydings of Maryland proposed it, but won only thirty-one votes for it. (He was defeated two years later in a close election in which the NRA was heavily involved.) In 1971 Ted Kennedy introduced a similar bill. He testified in his own behalf before the House Judiciary Committee the following year, and proposed the bill in the Senate Judiciary Committee, but got nowhere. In 1972 the Senate did pass Birch Bayh's Saturday Night Special bill. Bayh's bill outlawed the sale of domestically produced cheap handguns, the so-called Saturday Night Specials. The 1968 gun-control bill had forbidden importation of such guns, but manufacturers got around it by importing the parts, then producing the guns in the United States. Kennedy offered his registration and licensing bill as an amendment to Bayh's bill in committee, and again when it came to the floor in August. "Firearms registration will tell us how many guns there are, where they are, and in whose hands they are held," Kennedy told the Senate. But he was defeated by a vote of 78–11. Perhaps some senators remembered what had happened to Tydings. Bayh's bill then passed, but the House never acted on it.

On his forty-first birthday, February 22, 1973, Kennedy reintroduced his registration and licensing proposals and the Saturday Night Special proposal as a single bill. There were no hearings, and the bill was almost certainly going nowhere as a separate bill. Almost exactly a year later Senator Javits, who had co-sponsored the new Kennedy effort, wrote him that he had been thinking of offering such a bill as an amendment to the Administration's death-penalty bill. In 1972 the Supreme Court had in effect struck down all death-penalty laws. The new legislation was meant to get around that ruling. Kennedy was opposed to the legislation and was not sure that it was, therefore, the best vehicle for seeking gun controls. Suppose the amendments were accepted— would he then vote for the bill, for the death penalty? In the end he decided to go along with Javits. He offered the registration and licensing Saturday Night Special bill on March 13, 1974, as an amendment to the bill. However, the registration and licensing section would apply only to handguns. Kennedy and Javits decided that had a better chance of being accepted than the broader bill, which had languished a year in Bayh's subcommittee. Senator John McClellan of Arkansas, manager for the death-penalty bill, urged the Senate to table Kennedy's amendments, suggesting that if the bill had merits it should be considered separately after proper hearings. Kennedy would not let the record show that the Senate was merely making a procedural decision. The voting would be on the merits, he insisted. He reminded McClellan, snappishly, that a few years back, when the Judiciary Committee had refused to act on some conservatives' bill that would have made it easier for owners of guns to buy .22 caliber rimfire ammunition, they had added their bill as an amendment to a tax bill.

I urged members and made the same argument just made by the senator from Arkansas; that is, why do we not follow the procedures of the Senate and go ahead and have some hearings, listen to the witnesses and all the rest. All we got out of that was about twelve or fourteen votes when I argued that we should follow the procedures of the Senate.

That goes to show, Mr. President, that we see in this body time and again that it is those who have the votes who are going to decide the issue. But we should not confuse it with procedures followed by the Senate because we have seen whether those who have stood in favor of altering or changing gun control laws are willing to follow any procedures of the Senate and whether it comes down to direct amendments on legislation, or no hearings, or whatever it may be. We have had all the hearings, as I have mentioned earlier in debate, on these particular provisions. It is not a new issue but one which has been heavily debated and discussed. I would hope that this bill will not be tied up on the question of procedures. It is a simple, a fundamental, and straightforward amendment that has been debated and discussed and on which there have been days and hours of hearings. Senators can make the decision on how they will vote on that basis.

The vote was 68–21 to table. Kennedy then proposed just the old Saturday Night Special bill as a separate amendment. Again McClellan made a motion to table and again the Senate so voted, this time 58–31.*

Nothing if not persistent, Kennedy was back with gun-control legislation in 1975. This time he proposed, with Adlai Stevenson III as principal co-sponsor, registration and licensing for handguns and handgun owners. Stevenson had unsuccessfully proposed that as a floor amendment in the 1972 debate on the Saturday Night Special Bill. In February 1975, the Crime Subcommittee of the House Judiciary Committee began hearings on a number of gun bills, the first such in seven years, the first ever not in direct response to the assassination of a national figure. Chairman John Conyers said he believed the 94th Congress would do "something [about] the problem of handguns." In the Senate Bayh said he would try again for his Saturday Night Special bill if the House moved first.

Kennedy-Stevenson was something of a moderate bill. There were other, tougher proposals. One, for instance, would outlaw the manufacture, sale, and transfer

---

*It wasn't all smashing defeats for Kennedy in his jousting with McClellan that day. He convinced the Senate to add two substantive amendments to the bill, over McClellan's vehement objections. The bill made the death penalty mandatory in kidnaping and hijacking when a victim was killed. Thus, if a plane hijacker killed one passenger he would have nothing to lose if he killed all the rest, and nothing to gain if he didn't. Kennedy proposed that the attorney general be allowed to waive the mandatory provision if it would lead to a trapped hijacker's releasing the rest of his hostages. The Senate approved that 49–40. Kennedy also got the Senate to make it more difficult to find an individual guilty of a capital crime. By a vote of 49–43 the Senate amended the bill with a Kennedy proposal to liberalize the mitigating circumstances that a judge and jury could take into account in deciding not to require the death penalty and to upgrade the degree of proof required from "preponderance of evidence" to "beyond a reasonable doubt." The House never acted on the death-penalty bill, so it died with the 93rd Congress.

of handguns. Attorney General Edward Levi suggested that all handguns be banned on streets in high-crime areas. And there were other proposals, nearly fifty of them. As this is written the situation in Congress seems to suggest that some sort of bill will be enacted by the end of 1976, perhaps even the Kennedy-Stevenson bill. If not, Kennedy is certain to keep at it. He takes the long view on issues like this. Even failures, in his own phrase, become "building blocks."

12. BEYOND THE
WATER'S EDGE

It is a rare senator who does not involve himself in foreign affairs. An opening on the Foreign Relations Committee is vigorously competed for. When Eugene McCarthy gave up his seat on the committee in 1969, he was regarded as bizarre. When Senator Edmund Muskie gave up his in 1975, after having worked so hard to get it finally in 1971, eyebrows went up. McCarthy was planning to quit the Senate in 1970, as it turned out, and Muskie, having just been named chairman of the new and powerful Budget Committee, had to give up something. He was senior and expert on Government Operations and Public Works, so his decision was the proper one. Most senators who want to can find a way to turn their eyes abroad by discovering a mandate in some subcommittee assignment. The Foreign Operations Subcommittee of the Appropriations Committee, the International Finance Subcommittee of the Banking, Housing and Urban Affairs Committee, the Foreign Commerce and Tourism Subcommittee of the Commerce Committee, and the International Finance and Resources and the International Trade subcommittees of the Finance Committee all have obvious responsibilities in foreign affairs. No member of any of those subcommittees has been more imaginative in interpreting his mandate to involve himself in foreign policy activity than the chairman of Refugees and Escapees Subcommittee of the Judiciary Committee, and the subcommittee was usually his device.

When Turkey invaded Cyprus in July 1974, for example, Kennedy promptly dispatched Dale de Haan, the staff director, Jerry Tinker, a permanent consultant, and Dr. Dennis Skiotis, assistant professor of Greek and Turkish history at Harvard, hired as a special temporary consultant. The team not only toured Cyprus, where fighting had led to many thousands of displaced civilians, but called on high-level Greek, Turkish, and American government officials in Ankara, Athens, and London. Their reports back to Kennedy prepared him for the delivery of several speeches in which he not only made specific recommendations for assisting the refugees but also urged policy decisions on the U.S. government not related to refugees. The subcommittee staff was back in Washington in mid-September, and had prepared a 116-page report by early October. Kennedy went beyond refugee affairs in a speech based on the report on October 20, at a testimonial dinner in New York for Archbishop Iakovos, Primate of the Greek Orthodox Church in the Americas. Greeks and Americans of Greek descent were outraged by the Turkish invasion, which was carried out in the name of the political rights of the Turkish Cypriots and to the detriment of Greek Cypriots. Greek-American members of Congress were already mounting an effort that would cut off military aid to Turkey, over the heated objections of President Ford and Secretary of State Henry Kissinger, who argued that the United States needed Turkey as an ally and should not offend her. Kennedy joined with the opposition. He told his New York audience, "I have shared your deep personal concern over the plight of your relatives and friends. . . . Whole villages and towns and cities [on Cyprus] . . . are empty of the Greeks who lived there. In understandable fear, and with only the clothes on their backs, they fled to safety from advancing Turkish forces. But many of their neighbors had died." The theme of concern for *refugees* was constant, but so was the theme of concern for *Greeks*, their humanitarian rights and their political rights.

Kennedy was accused of trying to make political capital for himself. There are more Greek votes in America than there are Turkish ones. Kennedy's rhetoric concerning the refugee problems on the island was certainly sometimes similar to what you would hear in the heat of an election campaign: "Although flatly denied in all quarters of the Administration, the evidence in the field suggests a perceptible 'tilt' in American policy towards Turkey. . . . Policy [was] coldly calculated to minimize disturbances within NATO." The study mission report was a dry, dispassionate, fact-studded, even technical essay for the most part, but it was not the press that panned out the few glowing, headline-making political nuggets. The press release issued by Kennedy's office on the day the report was made public began, "Senator Edward M. Kennedy, Chairman of the Subcommittee on Refugees, today charged the Ford Administration with 'a cynical use of tax dollars in support of policies which prolong the Greek refugee problem and the Turkish occupation of Cyprus.' "

There was also a vein of politics running through Kennedy's attacks on the Nixon Administration the previous year, when the elected Communist government of Chile was overthrown by a right-wing military group. The Nixon Administration at least approved of what happened, and there were even suspicions, never proven, that it may have conspired to bring about the change in governments. The coup was bloody. President Allende was slain. Kennedy's criticism came from the platform of the subcommittee again. He held hearings on "Refugee and Humanitarian Problems in Chile" in September 1973 and again in July 1974. The September hearings, a one-day affair, came only seventeen days after the coup. Kennedy's opening statement included this: "The people problems in Chile today raise troubling questions over the administration's casual decision to recognize the military regime—and over the intent and purpose of American policy." And: "I voice my dismay over the personal tragedy of Mr. Allende. The best our government was able to do was issue a State Department release two or three days after his death. I think this is a tragic indictment given the circumstances surrounding his death." Kennedy was merciless in his cross-examination of State Department witnesses who came before the committee, interrupting, almost badgering. At one point he expressed indignation at the fact that the Nixon Administration had cut off aid to Chile after President Allende came to power in 1970, but had not cut off aid to "military regimes in Latin America," and was probably going to resume assisting Chile now that Allende was gone.

In 1971 Kennedy certainly sounded political when he barged into the Northern Ireland conflict. In October, Kennedy and Senator Abraham Ribicoff of Connecticut introduced a resolution urging the British to withdraw immediately from beleaguered Ulster. Kennedy had been working with representative (later governor) Hugh Carey of New York on a similar resolution. When he heard Ribicoff was way ahead of them, he asked Ribicoff if he could add his name to the resolution. Ribicoff agreed, and though he was clearly the principal advocate of the proposal, it was Kennedy who drew the fire of senators and commentators. "A flagrant appeal for Irish Catholic votes," said one senator. Even the British prime minister attacked him for a speech Kennedy made at the time— "an ignorant outburst," said Heath. The following February Irish foreign minister Patrick J. Hillery came to the United States seeking U.S. pressure on Britain. Thirteen Catholic demonstrators had been killed in Londonderry by British soldiers. Hillery first went to the State Department for a meeting with Secretary William Rogers, then to the Hill to see Kennedy and other members of Congress. Later in the month Kennedy went before a House Foreign Affairs Committee subcommittee on Europe to urge the Administration to "end its policy of silence." He warmed to the subject, condemned Britain, calling Ulster its Vietnam, Londonderry its My Lai. He again called on Britain to withdraw its troops from Ulster, and again was widely criticized for playing politics with the issue.

And also in 1971 and 1972, there was evident politics in Kennedy's attacks on President Nixon for his handling of the serial crises those years in South Asia. In the spring of 1971, the Pakistani Army stationed in the eastern half of that divided nation cracked down brutally on the political organization there that was demanding independence for the eastern region. By summer nearly 10,000,000 refugees had fled into India. Cholera and other diseases caused thousands of deaths and the prospects of tens of thousands more. Indian prime minister Indira Gandhi urged Pakistani prime minister Yahya Khan to settle his differences with the separatists so that the refugees could return home, and at the same time she recognized the new, self-proclaimed government-in-exile of Bangladesh. Tensions mounted between India and Pakistan, resulting in a two-week war in December. The U.S. role was officially neutral, but, as a leaked memo later revealed, policy-makers were instructing officials and diplomats to "tilt" toward Pakistan. Kennedy and other liberal senators were severely critical of the tilt; Kennedy particularly, since he had tilted the other way long before the war broke out.

The refugees subcommittee held hearings on the problems facing India in June and July 1971. Kennedy said famine loomed. State Department witnesses rebutted him. One said "those who ought to know" had assured the department that there was sufficient relief food for several months. As often happened in these hearings, the battle was for the headlines. Kennedy won when he followed this difference of opinion several days later by making public secret State cables, including one from the counsel in Dacca to Secretary Rogers that said, "The specter of famine hangs over East Pakistan, and prospects for averting widespread hunger, suffering and perhaps starvation are not, repeat not, good." A department spokesman could only reply that Kennedy was making it difficult "to carry on a constructive dialogue . . . when we abuse our confidential communications this way." Kennedy decided on the spur of the moment to go to India and Pakistan. He arrived in August to find he had become "a particular hero," in the phrase of a Washington *Post* reporter, for his attacks on U.S. policy. He was a particular hero to the refugees, but a villain to government in Dacca. He was denied entry into East Pakistan. Based on his touring of the refugee camps in India, he blasted Pakistani policy as "genocide." Later, after the India-Pakistani War and after Bangladesh had successfully asserted its nationhood, Kennedy paid his visit to Dacca. That was in February 1972. The United States had not yet recognized the new nation. (It would in April.) The trip was like an American political campaign. Kennedy had his wife and Robert's son Joseph with him.

Autograph-seekers by the dozens and admirers or simply celebrity-seekers by the hundreds mobbed him wherever he went. More than 8000 students overflowed a lecture hall at Dacca University. Garlands of flowers were thrown at him. Kennedy told the crowds pointedly, "The people of the world recognize you." He compared Bangladesh to early America. It was an emotional and emotion-generating tour. Not that that was all there was to it. A State Department official who was involved in the Bangladesh refugee assistance program, and who thinks the department did an excellent job with "the largest, most desperate refugee situation in history," and who is not an admirer of Kennedy, told me that Kennedy did force the Administration to spend more money than it would have otherwise, and did help and spur the volunteer agencies involved to raise more private funds.

Kennedy has become a hero for people like the dispossessed of Bangladesh. The more he comforts them, the more that role is recognized and exalted, and the stronger Kennedy becomes with those American voters and opinion-makers who believe that some American must play such a role. But it seems to me that to assess Kennedy's involvement in refugee problems and the foreign-policy decisions that grow out of it from the perspective of how many votes he may win in the United States is wrong. In the first place, as Senator Ribicoff said in the contretemps over Ulster, Kennedy already has the Irish Catholic vote. He already has the support of the liberals, who give humanitarian considerations a high priority, because of his general political outlook. He could throttle down to a crawl his efforts in behalf of the refugees of the world and still expect those people to support him because of other issues.

There really isn't anybody else to turn to on the refugees' issue. I believe Kennedy is the champion of refugees and the rest of the world's poorest, most miserable people for two reasons. One is that he and his staff have developed the expertise to deal with the problems of extreme misery and poverty, and feel an obligation to employ it. The other is that Kennedy sympathizes with the *victims* of the world.* Not just those who are victimized by unpopular political

*The first close-up look I ever had of him convinced me of this. In May 1974, I arranged to travel with Kennedy during a two-day visit to Georgia.

currents. He has been speaking in behalf of the Palestinian refugees since a trip to the area in 1966. And not just those victimized by politics of any sort. Very likely his next major effort in this general field will be in behalf of the poor of the world who are victimized by nature and geography, the desperate poor of the Fourth World, the poorest of the poor. In mid-1975 Kennedy got enough money from the Senate to send De Haan and Tinker, and Dr. S. Philip Caper of the Health Subcommittee, and eight academic experts on community health, nutrition, and population dynamics on study missions to Africa, the Middle East, and Asia to assess world hunger and health preparatory to a new series of hearings.

Perhaps the proper political criticism of Kennedy is not that he seeks out international causes that will help him with voters at home, but that he is committed to an international constituency whose own best interests may not always coincide with those of the United States. Are the poor of the world the best allies? Does his commitment to the world's victims affect his approach to traditional foreign-policy considerations? The best way to answer that is to quote his most recent "major" foreign-policy statements. As a senator his views on foreign policy have not had much, if any, direct impact on generalized policy-making. The Foreign Relations Committee still guards its territory on the big picture. And the president is even more jealous of his prerogatives. Indirectly and over the long run, Kennedy as a senator may have influence on foreign policy because he is regarded by presidents as a possible challenger, and because he has

---

The only other journalist on the trip was Hunter Thompson, the legendary drug- and alcohol-powered reporter for *Rolling Stone*. We rode in a Georgia State Patrol car with Kennedy and aide Paul Kirk from Atlanta to Athens early one Saturday morning. Kennedy was to give the Law Day speech at the University. Running late, Kennedy kept urging the trooper to hurry, so that soon we were hurtling over the two-lane blacktop road at 85 and 90 miles an hour. All the while Thompson, who I assumed was as irresponsible a journalist as he portrayed himself to be, was interviewing Kennedy, who I assumed was as superficial as he was often portrayed to be, on the problems of the Fourth World. It was a bizarre half-hour or so, the car hurtling through the red clay hills, the surprisingly professional and probing questioning by Thompson, the obviously expert and compassionate answers by Kennedy.

power to influence other senators' home-state constituencies. He does the latter, if he does it, by having access to his own national constituency through the media.

Like most senators, Kennedy has always made speeches on the floor of the Senate or in other arenas on significant developments in the field of foreign affairs, with no particular expectation of results. It is expected of them. In the 1960s he was already experimenting with the reaction to his advancing new ideas. In 1966 he and George McGovern became the first two senators to advocate publicly and forcefully a new policy toward Red China. He was one of the first senators to call for resuming relations with Cuba. In the 1970s he has been working with intensity at becoming a creative force in foreign policy-making, investing time and energy (and money) in the effort. In 1973 he hired Dr. Robert E. Hunter, a former professor and journalist who had written speeches for Hubert Humphrey and worked at the Lyndon Johnson White House, as a full-time adviser on foreign policy. Richard Holbrooke, managing editor of the slightly antiestablishment *Foreign Policy* magazine, introduced them. Kennedy told Hunter, as Hunter later recalled it, "I need an adviser who has experience in arms control, European security, the Middle East, economic development." Kennedy was obviously looking to the next decade's presumed challenges. "Kennedy said to me," Hunter continued, "that regardless of whether he ran for president, he was going to devote more time to foreign-policy issues. He said he had a national audience and would be listened to. He wanted a man who would keep contact with the foreign-policy community, give him things to read he might not ordinarily see, write speeches for him."

In addition to being able to afford a special assistant for foreign-policy matters (because of his control of so many subcommittee staff slots), Kennedy also has that advantage over other senators of having national standing. And he has international standing as well. When he travels abroad, he gets red-carpet treatment. In 1975 he took his wife and some other family members on a tour of the Middle East. *Newsweek* described the attention he received as similar to that a president would be accorded. In 1974 Kennedy visited nine European and Middle Eastern nations, and in eight he met with the head of state. The American press had a field day with the Moscow stop on the trip. On April 22 the Washington *Post* had a story on the front page under this headline: KENNEDY IRKS SOVIET HOSTS/EXPELLED FROM MOSCOW U. AFTER FRANK TALK. An Associated Press dispatch detailed how Kennedy had asked students there some questions about Russian accomplishments. (He often asks campus audiences questions or invites them to ask him questions following a speech.) According to the AP this was unheard of in the Soviet Union. Some in the audience denounced his "provocation," others laughed at his gaffe, and finally officials rushed him from the stage, saying that he was ill, though Kennedy insisted he was not. The story, AP later admitted, had been hyped up by editors in New York. It didn't happen that way, quite. In any event, the story produced more headlines and editorials than anything else Kennedy did on his tour, including his four-hour meeting with Leonid Brezhnev—an unprecedented gesture to a private visitor, which Kennedy was.

Kennedy defined his view of the world in a series of speeches in 1974. At Moscow University (in a speech also overlooked or ignored by much of the press) he suggested that the United States and Russia had mutual interests in ending the arms race, in keeping peace in the Middle East (he urged "a more active Soviet role" there) and elsewhere, and so on. It was a polite speech, in support of going beyond detente, suggesting that Russia could move toward greater cooperation with the United States, nonsuperpowers, and, eventually, China. Five months later, on September 13, with a new president in power barely a month, Kennedy spoke to the Los Angeles World Affairs Council. He stressed several themes. The first, as always when he spoke of world affairs, was halting the nuclear arms race. The Strategic Arms Limitation Talks were scheduled to resume the following week in Geneva. Kennedy proposed:

First, there should be full public disclosure by the Administration of nuclear weapons doctrines and programs on both sides, and an effort to reduce Soviet secrecy.
Second, there should be an end to building unneeded

new weapons systems—then justified as "bargaining chips" —and a search for mutual restraint.

Third, there should be mutual avoidance of arms programs—such as new, silo-busting missiles and warheads— that could call into question the doctrine of mutual assured destruction.

Fourth, arms control could be separated from the cycle of summit meetings, in order to reduce pressures to reach agreements for dramatic impact.

Fifth, we should develop a new view of the political role of the SALT talks, to emphasize other means of developing relations between the superpowers.

Kennedy also proposed that something be done about "another nuclear problem," the spread of nuclear weapons beyond five permanent members of the United Nations Security Council. The superpowers should halt *all* testing of nuclear weapons (they had halted testing in the atmosphere, space, and under water in 1963, and in June 1974 had halted some underground testing). This would set an example of restraint, Kennedy said. He also advocated restraint on peaceful nuclear explosions. The second theme in his speech (which Kennedy described as an *agenda* for President Ford) was greater cooperation with Russia and all other powers in dealing with "the crisis in the international economy, and the growing economic ties that increasingly bind nations and peoples together." What he had in mind, he said, was a national and international attack on inflation, a reform of the "great institutions of international economic cooperation." The traditional monetary and trading systems had not adapted to the massive shifts of dollars from industrial nations to the oil-producing states. There had to be a new international mechanism to manage trade in energy and other raw materials.

[That] commands a major shift in attitudes, both here and in other industrial countries. The simple fact is that we Americans must now live more fully in the outside world than ever before, relating to the acts of other nations, as well as helping to shape the overall structure of international relations. In energy this means acting in concert with other oil-consum-

ing states—rich and poor. . . . But it also means working with
the oil-producing states, themselves. . . . We need to encourage them to spend as much as possible on their own economic development. . . . We need to stimulate the flow of
investments back to the industrial countries. . . . We need to
encourage the flow of development funds from the oil-pro-
ducers to the "Fourth World" of nations most affected by the
rise in oil prices, and we must set the example ourselves. And
most important, we must act now to draw the oil producers
more fully into the world economy and encourage them to
play responsible roles on behalf of all nations.

Kennedy repeated this stress on the two themes in a
speech he called "Beyond Detente" delivered in Vienna in
November, and in an article of the same title written for
Foreign Policy that same fall. In May 1975, when he toured
the Middle East, he stressed the economic cooperation
theme, and in a speech at the University of Teheran, he told
the oil producers that he opposed those in the consuming
nations who would seek a "confrontation . . . seeking to drive
the price of oil down through reverse embargoes, or through
excluding the [oil-producer nations] from the benefits of
Western technology." At the same time, he urged the producing states "to recognize our joint responsibilities for continuing to share our abundance with others, whether the
food of the United States or the oil of Iran."

Kennedy, who has long been politically close to and
supported by the American Jewish community, has been
criticized by some who follow foreign affairs for beginning
to tilt a little away from Israel. Hunter has been accused of
being an Arabist. Kennedy says his views have not changed.
In a speech at Beersheba, Israel, in November 1974, the
senator said:

There will be no easy solutions in negotiating the peace. But
as the way unfolds, I can assure you of this: the United States
must and will continue to provide the assistance that Israel
needs to defend itself. We will not be deterred by the eco-
nomics of oil—but will continue in our attitudes and actions
to keep this separate problem apart from the process of
peace. Our commitment to Israel's independent future will

endure—as will our commitment and our efforts to help find
an end to the conflict. And we will seek to persuade all outside powers—including the Soviet Union—to move in the
direction of peace. For no nation can profit in the Middle
East when the dogs of war are unleashed.

As for Hunter's being an Arabist, I asked him. This is
his reply: "No. I'm not. I have no ax to grind in the Middle
East. I am a Middle East specialist, but that's all. I don't
speak Arabic. It is true that in my writings I haven't been as
unsophisticated about Israel as Americans in general have
been." Another senator says that Kennedy has begun to get
a "broader spectrum" of advice on Israel since Hunter
joined the staff. If that is true, as of this writing (summer
1975) there is no public evidence that the advice has led to
any change of heart on Kennedy's part. Lobbyists for Israeli
interests say if anything Kennedy and Hunter have "bent
over backwards" to offset the suspicions of Hunter. But they
quickly add they wish Kennedy were "more positive" in his
support of Israel within the Senate. "Jackson, Humphrey,
even Muskie are more helpful to us there," one says.

Slowing down the arms race and halting nuclear
testing have been at the heart of Kennedy's ideas about
foreign policy since before he entered the Senate. These
ideas are central to most liberal Democrats, of course, but
in Kennedy's case there is an added dimension—it is a fallen-
standard issue. President John Kennedy's legacy to the nation includes the first significant stride toward a final halting
of nuclear weapon development. In a speech at American
University in the spring of 1963 Kennedy unilaterally ended
U.S. weapons testing in the atmosphere, and in the summer
of that year the United States, Russia, and Great Britain
signed the partial test-ban treaty (banning tests in the atmosphere, space, and under water). "My exposure to this issue
was sensitized by both the American University speech—
which I think was magnificent, and would think so even if
it hadn't been my brother—and by the Cuban missile crisis,"
Ted Kennedy said years later. The missile crisis confrontation occurred in the last month of his first campaign for the
Senate. "My entrance into public life was in the shadow of

that. It had a very profound impact upon me." Kennedy
spoke, wrote, and voted in support of extending the ban to
all testing throughout the 1960s, and in the 91st, 92nd, 93rd,
and 94th Congresses proposed and actively (but unsuccessfully) lobbied for Senate resolutions supporting either
moratoriums on all testing or prompt signing of a comprehensive test ban treaty.

The Nixon Administration also favored a treaty. The
difference between the liberal Democratic position and the
Administration was that the former believed on-site inspec-
tion, which the Russians would not agree to, was unneces-
sary, while the latter believed it was vital. Kennedy was
always with the liberals on this. A good indication of how
strongly he felt about the general issue of arms control was
his rather constant and at times lavish praise for President
Nixon's efforts in this field. Even after Nixon had resigned
in disgrace Kennedy was still praising him (in almost Nixonian hyperbole) for the Strategic Arms Limitation Talks,
which he said "must be considered one of mankind's great
political triumphs—one of the great testaments to man's
ability in crisis to reach out for sense and sanity."

That statement came in a speech to the Arms Control
Association in Washington in April 1975, at a Kennedy-
hosted meeting previewing a review conference on the fifth
anniversary of the nuclear nonproliferation treaty, another
Nixon accomplishment. Kennedy used the occasion to flesh
out his earlier sketches of the need for halting the spread of
nuclear weapons to additional nations. He proposed an
eight-point program: a comprehensive ban on nuclear testing; greater efforts to end the superpower arms race; agreement by the superpowers to "play down" the significance of
nuclear weapons in assessing national power; an agreement
by nuclear powers never to use such weapons against countries without such weapons; an extension of the nuclear free
zone to the Middle East and Africa; restraints on the sale of
and supply of conventional weapons; efforts to control
peaceful nuclear explosions; efforts to meet the security
needs of countries that might otherwise build the bomb.
Kennedy insisted that his program was not one that the
nuclear powers would "do *to* the nonnuclear states. Rather
it must be something that all nations do *together* in their

common interest." Whether nonnuclear states will see the eight points in the same light is uncertain.

How influential Kennedy has been in the general area of foreign policy or the specific area of arms control is hard to measure. Until as late as 1975, probably not very. I would guess, based on interviews with senators, congressional staff members, bureaucrats, and journalists who specialize in this area of activity, that the situation would be about what it was as of summer 1975 (excepting only humanitarian aid levels and activities) if Kennedy had never become involved. However, late in 1974, Kennedy and senators Charles Mathias and Walter Mondale began an effort that might have some direct and significant influence on the course of the world's progress along the path of control of nuclear weapons. Ironically, these three liberals found themselves somewhat in the position of coming to the rescue of President Ford and Secretary of State Kissinger under fire from some traditional liberals in the arms control debate—who were led by that old cold-war warrior, Senator Henry Jackson.

The Strategic Arms Limitation talks had led to one great Nixon triumph, a 1972 agreement with Russia to limit the number of defensive missiles either country could deploy. According to a study of arms-control diplomacy in *Science* magazine, that success was partly due to the 1968–69 Senate debate on the ABM. The next phase, which President Nixon did not survive in office long enough to see through, was to be a limitation on offensive weapons. On November 24, 1974, President Ford and General Secretary Brezhnev announced at Vladivostok that they had reached agreement to limit the number of offensive weapons. Kissinger hailed the communiqué as a great breakthrough. But a few critics immediately pointed out that the Vladivostok accord set such a high ceiling on the number of strategic weapons the two nations could deploy that both would have to continue in the arms race for perhaps the ten-year life of the agreement. Russia could add two warheads a day to its arsenal for the next ten years, according to one calculation. The liberal goal of achieving a stabilizing equality of weapons between the two superpowers by having one reduce its arsenal to the level of the other or one build up to the other's existing level was put aside in favor of a goal of achieving equality by allowing both to build up to a much higher level. Any hopes that the two countries would not actually arm up to the ceiling seemed dashed when President Ford said the United States had "an obligation" to build up to the level in the accord.

Senator Jackson led the immediate congressional opposition to the proposal. As a somewhat hawkish expert on weapons, he was a respected and powerful figure on Capitol Hill. On November 26 and again on December 6 he attacked the agreement for allowing too great an increase in the number of weapons on both sides. In the second statement, he called on the Administration to renegotiate lower arms levels. The next day Kissinger warned that if Congress insisted on changes in the agreement "serious consequences" could result. However, on December 10, Kissinger and the Russians agreed to a change in the official Vladivostok *aide memoire* which made a basic change in the communiqué. The latter had said further negotiations would deal with arms reductions after 1985. The change said reductions could be negotiated before then.

Shortly after the communiqué was published, Kennedy and aide Robert Hunter explored what role they could play in the Senate. As usual, Kennedy began by seeking advice from experts outside of government, academics and former government officials. He or Hunter talked to a few on this list promptly (and the rest later): Paul Doty of Harvard, Richard Garwin and Jerome Wiesner of M.I.T., Paul Warnecke of the Center for Defense Information, Tom Halstead of the Arms Control Association, Henry Owens at Brookings, Richard Holbrooke of *Foreign Policy* magazine, Averell Harriman, and several others. The question Kennedy put to them was, Should he endorse Vladivostok, or follow Jackson and take a tough line? His philosophic instincts told him to go with Jackson, his legislative and political instincts not to, I would guess. At any rate, the advice he got back from the experts, according to Hunter, was "almost unanimous" that it was unlikely that the Senate could force Russia (or the Pentagon) to accept much lower numbers for delivery systems and warheads in a short period of time, and that even trying to might scuttle the accord, which, slight as it was, was a step in the right direction. The question then was to decide on how to both support the accord and keep up pressure for real nuclear-arms reduction. The answer seemed to be an idea senators Walter Mondale and Charles Mathias were advocating separately, to get the Senate to approve a resolution supporting Vladivostok in the framework of a formal call for reductions. "At the time of the Vladivostok communiqué," Kennedy explained later, "I had the same kind of reaction that many others had, that the ceilings were much too high, particularly given the kind of statements that the Secretary of Defense was making that there needed to be major build-ups. But at the same time I wanted to see if we could find a way to get major support for it. That meant putting a different interpretation on it."

Mathias had prepared a rough draft of such a resolution. "Kennedy, Mondale, and several other senators expressed interest in joining me," Mathias said. The three senators became a team, because, as Mathias put it, "These two were willing to do the hard and time-consuming work on drafts." A final version of the resolution was introduced on December 12. The key section said, "It is the sense of the Senate that the President should make every possible effort to negotiate further nuclear arms limitation and reduction measures *as part of the final accord carrying out the Vladivostok agreement*" (emphasis added). Those measures should include lower numbers of allowable delivery vehicles and warheads, a limit on missile test flights, and the insistence that the Vladivostok agreement be submitted to the Senate in the form of a treaty. Kennedy's press release on the 12th and a Mondale statement put them, if not Mathias, closer to Jackson than to President Ford.

The resolution died with the 93rd Congress, and the three senators and an unhappy Kissinger began negotiating a new resolution. Before they could reach agreement, Russia had broken off the 1972 trade agreement with the United States, citing interference in the form of the 1974 Jackson amendment requiring freer emigration for Russian Jews as a part of the trade agreement. The same day Kissinger made that announcement, January 14, Defense Secretary James Schlesinger announced a Russian deployment of new missiles ahead of the previously assumed capability. Detente seemed to be in jeopardy. That same day or the next the three senators and Kissinger agreed on the new resolution. It was a far cry from the December version. Kissinger had persuaded the senators to change the language of the key section to: "It is the advice of the Senate that the President should make every possible effort (a) to complete the negotiations resulting from the Vladivostok agreement in principle; (b) *in addition,* to reach further agreements" (emphasis added). In other words, Vladivostok would still have those high ceilings and the President would not be instructed to lower them in that agreement. The senators gave up on missile test limits and the treaty requirement, too, though there would still be Senate review. What the senators got from Kissinger in return (in addition to a warm public statement) was acceptance of this language in another section of the new resolution:

> The Vladivostok Agreement establishes limits within which the United States and the Soviet Union may deploy strategic forces, but . . . any deployment of United States strategic nuclear weapons, up to the limits established by the Vladivostok Agreement, should be based solely on the actual needs of United States security.

So no president could say he was obliged to build up to a ceiling just because there was a ceiling, as President Ford had said.

Senator Jackson, meanwhile, continued to fight for a much tougher agreement. In March 1975, quoting from a song "One Man's Ceiling Is Another Man's Floor," he warned that the levels of strategic weapons allowed in the Vladivostok agreement could easily become a floor for a post-1985 arms race if Russia and the United States built new weapons up to the numbers. He proposed that each side designate 700 of its present strategic delivery systems, which would have to remain unmodernized, and would therefore be natural candidates for a "program of reductions" after 1985 as they became increasingly obsolete. What Congress will do remains to be seen, and on whose side traditional liberal disarmament groups will end up.

Kennedy argues that his way is best, because it is most likely to pass the Senate and least likely to cause the Russians to give up on even the beginning that Vladivostok represents.

Whatever the outcome of the Kennedy-Mathias-Mondale effort, and however it is assessed, Kennedy would probably count as a more important contribution to slowing down the arms race (if it is slowed down) his efforts as a senator to get the full Senate more involved in the debate and decision-making on weapons and weapons policy. Until 1969, weapons-system decisions were made in the Senate Armed Services Committee, then ratified on the floor as a matter of course. Chairman Richard Russell wielded his great power throughout the 1950s and 1960s in an almost authoritarian manner. The usual explanation for this was that the debate on sophisticated atomic-age weapons systems was too sensitive and too complicated for a full-scale floor debate in either chamber of Congress. That security considerations were involved was obvious, if overstated, but the argument that the subject matter was too complicated was curious. Senators are supposed to understand complicated and technical matters. The point of the committee system is that it develops experts who can explain such things to their colleagues. Furthermore, in the case of military affairs, the Senate Armed Services Committee under Russell had maintained one of the smallest staffs of any committee. Though the staff members were competent and hard working, they were not experts.

In 1969 Russell relinquished the chairmanship to become chairman of the Appropriations Committee. John Stennis of Mississippi took over Armed Services. Stennis had put together his own staff on a subcommittee he had headed for years. Some of those members had developed more expertise than Russell's men had, and Stennis entered the chairmanship somewhat more willing to make the process of authorizing weapons systems and other military needs more open. Not as open as it turned out to be, however.

In 1968 the Armed Services Committee brought to the floor an authorization bill that included in it the funds for preparing sites for a new antiballistic missile system. The amount was only $227.3 million, and President Johnson

amount was only $227.3 million, and President Johnson
claimed that the system, which he described as only a "thin"
one designed to defend against an irrational attack by the
newly nuclear- and missile-armed Chinese, would cost an
eventual five billion. However, his former Secretary of Defense, Robert McNamara, had prophesied that once begun
the system would be expanded to a $50 billion defense
against Russian missiles and missile capabilities. Senate debate by advocates of the thin system in June made it clear
that Sentinel was just the beginning of a bigger network.
This was too much for Senate liberals, and two of them,
Philip Hart of Michigan and John Sherman Cooper of Ken-
tucky, launched a fight against authorization of the $227.3
million. Russell led the floor fight against them. He had powerful support from the Administration. But for the first time
in memory, a Defense Department strategic-weapons request with Armed Services Committee endorsement en-
countered serious opposition, as Senate Majority Leader
Mike Mansfield, who supported Cooper and Hart, pointed
out. After five days of debate, mostly philosophical, in which
the liberals foresaw an accelerated arms race, Johnson and
Russell prevailed. The Cooper-Hart amendment to delete
the funds from the overall military procurement authorization bill failed on June 24 by a vote of 34–52. Robert
Kennedy had been killed two weeks before. Ted Kennedy
neither participated in the debate nor voted on the amendment.

　　One of the three sites to be prepared for the Sentinel
system was at Reading, Massachusetts, near Boston. The
army began meetings in nearby Lincoln and Andover to
discuss the program. Nearby residents would have none of
it, however, and as 1968 ended, the Kennedy office in Boston
was inundated with constituent complaints. Kennedy assigned his then chief legislative aide, Dun Gifford, to investigate. To both of them it was still a local issue. Gifford called
on Jerome Wiesner in Cambridge, president of Massachusetts Institute of Technology and a former science adviser to
President John Kennedy. He opposed the ABM system as
probably ineffective and certainly a spur to the arms race.
Gifford had a high security clearance from his Navy days.
Senator Stennis let him study the Administration's classified

material sent to the Armed Services Committee to justify the new request for funds. By the end of January, Gifford had reported to Kennedy that the system was too expensive, wouldn't work, exposed nearby population centers to retaliation, and would seem to the Russians to be an aggressive act. On January 31, Kennedy sent a letter to the press, and reaped a publicity bonus within a week, when Laird announced that he had ordered a temporary halt of construction and a review of the system. Within a month President Nixon announced that he was completely changing the concept of the Sentinel system from one of protecting cities from the Chinese to protecting American missiles from the Russians. It was a pretty good political ploy. President Nixon could more confidently promise that the system would never rise in cost to the awesome fifty billion dollars predicted by McNamara, and also move the sites from suburban locations.

It was not just Kennedy the President was responding to. Senators Cooper and Hart were back in the forefront. By the time Kennedy mailed his letter to Laird, Hart thought he could already count on more than the thirty-two votes his amendment had won in 1968. Even after the President substituted what he called Safeguard for the old Sentinel, the Cooper-Hart forces thought they could make a good fight of it in 1969. Kennedy and Gifford weren't so sure. Gifford, in fact, thought Safeguard might breeze through with no more than twenty votes against it. That estimate led Kennedy to make his crucial decision in the ABM maneuvering, the one that led to his principal contribution not only to that debate but to subsequent Senate consideration of military-weapons systems. He told Gifford it was just unacceptable to let a system as bad as Sentinel be approved by a large margin after an extended debate. He said Senate liberals lost arguments with the Pentagon because they didn't have *facts* and the Pentagon did (though some of them weren't *true* facts). They, the liberals, would have their own facts this time. Kennedy got Wiesner and Abram Chayes of Harvard, a former State Department counsel, to prepare a study of the ABM system. On February 19, Kennedy announced that he had initiated the study and that he would transmit it to the committees of Congress considering the authorization bill.

It looked as if Kennedy were jumping onto a real bandwagon. The Senate Foreign Relations Committee beat the Armed Services Committee to the punch and began its own hearings on the overall procurement bill on March 6 (two weeks before Stennis began). Both committees gave more than equal time to critics of the ABM system and other expensive Pentagon programs. The Wiesner-Chayes project meanwhile became a book, with chapters by twenty-two experts in the various fields of national security.* In mid-May Wiesner testified on the main findings to the Senate Armed Services Committee. Those findings paralleled Kennedy's (and other senators') earlier objections to the system, and also included some highly technical and impressive criticisms of the system's missile components, radar, and computer. This was not the sort of rebuttal to Pentagon expertise the committee was used to.

The book itself had become a *cause célèbre,* not because of its weighty arguments against the system, but because Kennedy, against the advice of a number of his colleagues, had written an introduction to it. The objection to his writing the introduction (which Harper and Row suggested would make the book sell) was that Kennedy, then the likely Democratic nominee for president in 1972, would seem to be challenging Nixon personally, thus politicizing an issue that should be lifted out of politics. Kennedy talked the matter over with other liberal senators (who opposed his writing it), some liberal lobbyists fighting ABM (who opposed his writing it), and his own aides and political advisers. The question of how his writing the introduction would affect him politically was discussed at length, and the staff conclusion was that it would not hurt the anti-ABM effort or his own political future. So he wrote it. In it he claimed that the Nixon system would cost $20 billion, or triple what Nixon said it would cost, and that made as many headlines as any of the technical arguments against the system that the book presented.

Kennedy himself was not involved in any of the day-to-day efforts to round up a majority in support of the new

ABM: An Evaluation of the Decision to Deploy an Antiballistic Missile System.

Senate floor fight, which lasted from July 8 till August 6 and included one closed-door session. Kennedy's Chappaquiddick episode came on July 21 and deprived him of both time and influence to invest in the last half of the effort. On the two crucial votes on August 6, the Cooper-Hart amendment and a substitute for it lost 50–50 and 49–51.

So it was a losing effort, "but if we lost the battle, we won the war," one participant said, referring to the fact that for the first time since World War II a major weapons system had nearly been defeated after a long debate. Senator Mansfield and Senator Stuart Symington, a member of the Armed Services Committee, made the same point. Mansfield predicted that things would never be the same again. Senator Stennis, for his part, expressed some resentment in private at what he regarded as shabby or dishonest work by the Pentagon in its justification of Safeguard, which was revealed by the experts Kennedy had enlisted in the ABM fight. Stennis remained a friend of the generals and admirals, and a supporter and advocate of strong national defense, but in the 1970s, his committee was much more skeptical in its reviews of Pentagon requests than it had been in the 1950s and 1960s, and the full Senate was more skeptical of the committee's conclusions than it had been in the past.

Kennedy's interest in military matters was quickened by the 1969 debate. He became a member of the military committee of the NATO interparliamentary organization, the North Atlantic Treaty Assembly, and educated himself on a range of military questions in meetings of the military committee in the early 1970s. By 1975 he had become vice-chairman of the committee. In early 1975, as the last chapter in Vietnam came to a close, Kennedy began thinking about the implications of the end of American involvement in Southeast Asia. He believed that a new era was beginning, and that decisions on military spending should be subject to more scrutiny than ever. A lot of expensive long-range plans had been held up in the Pentagon while the war in Vietnam was staking its claim on funds. Now those plans and the weapons systems involved were coming front and center. In March Mark Schneider, Kennedy's aide who included military matters in his charge, wrote the senator a memorandum proposing a new look at military spending proposals.

dum proposing a new look at military spending proposals. Kennedy agreed, and arranged a dinner at his home in early April. Barry Blechman of Brookings, Joseph Woolsey, a Washington lawyer who had formerly worked for Senator Stennis, Morton Halperin, a former Pentagon official, Eugene LaRoque, a retired admiral, Schneider, and Robert Hunter, Kennedy's foreign-policy adviser, met there to go through the Administration's 1976 Department of Defense budget requests. A consensus quickly developed among the experts that there was no justification for any large increase in spending for procurement and research. Kennedy decided to see if other senators were willing to join in a major, concerted effort to reduce spending and kill some of the specific weapons programs proposed.

Later in April, or on May 1, Kennedy and Senator Alan Cranston of California sat together on the floor of the Senate and discussed the upcoming debate on the procurement bill. Cranston was an informed and dedicated critic of defense spending. He had been one of the leading advocates of Pentagon cuts in the new Budget Committee. The two senators decided to get together a larger group of liberals and make a headline-catching, days-long campaign against the bill. A few days later they met again to discuss their plans in the cloakroom off the Senate chamber. The "team" soon included the three freshmen Democrats on the Armed Services Committee, John Culver of Iowa, Patrick Lahey of Vermont, Gary Hart of Colorado; the ranking Democrat on the Committee, Stuart Symington of Missouri;* long-time

*Symington, who was retiring from the Senate at the end of 1976, had become the liberals' favorite defense expert. He had been elected to the Senate in 1952. He had been Secretary of the Air Force before that. He served on Armed Services and Foreign Relations. Over the years he had become increasingly skeptical of the national security establishment. And he liked to assist his youthful colleagues. He was acting chairman of the Armed Services Committee when William Colby was nominated chairman of the Central Intelligence Agency. There was little opposition to Colby, but Kennedy objected strongly. He knew of Colby's work in Vietnam through his own refugees hearings. Symington let Kennedy sit in on the confirmation hearings and conduct the principal cross-examination of the witness. Kennedy grilled Colby for four hours one day. He brought out a good bit of detrimental information, but only he and twelve other senators voted against confirmation when it came before the full Senate.

Wisconsin; his Wisconsin colleague, Gaylord Nelson; Maine's William Hathaway; and South Dakota's George McGovern and James Abourezk. A few of these just happened to be in the cloakroom, came over to see what was gathering a crowd, and asked to be included in the debate strategy.

The senators involved told their staffs to begin working together to come up with a coordinated procedure for the debate. By mid-May, Kennedy and Cranston were leading a platoon of senators. Birch Bayh of Indiana, Thomas Eagleton of Missouri, Mike Gravel of Alaska, Adlai Stevenson III of Illinois, John Tunney of California, Charles Mathias of Maryland, Jacob Javits of New York—liberals all, Democrats all except Mathias and Javits. Those and the original cloakroom group (or staff representatives) met in a Capitol office May 13, at the invitation of Cranston, for a pre-debate briefing. After Kennedy led off and Cranston and Culver followed up, there was heated give-and-take, resulting in a decision to add foreign-policy considerations to the debate, to stretch it over at least five days, and to delay its beginning beyond the date already tentatively set, May 20, so that more time would be available to study the Armed Services Committee report and the House debate on the same bill. Kennedy and Cranston prepared a letter to Mansfield urging a delay. The majority leader told them to work it out with Stennis. Stennis objected. He foresaw a long, wearying, confusing, and just conceivably overwhelming debate. But he bargained with the liberals and eventually agreed to a postponement till after the Memorial Day recess. What he got in return was an unusually specific unanimous-consent agreement to limit time on each segment of debate, on the total debate; and he got a look at the amendments to be proposed in advance. The agreement named Kennedy as the manager of time for the critics, though he and Cranston agreed to work that out in tandem.

At that point the two liberals went a step further. They decided that a "Great Debate," as they and the Associated Press now called it, on defense and foreign policies in the post-Vietnam era might not seem so great unless there was something like as much effort made on the other side as on the critics' side. Kennedy and Cranston (and Javits) enlisted several conservatives, including Barry Goldwater of Arizona, James McClure of Idaho, and Harry Byrd, Jr., of Virginia, to join them in signing a "Dear Colleague" letter to every senator, calling their attention to what they hoped would be the most significant Senate debate on such matters since the ABM fights. And things started off as if, indeed, the Kennedy-Cranston production would be all they had hoped it would be. There were to be two days of general debate, Monday and Tuesday, June 2 and 3, followed by three straight days of voting on amendments—specific cuts in spending. All Monday afternoon, some twenty senators stayed on the floor participating in or listening to the debate. That is very unusual in the Senate. Also there was an unusual amount of give-and-take. Senators debated rather than just reading prepared speeches. Kennedy had his speech printed in the *Congressional Record,* but did not deliver it, using his time to contest with the conservatives instead. But the next day it was back to business as usual. Only a few senators devoted much time to the debate. Others drifted in, made speeches, drifted out. This was probably because the immediate outcome of the debate was plainly going to be in favor of the conservatives on every particular. Senator Stennis had begun debate with this: "My main point is that with conditions as they now are it is just wrong to be lessening our preparedness or unilaterally withdrawing our forces beyond the strength which we have tried to build into this bill." And that was the post-Vietnam mood of the Congress, if not of the nation.

The *New Republic* grumped of the great debate that "It was not even a *good* debate most of time," and Kennedy and Cranston sadly agreed. Cranston said at the end of Tuesday's session, "What we have accomplished is not all that we hoped, but it is something, and I think it sets the stage for a more effective participation by the Senate in very important decision-making in foreign policy and in defense."

Kennedy added, "In this debate we [sought] to understand the distinction between commitments which directly relate to our security and require the availability of military power and those which do not. We really have not been able to achieve, in this sense, a very precise and clear consensus. But I do think it has been helpful." The *New Republic* conceded a little: "The affair was far from a failure.

Worthwhile floor debate did take place, enough to suggest that the Senate could become a constructive forum. . . . Senate debate settles nothing. Votes on amendments are the normal focus of Senate action. Yet seeds planted during the two-day Senate defense debate may germinate and grow into something worthwhile." The seeds sure didn't sprout in the next three days. Symington's amendment to cut the committee bill from $25 billion to $23.8 billion lost, 38–58. Eagleton's amendment to delay the airborne warning and control system aircraft program lost 38–58. McGovern's amendment to delete funds for the strategic B-1 bomber lost 32–57, Kennedy's amendment to delete funds for procurement of Minuteman III missiles lost 32–57. The bill passed 77–6.

Kennedy and Cranston voted for the bill. Kennedy seemed more upset by the fact that procedure fell short than the fact that the vote totals did. One day senators William Brock and Howard Baker, Tennessee Republicans, came to the floor to deliver speeches siding with the conservatives. Neither stayed to participate in the debate, which both criticized—Brock sneered at it as "a nondebate." Kennedy, wounded, criticized them not for their views on defense spending and foreign policy but for their views on the debate. "I know there were some members earlier who made comments about the nature of this exchange. I found that some of them just drifted into the chamber, made their comments, even read from formal statements, then drifted away, even though they had made some observations about the character and nature of the debate." He sounded as testy as Dick Russell ever did when he thought the Senate was not living up to his vision of it. And his indirection was in the best Club tradition.

13. WATERGATE:
FINE KENNEDY HAND

D: I am convinced that [Senator Sam Ervin] has shown that
    he is merely a puppet for Kennedy in this whole thing.
    The fine hand of the Kennedys is behind this whole
    hearing. There is no doubt about it. When they consid-
    ered the resolution on the floor of the Senate I got the
    Record out to read it. Who asked special permission to
    have their staff man on the floor? Kennedy brings this
    man Flug out on the floor when they are debating the
    resolution. He is the only one who did this. It has been
    Kennedy's push quietly, his constant investigation. His
    committee did the [unintelligible] subpoenas to get at
    Kalmbach and all those people.

P: Uh huh.

D: He has kept this quiet and constant pressure on the
    thing. I think this fellow Sam Dash, who has been se-
    lected counsel, is a Kennedy choice. . . .

P: Yes, I guess the Kennedy crowd is just laying in the
    bushes waiting to make their move.

So John Dean (D) and President Richard Nixon (P)
mused in the Oval Office early on the morning of February 28, 1973. There was a great deal of untruth in what
was said. Chairman Ervin of the Senate Select Committee on Presidential Campaign Activities was no puppet.

Sam Dash, who Ervin had selected to conduct the investigation of the Watergate break-in and its aftermath, was not a Kennedy man. But the "fine hand" of Senator Edward Kennedy did prepare the way for a select committee investigation of Watergate, did bring pressure for the creation of the committee. If Kennedy had not been what he was—a Kennedy, a party leader, a national celebrity, a potential president—he, not Sam Ervin, would very likely have run the select committee.

Ted Kennedy and Dick Nixon had first met in the mid 1950s, when the former was a student at Harvard and the latter was vice-president. Kennedy came down to Washington on the overnight train to visit his brother. John Kennedy's Senate office was adjacent to the Vice-president's. Ted Kennedy got to his brother's office before it opened. He was sitting on the floor waiting for the first secretary when Nixon came by. The Vice-president invited Kennedy in to chat. Kennedy found him pleasant then, but apparently he later came to dislike Nixon. I base that conclusion on the many harsh things Kennedy has said about Nixon in political speeches, on secondhand accounts of Kennedy remarks about Nixon to friends, and on his comments on Nixon in interviews. For instance, I asked Kennedy about a few lines in William Safire's "inside the White House" book, *Before the Fall*, which suggested that after Chappaquiddick Nixon called Kennedy aside at a White House meeting with congressional leaders and gave him helpful private advice on how to handle the crisis. "I appreciated the gesture," Kennedy said soberly, then exploded into hearty derisive laughter. "Although the fact that it was in the papers that afternoon . . . !" I asked him if he disliked Nixon, "as many people say." He replied, "Some people say I dislike him because he ran against my brother for the presidency. But Hubert Humphrey ran against both my brothers, and I have the greatest affection for Hubert." That seems to me a partial answer that can be interpreted to mean the opposite of its surface meaning. It wasn't those particular people or that particular narrow reason for dislike that I was asking about. Another time, asked if he resented Nixon's success, Kennedy said he had no "deep-seated" resentment against it. I asked Kennedy if the Watergate investigation and its aftermath were "personal" to him. "Not really," he said, in the shoulder-shrugging equivocation that phrase so readily lends itself to. I believe that at least in part he was motivated by a personal dislike of Nixon. It could hardly be otherwise. Some of the White House "horror stories," as John Mitchell called them, that the Watergate mentality and characters produced involved Ted Kennedy and John Kennedy in a direct and personal way. For example, E. Howard Hunt, Jr., the White House consultant who was indicted and convicted for conspiracy in the break-in at the Democratic National Committee headquarters in the Watergate office building, had not only fabricated State Department cables that implicated John Kennedy in the assassination of South Vietnam President Ngo Dinh Diem, but had also begun a dossier on Ted Kennedy and Chappaquiddick.

Nixon and Nixon staff at the White House in 1971 and 1972 may or may not have been personal in their opposition to Edward Kennedy, but they did oppose him and sought to do him in. The President and his men believed that Kennedy—not Muskie, not McGovern, not Humphrey—would be the Democratic presidential nominee running against Nixon in 1972. In the summer of 1971, Charles Colson, the President's counsel, ordered Hunt to go to Rhode Island to interview Clifton deMotte, who had done public-relations work for a motel in the Cape Cod area. Hunt tried to enlist deMotte in his investigation, and asked him if he already knew of any derogatory information about the senator. DeMotte refused to join Hunt, or "Edward Warren," as the CIA-disguised and ID-ed investigator called himself. There were other and earlier White House-directed attempts to uncover damaging Chappaquiddick-related facts about Kennedy. Tony Ulacewicz's first assignment, in 1969, was Chappaquiddick. Ulacewicz was not on the White House staff, but took his orders from John Ehrlichman's investigator, Jack Caulfield, and his salary from Herbert Kalmbach, President Nixon's personal lawyer.

Colson, H.R. Haldeman, and others were also convinced that there was a link between Kennedy and McGovern; that the latter was a stalking horse for the former, and that both were linked to peace groups and even foreign groups. Haldeman once ordered a twenty-four-hour-a-day surveillance of Kennedy, which was only called off when it was decided that the shadows might be apprehended as suspected assassins. According to Bernard L. Barker, one of those arrested, the actual fateful break-in itself was justified to the burglars in terms of information linking Kennedy and McGovern to the Cuban government. Kennedy was aware of the existence of this attitude in the White House, if not of the details.

Despite all this, it was almost surely professional, not personal, considerations that turned the fine Kennedy hand in the direction of investigating Watergate.

The five men arrested on Saturday morning, June 17, 1972, in the Democratic offices in the Watergate complex had cameras and electronic surveillance equipment with them. On Monday, the Supreme Court ruled, 8–0, that the federal government was acting unconstitutionally when it conducted electronic surveillance, including wiretaps, of domestic political radicals and other criminals without a court warrant. The Nixon Administration had claimed the right to do this. In 1971 Kennedy, in his role as chairman of the Administrative Practice and Procedure Subcommittee, had inquired of the Justice Department about the number of wiretaps and bugs in operation without court orders. The answer provided by an assistant attorney general used different figures from those cited by the President in a speech to newspaper editors, and different too from those used by the solicitor general. This had raised suspicions in Kennedy's mind and in that of the subcommittee chief counsel at the time, James Flug. The Watergate break-in and the Supreme Court ruling followed by less than two weeks Senate confirmation of Richard G. Kleindienst as attorney general. Kennedy had tried and failed to get the Senate to send that nomination back to the Judiciary Committee. He claimed not enough was known about Kleindienst's involvement in several questionable Justice Department actions, particularly but not solely the decision to settle out of court an antitrust case involving International Telephone and Telegraph. During long and bitter hearings Kennedy and a few other liberals on the Judiciary Committee became convinced that the department had been engaged in a lot of unethical and perhaps illegal activities.

It was Kennedy's persistence in questioning Kleindienst about White House involvement in that matter which led to Kleindienst's eventually pleading guilty to a charge of not truthfully testifying to the committee, a misdemeanor for which he received a suspended jail sentence and a fine. He could as easily have been charged with perjury. Kleindienst was asked early in his testimony if he had received orders from anyone on the White House staff to drop the ITT case. He answered in a way that clearly suggested he had not, but that avoided dealing with the question of whether he had received orders from President Nixon; as in fact he had. Thereafter when he was asked about "White House" instructions he answered as if assuming that only the staff was meant. Kennedy kept coming back to it. He had been well briefed on the subject, as a good prosecutor must be. Though he had no direct knowledge that Kleindienst was lying, his inquisitor's instinct and his preparation led him to keep it up.

The best attack in a situation like that is to keep asking the same question over and over, slightly rephrased each time. If you're lucky the witness will either get caught with a contradiction or evasion, or, in exasperation, flatly lie. Kleindienst did the latter.

"Senator Kennedy," he said to about the tenth question of whether there was White House pressure on him, "as I have testified fully: in the discharge of my responsibilities as the acting Attorney General in these cases, I was not interfered with by anybody at the White House. I was not importuned. I was not pressured. I was not directed."

"I think if you look at the ITT hearings, and the Gray hearings, and the Richardson hearings," says Senator John Tunney, also a member of the Judiciary Committee (referring to committee confirmation investigations of Kleindienst, acting FBI Director L. Patrick Gray, and Attorney General Elliot Richardson, all of which were in one way or another related to the broader Watergate story), "you realize that Ted Kennedy was attentive to duty, that his questions demonstrated a tremendous amount of preparation and excellent staff work." Former senator Joseph Tydings, another liberal Judiciary Committee member and a former corruption-busting U.S. attorney, gives Kennedy the highest marks for this talent. "Cross-examination . . . this is *home-work*. You must be able to catch a witness when he says something slightly different from what the record shows he said before. Teddy does that well." Kennedy was certainly doing his homework during the Kleindienst hearings, every night taking home thick looseleaf notebooks prepared by the staff of the Administrative Practice and Procedure Sub-committee.

One Judiciary Committee member, asking anonymity, gave this assessment of Kennedy as inquisitor: "He does prepare himself better than almost every other senator I know. But he lacks one thing. He lacks the killer instinct. Can you imagine what Bobby Kennedy would have done to Kleindienst or Gray? I loved Bob Kennedy. He had the greatest moral presence I've ever seen. He was a force for good. But he was a shark! Teddy's not above sticking it to somebody a little bit. He certainly has the Kennedy trait of a long memory. But he's more considerate of his enemies, more humane."

By the time the Kleindienst hearings came to an end, Kennedy's suspicions about the Nixon White House were such that, in Flug's phrase, "We were ready to believe anything." Then the Watergate story broke. "We knew immediately that was high-level stuff," Flug said. "We decided to use the Supreme Court ruling as a wedge for getting into this. We asked Kleindienst to testify. He refused. We asked [Robert] Mardian [former assistant Attorney General, then at the Committee for the Reelection of the President]. He said 'no.' We speculated that this was putting some fear into them at CRP, since we let it be known that we were interested in the break-in as well as the court ruling." The hearing produced nothing of interest. Some members of the subcommittee staff wanted to look specifically and exhaustively into the Watergate break-in, but Kennedy opposed that that summer, apparently because he feared it would look too political, and would damage him.

The summer of 1972 rolled on, with the Washington *Post* reporting that there were links between the Watergate burglary and other dirty political tricks and the Committee for the Reelection of the President and the White House. Flug's staff was clipping these and other stories for a Watergate file, but nothing more. It was assumed that the other investigations then under way would turn up something, if there was something. The Justice Department was preparing its grand jury case against those arrested in the break-in. A federal judge had before him an invasion-of-privacy civil suit filed by Democratic National Chairman Lawrence F. O'Brien. The House Banking and Currency Committee was considering an investigation into Nixon campaign finances, which would have led experienced investigators to Watergate. And there were others. Then things began to happen in rapid-fire order. On September 15 the Watergate grand jury brought back narrow indictments of just the original seven defendants, and no indication that there was any intent by Justice to look for higher-ups. On September 20 O'Brien's suit was effectively killed. On October 3, Republicans and conservative Democrats on the House Banking and Currency Committee killed that probe. Kennedy immediately wrote Sam Ervin, suggesting that his Constitutional Rights Subcommittee investigate the affair. Ervin replied on October 10 urging Kennedy's Administrative Practice and Procedure to investigate. The North Carolinian was upset about delays in trying the burglars, as were many other people, who saw in the delay a political decision by the Justice Department to avoid doing anything that might harm President Nixon's reelection chances.

On October 12 Kennedy wrote all members of the subcommittee that the staff had started an investigation of "alleged political espionage activities involving the major parties and their campaign organizations. As the facts now appear, the matter does fall within the subcommittee's long-standing specific interest in wiretapping and bugging, as well as its general mandate to study the investigative and enforcement practices and procedures of federal departments and agencies." He said he wanted to issue subpoenas and perhaps hold public hearings. All the other Democrats on the subcommittee—Tunney, Burdick, Bayh, and Hart—approved. The three Republicans—Thurmond, Mathias, and Gurney—did not. Gurney threatened to go to the full committee to halt what he called "a partisan political attempt to keep the Watergate affair alive." But he didn't. Kennedy's reply was a letter to all subcommittee members saying he had the chief counsel, three assistant counsels, and the chief investigator of the subcommittee working full time on the assignment. He said Senator Ervin had offered staff assistance, as had other House and Senate committees. "I can assure you that the inquiry will proceed in an orderly, professional, lawyerlike manner," he concluded.

Flug and his staff began issuing subpoenas in the Segretti area. Donald Segretti was being fingered in the Washington *Post* stories as a key figure in a well-financed, well-coordinated, White-House-staff-directed campaign of political espionage and sabotage. A *Post* story to that effect appeared on October 10. "Almost immediately it became clear to us that Justice hadn't done anything," Flug later said. It also became clear to the investigators that the trail led high up, and that it would be impossible for them not to appear to be *Democratic* agents snooping after *Republican* culprits. The inquiry could be made to seem just more politics. No one, apparently, said in so many words to Kennedy that he ought therefore to drop or play down the whole thing, but there was an unspoken assumption that that might be safest. On the other side, supporters of George McGovern, who was then running far behind President Nixon in the presidential race, according to all polls, were urging Kennedy and his staff to go public with all the derogatory evidence they found as soon as they found it.

Kennedy and his investigators resisted both pressures. "He let us know he had faith in us to do the right thing and let us go," recalled Flug. "So we had faith in him. We knew we could be as tough as we had to be and he would back us up." About the only concession to appearance that anyone made was Flug's decision to shave off his beard, so he would not look like a bomb-thrower to those he was interviewing.

Late in October, Senate Majority Leader Mike Mansfield was in Montana campaigning for his colleague Lee Metcalf. He told an interviewer that he had decided the Senate would investigate the Watergate break-in and sabotage of Democratic candidates' campaigns. The latter seemed to offend him more than anything else. His sense of fairness and decency in politics focused on stories of planted false accusations against Muskie, Humphrey, and Jackson involving racism and sexual deviation. Mansfield told the reporter he thought Senator Ervin or Kennedy, whom he knew to be investigating the allegations, would be the logical choices for chairmanship. A day later he was making the pledge of an investigation in speeches. But he had dropped Kennedy's name and was mentioning only Ervin. Kennedy recalls talking to Mansfield about the results of his own probe, but doesn't remember when or how much detail he went into. Mansfield recalls that he decided to get a Senate probe of Watergate and other suspicious events on the basis of press reports.

So the fine hand of the Kennedys was not as directly at work as President Nixon and John Dean thought.* Clearly Kennedy prepared the way for Ervin. His staff provided the later Watergate Committee with a great deal of assistance, worked with it on an almost daily basis well into 1973, turned over to it evidence such as telephone and financial records of Segretti and Herbert Kalmbach, and, as Kennedy wrote Ervin in June, "a complete and detailed set of memoranda on information obtained and recommended leads."

Mansfield had dropped Kennedy from his speeches for the obvious reason that a Kennedy committee would invite skepticism from much of the public and enmity from the legion of Kennedy detractors. So much attention would be devoted to Kennedy that it would be difficult to focus the spotlight of guilt on whoever turned out to be guilty. Nixon knew that, and his and Dean's comments in the Oval Room may have been in part wishful thinking. H.R. Haldeman had written Dean a memo two weeks before urging a White House investigation of "the peace movement which leads directly to McGovern and Teddy Kennedy. This is a good counteroffensive. . . . We have to play a very hard game on this whole thing and get our investigation going as a counter move." Even honorable men would have been the unwitting allies of that hard game. So the decision to turn the investigation over to Ervin and a select committee of noncontroversial senators was undoubtedly the correct one.

The Ervin Committee hearings appalled many

---

*Unless Flug leaked to the press the stories Mansfield read. He says he did not, and he does not have a reputation among reporters as a leaker.

professional investigators and lawyers. The chairman became a national hero, but not because his committee proceeded "in an orderly, professional, lawyerlike manner."
The Kennedy subcommittee probably would have done it
better and faster. Kennedy, Hart, Bayh, Burdick, and Tunney; Thurmond, Mathias, and Gurney (who was on the Ervin
Committee) would have done a better collective job of cross-
examining the reluctant witnesses, and except for the glit-
tering distortion caused by the presence of Kennedy as
Kennedy, the subcommittee would have provided fewer
theatrics. It is ironic that Kennedy glamour overcame
Kennedy competence and kept him from playing a major
role in the major event of modern constitutional government. Or, rather, *the* major role. As a member of the Judiciary Committee, Kennedy was still able to get involved in
the Watergate story in a major way.

L. Patrick Gray III had been acting director of the
FBI since the death of J. Edgar Hoover in 1972. Thus he was
in charge of the FBI when the Segretti sabotage had occurred (some of it based on the use of FBI files, according to
the *Post*), and during the Watergate investigation. Now he
had been nominated as permanent director. When the
Judiciary Committee began questioning him, a lot of attention was focused on those subjects. Kennedy passed on the
first day of Gray's hearings. But the next day he began to use
the knowledge he had acquired during his subcommittee's
investigation. He closely questioned Gray about Segretti's
phone calls and about wiretapping. When Gray returned for
a third day of questioning on March 6, Kennedy bore down
on him about White House involvement in the Watergate
investigation. It was rough on Gray. That was the day John
Ehrlichman made his famous remark about Gray to John
Dean to the effect that Gray was to be left hanging before
the committee without White House support. "Let him
twist slowly, slowly in the wind."

The next day Gray stopped twisting long enough to
drop a bomb. He had been unable to answer some of Kennedy's March 1 questions with specificity. Under pressure
from Kennedy he agreed to look up some details and insert
a statement in the hearings record later. On the 7th he did.
His statement was more responsive than Kennedy dreamed

it would be. Gray admitted that the early FBI investigation showed that Segretti had been in frequent telephone touch with the White House and with White House aides at home. He said that the investigation had shown that Kalmbach admitted having paid Segretti, usually in cash, from Nixon campaign funds. Gray thus confirmed for the first time that some of the worst charges against the White House reelection effort were true—and that the FBI or the Justice Department had at best done an unprofessional job in following all the leads that were developed, and had at worst been involved in a coverup. The ground began slipping out from under Richard Nixon's feet that day. (A few days later Judge John Sirica made public a letter to him from James W. McCord, Jr., the security coordinator for the Nixon reelection committee, who had been arrested in the Watergate burglary. McCord said perjury had been committed at his trial, that political pressure had been applied, that he wanted to talk to Sirica because he didn't trust the FBI or the Justice Department. The ground really rumbled now, and didn't stop until after Nixon had resigned.)

The Kleindienst resignation, announced by Nixon on April 30, led to the appointment of Elliot Richardson as attorney general. Kennedy and Senator Edward Brooke introduced Richardson to the Judiciary Committee with praise. The Boston Brahmin Richardson had already made a public pledge to appoint a special Watergate prosecutor. It was on this point that most of the liberals on the committee, Kennedy included, were most insistent. Hart and Ervin said they wanted the special prosecutor to have "final authority." Richardson said the attorney general had to keep that. Kennedy did get Richardson to agree to let the special prosecutor make his own decisions, such as on granting immunity to witnesses, without advance notice to the attorney general. He tried to get him to agree to retain the power only to fire the special prosecutor. Richardson refused, but said he would instead prepare a detailed charter spelling out the duties and responsibilities and freedom of the special prosecutor. He did that, and chose Archibald Cox for the job.

Cox was a Harvard law professor and former New Frontiersman. He had been John Kennedy's solicitor general. He was close enough to Kennedy to cause them both some embarrassment later. On October 20 Nixon fired Cox for refusing to obey an order not to pursue certain evidence —White House tapes—in the courts. That led to a "firestorm" of public outrage, as White House Chief of Staff Alexander Haig labeled it. Kleindienst had told Cox in confidence before he was fired that Nixon *had* intervened in the ITT case. Three days after he was fired Cox told Kennedy and Senator Hart, in the presence of two of their staff members, at Kennedy's Virginia home. Someone leaked the story to the press. Cox blamed himself, but all three principals were portrayed as irresponsible. "An inexcusable breach of confidence," said a White House statement. However, Nixon was still the net loser in the court of public opinion.

An even worse public-opinion blow to Nixon occurred a week and a half after Cox was fired. On October 31 it was disclosed in Sirica's courts that two of the famous tapes, the existence of which had been disclosed before the Ervin Committee the previous summer, were missing. The firing, the revelation earlier of tampering with the Justice Department, McCord's statement, and the apparent tampering with evidence led to the first serious talk of impeachment of the President. Representative Robert Drinan of Massachusetts had introduced the first resolution of impeachment in August, but no action was taken on it. A flurry of twenty-two resolutions descended on the House Judiciary Committee after October 20. On November 15 the House voted funds for a House Judiciary Committee staff investigation of the impeachment question. Senators, who would be the judges in an impeachment trial, kept their own counsel pretty much.

In September, when the President indicated he might not comply with a Supreme Court order to turn over all the tapes to the Special Prosecutor unless *he* considered the order "definitive," Kennedy had taken to the floor to say in a lengthy speech, "If this country stands for anything, it stands for the principle that no man is above the law. If President Nixon defied a Supreme Court order to turn over the tapes, a responsible Congress would be left with no recourse but to exercise its power of impeachment." That was one of the first, perhaps the first such statement to be made on the Senate floor. A dozen other senators listened quietly as he spoke, including two of the President's still staunch supporters, Barry Goldwater and John Tower. Neither replied to Kennedy. After the speech Tower told reporters he doubted if disobeying a court order was an impeachable offense. Kennedy told reporters that if Nixon got away with that, "It would be Chile, really, without the bloodshed" (a reference to the military coup that had just taken place in that country).

The Watergate-impeachment period was a peculiar one for Kennedy. Seldom in his career had so many contradictory pressures buffeted him. More than most senators he played a multiple role during the crisis: he was a Kennedy, a party leader, an aspiring presidential candidate, a senator, a member of the Judiciary Committee. He seems to have resolved the conflicting pressures in the direction of the latter two roles. He seemed most comfortable with them.

"He first decided that it would be counterproductive to be a leader in the impeachment movement," Carey Parker says of the earliest period. "He couldn't deal with the merits of the argument, since as a senator he would have to vote on it if it came to that." Parker says Kennedy also felt originally that it would have been counterproductive to play a leading role in the impeachment trial in the Senate, if one were held. "That would have inflamed it," he says. It is easy to imagine the counteroffensive that would have been mounted against Kennedy by Nixon defenders if he were to emerge a leader. Senator Goldwater had long ago expressed outrage at Kennedy's criticism of the moral implications of the White House role in the Watergate constellation of sins. Senators had not attacked Kennedy's morals after Chappaquiddick, so how dare he attack Nixon's morals now? he said. That reflex would doubtlessly have occurred even among some senators and others who were not out to exonerate Nixon.

Parker didn't say so, but Kennedy leadership in an impeachment trial would also have been counterproductive to Kennedy. He could have been hurt politically if he were perceived as playing a political game for himself or his party. Parker, Press Secretary Dick Drayne, and Kennedy discussed this at least once. On September 18, five days after the Senate speech, David Broder wrote in the Washington

Post that Vice-president Agnew, under investigation in a corruption case, was going to resign. Kennedy and his two aides met to discuss the implications. "Naturally we talked about how all this [resignation, new vice-president, impeachment, new president, etc.] would affect Kennedy in 1976," said Drayne. "You don't calculate your stand on that. It's cynical, irrelevant and, furthermore, you'll probably get caught." But you take it into account. The broad decision on that score was to lay low, when possible. The narrow decision was to call for a strong vice-presidential nominee when Agnew did resign. "The last thing the country needs is a caretaker vice-president unable to enjoy the confidence of the country he may be called to lead," Kennedy said when Agnew did resign the following month. Presidential aspirant Kennedy may or may not have preferred a caretaker, who would have also been a caretaker *president* in the event, thus allowing Kennedy to avoid having to run against an incumbent president if he ran in 1976. But he almost had to say the other, even if he felt it was best for the country to install a caretaker in the circumstances. A large segment of the public would perceive that Kennedy favored a caretaker for that selfish reason, no matter how eloquently or logically he presented his arguments.

When the firestorm broke on October 25, Kennedy called a number of aides and advisers to his Virginia home to discuss what to do. All Sunday afternoon Kennedy discussed the situation with Parker, Jim Flug, and other AdPrac staff members; also Burke Marshall, Steve Smith, Milton Gwirtzman. Then he left to attend a meeting of the liberals on the Judiciary Committee. The outcome was a decision on the liberals' part to press Eastland for hearings on the firing of Cox, and to use those hearings to follow the trail to Nixon's guilt. Kennedy's statement on the firing of Cox was a tough one. He said there was evidence Cox may have been fired not because of the dispute over the tapes, but because he was "too hot on the White House trail." He said this was obstruction of justice, an impeachable offense. Kennedy did not feel reluctant to speak out now, or later in the hearings, I gather because he felt that as one member of the committee charged with the responsibility to investigate the events of the crisis his remarks would be part of a chorus. He was just doing his duty. His senatorial seniority and peer support were protective coloration when he moved and acted against the background of the committee. A good example of that came November 6, when Elliot Richardson testified. Richardson had resigned as attorney general rather than fire Cox. Kennedy delved into a sensitive area. He quizzed Richardson about whether President Nixon had shown signs of psychological strain in the months leading up to the firing of Cox. Richardson equivocated. I doubt if Kennedy would have raised that issue elsewhere. But it is interesting to see that his early resolve to maintain a low profile was so short-lived. He may have decided that while it might be harmful to him to be in the thick of it, it might be equally or more harmful to appear to be ducking his responsibilities. Or he may just have decided that weighing all the political factors accurately was impossible in this unprecedented situation and so he might as well follow his instinct to *always* be at the center of things.

Kennedy came to the conclusion at the end of 1973 that the Senate was going to be faced suddenly with the responsibility to try a president, and would not be prepared for it. Senator Mansfield was extremely reluctant to begin preparations for a trial. He rightly felt that this would look as if the Senate leadership had preconceived notions about Nixon's guilt even before the House Judiciary Committee had drafted or voted on articles of impeachment. Kennedy and Phil Hart went to Chairman Eastland to get the committee to start a quiet preparation. But the parliamentarian indicated that he would rule to let the Rules Committee, not Judiciary, decide on procedures for a trial. The two liberals went to Mansfield suggesting that the leadership begin preparations, but he rebuffed them. So Parker and staff assistants to Hart, Senator Ribicoff, and Senator Javits, all of whom shared the belief that the Senate might end up going into the trial unprepared, began meeting to prepare their senators for what they expected to be informed leadership roles in the trial, if there were one. There were some two dozen of these meetings involving just the Hart and Kennedy staff members, plus other combinations. Briefing papers flowed to the senators. If the House had impeached Nixon, those four senators undoubtedly would have played the major roles in shaping Senate policy on how the trial would have been held. When Mansfield finally ordered the Rules Committee to begin a study, the staff members had accumulated a list of 106 questions that the Senate had to answer, which they forwarded to the committee.

What would have happened if Nixon had gone to trial? Would Kennedy have moved front and center? I think so. From the startling beginning to the shattering end of Watergate, the fine hand of the Kennedy apparatus was always there, actively, even eagerly at work; but not in the sense that Dean and Nixon meant. He was not manipulating people or events. There were no puppets. He could have and would have forced a Senate investigation if Mansfield had not. He would have been one of the ten or so best-prepared senators in the maneuvering and debate both on the nature of the trial and the substance of it. The AdPrac investigation had prepared him for the latter; those Carey Parker meetings with the three other senatorial staff aides prepared him for the former. In both areas, Kennedy had a long head start on most other senators. In that sense, he was very much the old-fashioned senator, getting a leg up on everybody else by looking ahead and by spending long hours at a specialized task made his responsibility by his committee assignments and seniority.

14. KENNEDY MEDICINE

In January 1971, Senator Kennedy, with Senator Sam Ervin at his side, began an assault on Richard Nixon that, like Watergate, led to a court's requiring the President to do something he didn't want to do. In this case the results were hardly as historic as those in the Watergate case, but they were of some consequence. Congress passed the Family Practice of Medicine Act in 1970. It was sponsored in the Senate by neither Kennedy nor Ervin, but Ralph Yarborough, a Texas Democrat who was chairman of the Health Subcommittee of the Senate Labor and Public Welfare Committee. The act, which authorized $225 million over three years to medical schools for training general practitioners, was not controversial. It was supported by the conservative American Medical Association as well as such liberals as Kennedy and Yarborough. The Senate passed the bill 64–1, the House 338–0. The bill arrived at the White House on December 14, 1970. Congress recessed for Christmas from December 22 to December 28. The President neither signed the bill into law nor vetoed it and sent it back to Congress so that it could attempt to override. Instead, on December 26, Nixon (saying that the bill took "the wrong approach,") claimed that he was pocket-vetoing it. The Constitution provides that "if any bill shall not be returned by the President within ten days (Sundays excepted) after it shall have been presented to him, the same shall become law, in like manner as if he had signed it, unless Congress by their adjournment prevent its return, in which case it shall not be a law." Kennedy immediately fired off a letter to the Justice Department saying that that language did not apply to "brief adjournments." Ervin called a hearing of his Subcommittee on Separation of Powers for the following month. He announced that he considered the act a valid law, and would seek to force the Administration to appropriate funds and administer it. Kennedy announced that he was going to court. He eventually got the case before judges, won it, and seemed to establish the principle that as long as Congress was more or less a year-round operation, as the modern Congress has become, the pocket veto is no longer constitutional. That took a while. It was 1972 before he filed the suit, 1973 before the case came up in the District Court in Washington, 1974 before there was an appellate decision.

On February 28 of the second year Kennedy, his wife Joan, sisters Jean Smith and Eunice Shriver, and sister-in-law Ethel Kennedy went to the court building for the arguments. Kennedy took no notes with him, only a slim, blue-bound copy of the Constitution given him by Senator Ervin. He had been well prepared, however, and unloosed a flood of statistics concerning the history of pocket vetoes and adjournments. Ninety percent of all pocket vetoes had come after World War II. Practically all were of minor bills. The Family Practice of Medicine bill was "the most important" ever pocket-vetoed. The five-day adjournment in which Nixon had vetoed it was the shortest in which a pocket veto had ever been exercised. As a co-sponsor of the bill in 1970, and chairman of the Health Subcommittee when he filed suit, Kennedy had been grievously injured. The Justice Department's Stuart E. Schiffer opposed his even bringing the suit. Kennedy had no standing, he argued. But the court agreed with Kennedy, both on his standing and the merits of his arguments. The Administration appealed, and the following year the Court of Appeals for the District of Columbia upheld Kennedy. That decision came in August 1974, the month Nixon left office. President Ford did not appeal the decision.* The act was duly printed (back-dated to December 25, 1970).

The bill's final enactment was a Kennedy triumph, and something of a rarity. Though he led many health-related bills through the Senate and on to eventual passage in the first five years he served as chairman of the Health Subcommittee, his true career in that field is best seen in the many losses he had to take, the compromises he had to settle for. The legislation he has seen enacted has not, for the most part, been very controversial. There has been a lot of it, but much of it was routine extensions or minor changes in health laws that have to be renewed periodically, such as the basic public-health law. That doesn't mean it has been easy work or legislation of no significance—or unrewarding to Kennedy. Several times in the course of the year from May 1974 through June 1975, I ran into Kennedy in the halls of the Capitol or one of the Senate office buildings. On nearly every one of those occasions he said something like, "We've been having hearings on the Food and Drug Administration [or some other health matter]. It's not the front page sort of thing but it's kind of interesting . . ." and discussed with animation and obvious interest some matter that wasn't even making the back pages.

Still, the most important thing Kennedy was doing in the health field in the years 1971–75 was losing battles. That was because he was taking on the most powerful special-interest groups in the doctors, medical schools, and phar-maceutical companies; because the public was not really ready yet to make drastic changes in health-care arrange-ments, or so it seemed; because the structure of the Con-gress was such that the chairmanship of the Senate Health Subcommittee was not *the* crucial position on *the* most im-portant health legislative proposal; and because on no other set of issues was Kennedy so far out front on that cutting edge for social change.

*After the appeals court ruling in August, President Ford pocket-vetoed an aid-to-the-handicapped bill during a thirty-one-day election adjournment, and Kennedy went back to court, in 1975, charging that the Ford veto was unconstitutional.

Kennedy became chairman of the Health Subcommittee in January 1971, rather suddenly, all things considered. He joined the subcommittee in 1965. He was junior man on a subcommittee that was rapidly growing in membership. (Today all but one member of the parent Labor and Public Welfare Committee are also on the subcommittee.) But in 1968 the chairman of the subcommittee, Lister Hill of Alabama, retired. In 1970, his successor, Yarborough, was defeated in his primary reelection campaign. That left only Senator Claiborne Pell senior to Kennedy. Kennedy had become a senator a day after he was elected in 1962. Gaylord Nelson of Wisconsin, who was elected the same day and who was also deeply interested in health matters, had not taken the oath till January 1963. By that margin, Kennedy got the chairmanship, Pell having decided to take the chairmanship of the Education subcommittee.

The first thing Kennedy did as chairman was to hold hearings on national health insurance.* That subject will be dealt with in detail later in this chapter. The second thing was to take on leadership of the effort to launch a highly publicized and somewhat controversial "war on cancer." In 1970, Kennedy's predecessor as subcommittee chairman, Ralph Yarborough, had got the Senate to create a National Panel of Consultants on the Conquest of Cancer. The panel was the idea of cancer researcher Dr. Sidney Farber, director of research for the Children's Cancer Research Foundation, Inc., of Boston, and Mrs. Mary Lasker, a long-time Washington lobbyist in behalf of an expanded federal effort in the field of health. The panel was headed by Benno Schmidt, a partner of J.H. Whitney & Co., New York. It recommended creation of an independent cancer agency whose head reported directly to the president, a comprehensive attack program, and expenditures of at least $1.5 billion in fiscal 1972–74, $1 billion a year after fiscal 1976.

*The very first thing he did was to hire LeRoy Goldman as staff director. Goldman was a former Health, Education and Welfare employee. In less than two months, Kennedy had doubled the number of professionals on the staff with the hiring of Stanley Jones, another former health bureaucrat. A month later Kennedy hired S. Philip Caper, a physician. By 1975, the staff had five professionals. This aggressiveness is part of the reason Washington *Post* reporter Morton Mintz could say later that the Senate was taking over leadership from the House on health legislation.

President Nixon was cool to the idea. In his State of the Union message he recommended just adding an extra $100 million right away (making the total $332 million a year), and promised to ask later for "whatever additional funds can effectively be used." A number of experts in the field didn't believe a lot of money could be effectively used. The Administration view was that cancer should continue to be the concern of the National Cancer Institute in the National Institutes of Health (whose head was several bureaucratic levels removed from the President).

After his January 22 State of the Union message, Nixon did not send a cancer bill up to Congress. Kennedy introduced his bill, which was based on the panel recommendation, on January 26, and scheduled hearings for early March. He was now talking about an assault on cancer similar in intensity to the program to land a man on the moon, and a cancer agency "modeled along the lines of the National Aeronautics and Space Administration." A Nixon spokesman told the Association of American Medical Colleges that the crash moon project had been undertaken after a significant scientific breakthrough had occurred, which was not the case in the effort against cancer. Kennedy's hearings began with opposition testimony from Administration officials, the Federation of American Societies for Experimental Biology, the AAMC, and the American Medical Association. The only significant institutional support for the Kennedy bill came from the American Cancer Society. Because of this, perhaps, the Administration calculated that there was no significant support for the bill in Congress.

The hearings came and went. In mid-May, as the subcommittee was preparing to begin at last the actual writing of its version of the bill, the so-called mark-up, the President suddenly realized that there was going to be a bill and that it was going to have Kennedy's name on it. He issued a statement on May 11—ten minutes after the subcommittee had gone into executive session to mark up the bill—saying that he was sending his own bill up immediately. He offered a bill that was, in the words of a health lobbyist, "a nothing bill." It did not match the Nixonian introductory rhetoric. "It is important," the President said, "that this program be

identified as one of our highest priorities, and that its potential for relieving human suffering not be compromised by
the familiar dangers of bureaucracy and red tape. For this
reason, I am asking Congress to give the Cancer-Cure Program independent budgetary status and to make its Director responsible directly to the President." This statement
(which was not true) came at a hastily called briefing for
reporters in the White House. Then Nixon turned the
briefing over to Health, Education and Welfare secretary
Elliot Richardson, who only a few months before had been
publicly expressing the Administration belief that cancer
research ought to be cut. Richardson carried on bravely.
This was not the first time that a president had reacted to
a Ted Kennedy health initiative so abruptly. In 1968, Lyndon Johnson ordered unprepared bureaucrats to brief the
press on his health program even as he was preparing to fly
back to Washington from Puerto Rico. Johnson had heard
that Kennedy was about to give a speech on health policy
and unmet needs in Boston.

   Peter Dominick of Colorado, the ranking Republican
on the subcommittee, introduced the Administration bill.
Benno Schmidt, acting as a consultant to Kennedy on the
cancer matter, and presidential aide Kenneth R. Cole immediately began negotiations aimed at rewriting it. The
ranking Republican on the full Labor and Public Welfare
Committee, Jacob Javits, was a co-sponsor of the Kennedy
bill. His aide, Jay Cutler, and LeRoy Goldman began working with the two bills. Essentially they just took the main
paragraphs of the Kennedy bill and pasted them into the
Administration bill. Schmidt took the finished version to
Cole. It carried the Dominick bill's number, so it could technically be called the Administration bill. Cole said it "con-
formed" with the President's "thoughts." Once again the
cancer agency would be independent of NIH, though still
technically within it. The bill passed quickly through the
subcommittee and full committee. The Senate passed it on
July 7 by a lopsided 79–1 vote. Only Gaylord Nelson voted
against it. He said he opposed creation of a separate agency
within NIH, and predicted that if cancer research achieved
that status, so would the NIH research effort in behalf of
heart and lung diseases. He foresaw the "dismantling" of

NIH.* Another liberal Democrat, Alan Cranston, expressed similar concern, but voted for the bill.

Kennedy had won an impressive victory in the Senate. Now the major obstacle to a new cancer agency became the House of Representatives. The chairman of the Interstate and Foreign Commerce Committee, Harley Staggers of West Virginia, supported the Kennedy bill, but the chairman of that committee's subcommittee on Public Health and the Environment, Paul Rogers of Florida, and almost all members of the subcommittee, were on record shortly after the Senate acted as either skeptical of or opposed to a new and independent cancer agency. One member, physician William R. Roy of Kansas, a Democrat, said before the subcommittee began its hearings in September, "My present feeling is that the cancer research effort should stay within NIH, not in a tenuous or theoretical fashion, but strictly within it." The subcommittee, full committee, and full House went with that view. In the bill the House passed on November 15, the "cancer-attack program" would be run by the National Cancer Institute of the NIH. The only concession the House made was to allow the president to appoint the NCI director, whose title would become associate director of NIH, with the advice and consent of the Senate. He would report to the director of NIH, but his budget would go directly to the president, with the NIH director and HEW secretary allowed to comment on it but not change it. NIH's other major research divisions, the National Heart and Lung Institute, and the National Institute of Neurological Diseases and Stroke, were also upgraded, their directors becoming associate directors of NIH. Thus, the effect of the House bill would be to leave the attack on cancer in the same relative bureaucratic position as before. More money was provided than had been previously: $1.59 billion in fiscal 1972–74, which was slightly more than the Schmidt panel had recommended, but even this act by the House was a retreat from what the Senate had done: open-ended authorizations. The House bill added an important new wrinkle. It

---

*In 1972 Kennedy introduced and led to passage a bill expanding the effort of the National Heart and Lung Institute, but leaving it in NIH without new status.

would increase the number of cancer-research institutions across the nation from three to eighteen.

Kennedy and the Senate faced a tough showdown in the conference. Rogers was newly elevated to chairman of his subcommittee, as Kennedy was, but he had been in Congress twice as many years. He was regarded as an aggressive and effective legislator. The House is often more successful than the Senate in conferences. That is especially true when technical legislation like health law is concerned. House members specialize more than senators do. They become more expert as a rule. In conference, knowledge is power. House conferees often stick together better than Senate ones do. Unity is also power in conference. Meanwhile, the White House had switched again and given an oblique endorsement of the House version of the bill. "The President approves this bill," a Republican representative said in the House debate, referring to the Rogers version. Finally, the Senate conferees expected the conference to be tough because the House had already defeated the Senate in a conference on an important health measure that year, the health manpower bill.

As it turned out, the House got its way more often than the Senate did in the cancer conference, but there was some compromise. The increased number of cancer-research institutions passed by the House was kept in the final version. The authorization adopted by the House was kept in. The Senate's independent conquest of a cancer agency within NIH was dropped in favor of the House's intensified cancer-research effort within NIH. However, the conferees agreed to the Senate's upgrading of the director of the cancer unit within NIH relative to the directors of the other disease institutes. Kennedy attended the conferences as chairman. He showed that he had done his own homework, and his knowledge of the legislation and the cancer-research effort seemed as great as Rogers's, according to lobbyists and others who are both knowledgeable and objective about what happened. But in the words of one, "Kennedy was preoccupied. He didn't seem really to care about fighting for any elements of the Senate bill. I don't think the details meant that much to him by then. He knew he wasn't going to get much political credit no matter what the result was. Kennedy's real contribution to the cancer effort came not in conference, nor in his hearings, nor in the Senate debate and voting, but in taking the old panel recommendation, the Yarborough bill, and making it his issue at the start. That forced the Administration to stop blocking the effort to greatly increase the cancer-research program. If Nixon had not been afraid that his rival, Kennedy, was going to get credit for a potentially popular major program, he never would have introduced even the bill he did. He would have opposed anything except the increase in funds under the old arrangement. And that would have been the end of it for that Congress. The House would not have initiated anything. Then Kennedy gave up the issue when Nixon's people made it clear that they wanted the issue for their own. I thought that was a very selfless, worthwhile thing Kennedy did. He said, in effect, 'Okay, you can have credit, put your number on my bill, but you have to take my bill as it is.' So the substance of what was in the original bill was his. That affected everything that happened after that. I do not believe Nixon would have done that if any other senator, one not regarded as a presidential rival in 1972, had been the chief spokesman for a major new assault on cancer."

It was after that unspoken deal, negotiated by Benno Schmidt and Kenneth Cole, and probably because of it, that Kennedy became "preoccupied" with other matters, and let other legislators and staff assistants shape the final version of the bill. When the authorization bill came up for renewal in 1974, Kennedy's role was even less active, though he was still regarded as leading advocate of the idea. By 1975 there was a growing public debate on the wisdom of the 1971 decision. A number of research scientists were complaining that there had yet to be a payoff commensurate with the expenditures. Studies appeared in a number of popular journals and newspapers pointing out that cancer death rates had not declined appreciably in the postwar era, not in the 1950s and 1960s, when cancer research first began to receive large amounts of federal aid, nor in the 1970s, when the amount of aid increased dramatically (to over $600 million a year by fiscal 1976) and the new bureaucratic setup began functioning. (Many of the leading critics of the war on cancer had been critics in 1971.) The criticism could best be summed up as a fear that politicians were overpromising cures for cancer in order to justify ever-increasing budgets, which took money away from other, more deserving, less spectacular research efforts—at the same time raising false hopes for many cancer sufferers. *The New York Times* referred to the cancer program as "cancer pork-barrel." Of course, as many scientists and politicians were still committed to the expensive war on cancer, and Kennedy was one. In June 1975, on receiving an award from the New York City division of the American Cancer Society, he chose to express his support of the program and to respond to the critics. "Those who fault the cancer program because there has been no dramatic downturn in death rates since 1971 simply demonstrate that they do not adequately understand the nature of what biomedical research is all about," he said. And: "The Congress has never been under any illusions about the difficulties involved in advancing the war on cancer. Each of us has known from the outset that much work remains in the area of fundamental biomedical research. . . . None of us thinks the appropriation of money per se guarantees the conquest of cancer. However, I know that without continued congressional support, this program will languish. I will not let that happen."

That conference on health-manpower legislation in which Paul Rogers and the House defeated Kennedy and the Senate had lasted ten full sessions. It was a classic case: Rogers was adamant, the House conferees were united, and the senators, exhausted and trying to juggle all those other balls senators keep in the air, finally conceded. The fight was largely one of details. On most of the major issues before them the members agreed. It was a question of how much should be spent in various categories. The final compromise was along the lines the House wanted. Kennedy and the Senate wanted to spend a good deal more. The bill was basically an extension of noncontroversial loan, scholarship, and construction-grant programs of the New Frontier and the Great Society. The principal goal on which all agreed was to increase the number of medical school students, and, if possible, to lead more of them to practice in rural and slum areas having trouble attracting doctors. (Provisions similar to those in the vetoed Family Practice of Medicine bill were rewritten into the new bill.) What was new about the 1971 bill was its provision for no-strings, per-student grants to health-professional schools for use by the schools rather than the students. These so-called "capitation grants" represented a major commitment of federal funds to subsidize the education of *all* medical students. Before the conferees met to smooth out the jagged edges of the two bills, the relative noncontroversial nature of the new approach was demonstrated by overwhelming votes of approval in both chambers. The House passed the bill 343–3 on July 1. On July 14 floor manager Kennedy told the Senate that the existence of a "crisis" in the health-manpower field assured that the body could "act with considerable consensus." It did, passing his version of the bill 88–0. Then, though the House prevailed on most points of contention, the Senate adopted the conference report on a voice vote, with almost no debate. The bill became law—and a disappointing law to Kennedy and some other liberals active in the health-care area.

So in 1974, when the act was due to expire, Kennedy decided on a dramatic new departure in financing medical education. The principal defect in the traditional approach was that doctors were not going into the areas where they were most desperately needed. Rural counties and urban slums, which had been losing doctors before the 1971 act, continued to lose them in the first years of the decade. This was one of the major medical problems of the times, in Kennedy's view. There were more than twice as many doctors per 100,000 population in some states than others. He began making it clear in hearings and speeches in 1974 that maldistribution of doctors would have to be dealt with more directly in the new legislation. He called it "a national disgrace." Other legislators active in the health field were also indicating that maldistribution was going to have to be tackled. For most members of Congress this was one of those tough political issues that almost always causes problems. On the one hand constituents in under-served areas were bringing pressure on Congress to do something. The more they heard people like Kennedy say that something could be done, the more they pressed, the more they were willing to accept drastic new measures. On the other hand, the medical schools and the American Medical Association were strongly opposed to anything coercive. And coercion was just what Kennedy had in mind. The 1974 Kennedy proposal confirmed the worst fears of the AMA and the Association of American Medical Colleges. In Kennedy's words, "It drove them right up the wall." The key section of the bill would require all students entering medical school, whether they accepted federal loans or scholarship or not, to agree to practice in medically underserved areas for two years after graduation. Medical schools would not receive capitation grants unless they agreed to require their students to sign the service agreements. Students could still get federal loans, and at a higher level of assistance than in existing law, but they would lose their licenses to practice if they did not honor their service requirement. In the past doctors who accepted scholarships or loans of this sort and then did not fulfill their obligation to practice in an underserved area simply had to pay back the loan. The Kennedy bill would end other old scholarship programs which did not require service.

The Kennedy bill would have been a highly controversial new departure even if that had been all it did. But it also attacked another problem of maldistribution, that involving medical specialties. In the view of many critics of the American medical community, there are far too many surgeons (and, as a result, far too much surgery) and far too few family doctors, pediatricians, and other practitioners, whose income is considerably less than that of surgeons and other specialists. But every suggestion that the government could "interfere" with the schools and students in making the decision as to what career a young doctor would pursue had been vehemently rejected. Kennedy proposed that a national council and ten regional councils survey specialty and region.

There was still another section of the bill that brought outraged criticism from the medical establishment: HEW would establish national standards for licensure of doctors and dentists. If states did not set standards as high as or higher than the federal standards, they would lose the right to issue licenses and the federal government would assume that responsibility. There were a few other slightly to signifi-

cantly less controversial sections of the bill. It was probably
the most drastic piece of health legislation ever to come out
of a full committee of the House or Senate, with the exception of Medicare. Some health professionals regarded it as
even more far-reaching than that landmark bill.

The committee passed the bill out to the full Senate
on September 3 by a 10–5 vote. The report prepared for the
majority (which means for Kennedy, since he controlled all
majority staff positions on the subcommittee) dismissed criticisms of its approach as well as substitutes for it. Voluntary
efforts had failed "dismally." It was time to be coercive. "For
without pressure and incentives from the public sector, history teaches us that it is reasonable to expect that the private
sector will continue to place its own interests first." Of a
substitute proposal by Thomas Eagleton of Missouri, a liberal Democrat, that capitation grants be replaced by federal
scholarships with service requirements, the Kennedy report
said that ending the grants would send costs up so that only
the very rich could afford medical school without scholarships. The result would be "voluntarism for the wealthy and
disguised compulsion for everyone else." It preferred compulsion for everyone. Of a substitute offered by Republican
Glenn J. Beall that would require medical schools to reserve
25 percent of the positions in each entering class for students
who would agree to serve in needed areas on a voluntary
basis, the report sniffed that the nation's needs required
more than a 25 percent effort.

That 10–5 vote was a clear signal that the bill was in
trouble. Labor and Public Welfare is the most liberal Senate
committee. The only three conservatives on the committee
—Beall, Robert Taft of Ohio, and Peter Dominick of
Colorado—voted No, and were joined by Eagleton and Harold Hughes of Iowa, also a liberal Democrat. The three liberal Republicans on the committee voted for it. Javits was a
co-sponsor.

When the Kennedy proposal came to the Senate, the
Republican strategy was to substitute the Beall bill. Its features included the 25 percent requirement and special
training grants and bonuses for medical schools that produced the most general practitioners and pediatricians, but
no licensing provisions or residency allocation. The Senate

scheduled debate on the two proposals on September 24. Kennedy—and Beall—counted, and found to no one's surprise that the Senate would take the Beall medicine but not Kennedy's. Kennedy began maneuvering to head off the Beall bill, knowing his own couldn't pass. His fear was that if the Beall bill became law, pressure to reform the medical-manpower situation would be relaxed. To get the sort of reform Kennedy wanted, every ounce of pressure was needed. If he couldn't get it in 1974, as he clearly couldn't, he might be able to in some future year—but not if the Beall bill had become law. The Rogers subcommittee in the House, meanwhile, was working on a bill that Kennedy found just as objectionable as the Beall approach. So delay and defense were called for. On September 24 Kennedy suddenly proposed a substitute of his own for both the Kennedy and Beall bills. This would have postponed major changes in the expiring 1971 legislation (now being funded on a temporary basis beyond its June expiration date) for at least one year and perhaps several. The Senate turned him down 33–58. Then the Senate approved Beall's bill by 81–7.

The House did nothing until after the November elections. Not till December 1974 did the Rogers bill go to the floor for a vote. The bill he had fashioned had broad support in subcommittee and committee. Instead of the compulsory feature of the Kennedy bill, the Rogers bill would require medical schools to spend 25 percent of the total of their capitation grants to train senior students in remote sites, such as rural clinics. Also, the schools could not qualify for capitation grants unless they could assure HEW that half their students went into residency training for family medicine, general pediatrics, or general internal medicine. Further, the schools receiving capitation grants would have to enter into agreements with students requiring them to eventually pay back the amount of the grant to the government. It was, all in all, more likely to achieve Kennedy's aim than the Beall bill. But he still objected to any measure less certain of results than his own. He told colleagues the Rogers bill was "too indirect" an approach to the maldistribution problem. He told Yale Medical School students in a major speech on December 2 that he expected to begin again in 1975 in the newly elected and lopsidedly

Democratic and liberal 94th Congress. The speech raised some eyebrows down in Washington. The House was expected to pass the Rogers bill, setting up the need for a conference to work out a compromise of that and the Senate-passed Beall bill. At which conference, of course, chairman Kennedy would lead the Senate conferees. A chairman and all conferees are supposed to work to get the Senate's views accepted by the House and, at least, to get an agreement. Here was Kennedy saying, "The new Congress will begin from scratch in January." Scratch one conference.

The House passed the Rogers bill by a vote of 337–23. There was almost no debate. The final days of the 93rd Congress were hectic, and it is conceivable that the failure of the conference to agree on a bill was not related to Kennedy's presumed desire for no bill. The conference met only once—on and off for seven hours on December 19. It was not the best day for such a conference. House members had to leave to vote on the confirmation of Nelson Rockefeller. Senate members had to leave to attend his swearing in. Kennedy had to leave to fight off efforts on the Senate floor to scuttle another health bill of his, one setting up new national health planning procedures. Kennedy says he did his duty by the Senate version of the manpower bill in conference. But one senator who was a conferee says, "At the very least, Kennedy was unenthusiastic. At the worst, he, well . . . leave it at unenthusiastic. I shouldn't say what I think was in his mind." A House conferee says Kennedy simply prevented any effort at compromise by bringing up extraneous issues, by stalling, and by trying to lead the Senate conferees, who as a group were more liberal than the Senate itself on health legislation, into taking a stand for some sections of his own bill, the committee version the Senate was known to be unwilling to accept.

The Republicans on the Senate Health Subcommittee had earlier labeled the original 1974 manpower bill a "doctor draft." "We cannot believe that a Congress which has helped to end the military draft . . . will support a civilian draft for the health profession." That was a dart aimed at Kennedy, who had led the Senate effort to end the draft. I've often wondered if in that conference Kennedy recalled the time the Senate conferees, led by those autocratic elders

Russell and Stennis, had in effect destroyed a pretty good
Senate bill reforming the draft by turning the conference
into a third house of Congress. That is what Kennedy was
doing in conference in December 1974, if his adversaries are
to be believed. The Yale speech makes them believable.

Next, Kennedy began hinting that he might take a
much different approach to part of the manpower problem.
In a speech to the Harvard School of Public Health in May
1975, he said, "Thus far I have preferred the continuation
and expansion of institutional support as the best way to assure the financial stability of the nation's health-professions
schools. But if the schools refuse to face up to the problem
of geographic maldistribution, I intend to propose that the
government stop giving them the money and give it to students in a wholly voluntary program."

Actually that was the sort of thing Senator Eagleton
had proposed in committee the year before. Kennedy had
rejected it then, saying it was no more voluntary than his
own proposal of that year. Representative William Roy, a
physician, had pushed a similar bill in the House in 1974. It
had proved attractive enough to force Rogers and his subcommittee to come up with a stronger bill than otherwise
would have been written. It might be that Kennedy's announcement about ending capitation grants was a tactical
move. At the time of the Harvard speech he still had not
introduced a new bill. In that speech he said he had not
changed his mind about federal licensure and restrictions of
specialty residences.

Expertise and a reputation for being "a responsible
type of senator," as Kennedy once put it, are no guarantees
of getting legislation enacted, even legislation that on the
surface seems unassailable. One of Kennedy's classic lickings
in this regard came in October 1972, in debate on the Social
Security amendments that would reform the welfare system
and make changes in Medicare and Medicaid. Kennedy,
then with nearly two full years' experience as chairman of
the Health Subcommittee, proposed that a study be made
by the Health, Education and Welfare Department of
whether chiropractors should continue to be reimbursed
under Medicare the same as other medical practitioners.

Kennedy complained to the Senate that chiropractors with only a high-school diploma and eighteen months' training in a school of chiropractic were treating people for serious diseases such as high blood pressure, anemia, gallstones, etc. Kennedy said his subcommittee had found that often patients who first went to chiropractors for serious problems turned to physicians only after it was too late, when the diseases had become untreatable, and the patients died.

Kennedy next tried humor, reading from a chiropractic textbook, with detailed instructions on how to talk to patients: "On the third [visit], the chiropractor is supposed to say . . . 'Your eyes are brighter.' . . . On the fourth . . . 'I hope you are feeling as good as you look.' . . . On the fifth . . . 'You are getting a spring in your step.' . . . On the eighth . . . 'Did you know you will live longer as a result of these adjustments?' " And so on. Then he turned to the textbook's section on collecting the bill. The *Congressional Record* does not indicate the true nature of the debate, except that at one point Kennedy is quoted as saying, "This is no laughing matter."

Kennedy recreated that scene for me two years later in an interview. "Even though you build a reputation around here so that when someone mentions your name, they know that that's going to be a responsible type of amendment, you can still lose and lose badly. We've had some losses, even on issues where I think that the majority of the members felt that the merits were on our side, but the pressures . . . I read this [the textbook] into the *Record* late in the evening, I remember, and the whole Senate was roaring with laughter. They realized how ridiculous this whole thing was, and it went to a roll call and we got only six votes."

An aide who was sitting with Kennedy at the time of the vote told me another anecdote. A liberal senator who almost always agrees with Kennedy on health matters came into the chamber just as the roll-call vote began. Told the vote was on a Kennedy amendment, he assumed it was something he could support. He passed Kennedy's desk. "Are you with me on this, ____?" Kennedy asked. "You bet," the other senator replied. By the time his name was called, however, he had learned exactly what the issue was, and voted with the huge majority opposed to Kennedy. (The vote was 66–6.)

One doesn't think of chiropractors as a powerful Washington lobby, but Kennedy ascribed his defeat to their influence. He sees them as a special interest much like any other. Another view is that it is their patients who create the political pressure to cause senators to vote so overwhelmingly against even a study of their efficacy in treating certain diseases. There are millions of patients. According to one expert in the health field, these are for the most part elderly people with modest incomes. They are a part of every liberal's and every Democrat's constituency—including Kennedy's. It is more noteworthy to me that Kennedy would take the lead in upsetting this part of his constituency than that he would in upsetting the chiropractors themselves.

In a somewhat similar way, Kennedy in 1975 offended a large part of his constituency by leading a Senate fight against an antiabortion amendment. In this case he won. Senator Dewey Bartlett of Oklahoma offered an amendment to a routine health-services and nurses'-training bill. The amendment would bar federal funding of abortions under the Medicaid program. Bartlett, a Catholic, objected on moral grounds, and originally on grounds that the program had cost too much. He said HEW had spent $40 to $50 million for abortions for the poor in 1973. Kennedy was floor manager for the bill. A Catholic with a large Catholic constituency, he had maintained a low profile on the heated abortion controversy. But on this amendment, he took the offensive. "Is the issue cost?" he asked Bartlett.

"The issue is cost . . . as well as the moral issue," Bartlett replied.

"The senator does not mind paying little money for abortions," Kennedy came back sarcastically, "but he does not like to pay a lot, is that what the issue is?" Bartlett turned to other aspects of his opposition. Kennedy and other senators who opposed the amendment argued that the bill was discriminatory to poor women who wanted abortions, that it might prevent Medicaid from providing birth-control assistance. Pressed in debate to state his own views on abortion, he said that he was opposed to it. Senator Javits introduced a tabling motion and the Bartlett amendment was killed by a vote of 54–36. Bishop Daniel A. Cronin of Fall River, Massachusetts, sent a letter attacking Kennedy to every priest in his diocese.

This was only one of many instances where Kennedy was on the winning side of legislative conflicts over health legislation. The planning bill referred to above was a major bill that replaced all traditional health planning and regional medical legislation, including the venerable Hill-Burton hospital construction law. The 1974 law set up a national network of planning agencies, which would be able to prevent unneeded hospitals and other such facilities from being constructed. Kennedy's Senate bill provided grants to states choosing to regulate doctors' fees. The House wouldn't go that far. But in conference Kennedy and the Senate did win approval of a demonstration project in a small number of states.

Another Kennedy success the same year was the creation of a presidential panel of advisers on biomedical research. It was patterned after a similar panel reporting to the president on cancer research which Representative Ancher Nelson had pushed through to enactment during the 1971 debate over the war on cancer. Kennedy also won legislative approval of new restrictions on research and experimentation on human subjects in 1974. This legislation resulted from dramatic hearings Kennedy's subcommittee conducted in which federal officials denied, then were forced to concede, such things as the existence of psychosurgery experiments in Veterans Administration hospitals.

Still another Kennedy success was the enactment in 1973 of legislation designed to encourage development of health-maintenance organizations. HMOs, as they are called, are prepaid group practices. Their supporters believe they provide better care for less money. Families pay a fixed amount to the group and receive all medical attention and treatment either at no additional cost or for only a minimal charge. This approach to medicine is directly contrary to the traditional fee-for-service approach supported by the American Medical Association and most doctors. A few HMOs were in operation in the early 1970s, but the start-up cost was high enough to require a subsidy, either from a private source or the government. In 1971 President Nixon proposed a federal subsidy, but soon the Administration wilted under extreme lobbying pressure from the AMA.

Kennedy in the Senate and Representative William Roy in the House pushed for larger subsidies. The Senate passed a $5.2 billion Kennedy HMO bill in 1972, but the Roy bill never got to the floor of the House. In 1973 Kennedy reintroduced a scaled-down ($1.5 billion) bill. Senators Javits and Richard Schweiker of Pennsylvania, both liberal Republicans, offered a substitute with a $700-million subsidy. When that amendment appeared likely to pass, Kennedy offered a substitute to his own bill which authorized only $852 million. The House then passed a bill with a much smaller authorization—$240 million, to be spread over five years rather than the three in the Senate bill. The conference led to a compromise closer to the House subsidy, $375 million in five years, but Kennedy and the senators won major concessions on nonmoney items, including the authority of the federal government to override state laws that hindered the development of HMOs.

To speak of this or that Kennedy bill is a shorthand device. Health legislation written by the Health Subcommittee usually has elements initiated by many of its members. But the shorthand is necessary, and not really misleading. "Kennedy *is* the Health Subcommittee," says Glenn Beall. "He controls the entire majority staff. It overwhelms the small minority staff." That means that the finished product of subcommittee efforts at drafting bills reflects Kennedy's views more than those of any other subcommittee member. In addition, Kennedy exercises his chairman's prerogative of putting his name on practically all legislation that emerges from the subcommittee. On one occasion that practice led to a contretemps senators usually avoid.

"Other chairmen who want to get involved in a member's pet project will just add amendments to the bill, but not Kennedy," says an individual who follows the legislative process closely (and who asked complete anonymity). "Kennedy gets the staff of Health to rewrite the whole bill with his idea incorporated in it, and then calls it his bill. He's the biggest thief on the Hill. The best example of that is the Nelson drug bill. Kennedy just stole that. Just stole it. Poor Gaylord worked on that for six years, holding the most important drug industry hearings ever, more informative than the old Kefauver hearings. He wrote his bill and Kennedy just took it as his own without hardly changing a line, a word, and put his own name on it. He's always doing that, and he always does it to the people he ought to be considerate of, the liberals like Mondale and Cranston, and Nelson."

The Nelson bill called for basic changes in the pharmaceutical industry, including its testing, advertising, and marketing practices, among other things. As such it was strongly opposed by the industry. But Nelson was not perceived by the industry as an effective legislator; a month after he introduced his bill in 1971 the chief counsel of the Pharmaceutical Manufacturers Association said he hadn't even bothered to read it. The bill died in the 92nd Congress. Nelson introduced it again in February 1973. That month Kennedy held hearings on human experimentation, including experiments with drugs, and became interested in legislation. He ordered his staff to prepare him a bill on the subject. The staff man who got the assignment, Dr. Lawrence Horowitz, studied the Nelson hearings and bill, among other things, and prepared a bill that closely followed the Nelson bill in many areas. He said later he thought that was customary practice, and assumed Nelson's name would be listed as a co-sponsor.

Kennedy said he did, too, and offered it to Nelson. There was a stormy meeting of the two senators. Nelson, up for reelection, waved a Wisconsin newspaper at Kennedy, saying that he was being criticized for his lack of effectiveness, that his long effort to reform the drug industry was just ready to be successful—and Kennedy was taking over his work. Kennedy said he wanted to work out an agreement with Nelson. Nelson said he didn't believe that. Kennedy lost his temper at that, and the meeting broke up with both senators quite angry. Thereafter the subcommittee held hearings on both bills.

The hearings themselves were fruitful, showing how the giant drug firms manipulated the public and many prescribing physicians. Ralph Nader called the series of hearings and another that followed "unprecedented" in their revelations. Still a later series of hearings, in 1974 and 1975, showing law regulation of the industry by the Food and Drug Administration, reaped a publicity bonanza too. But neither drug bill was acted on by the subcommittee, and both died with the 93rd Congress. According to one close follower of the Kennedy-Nelson conflict, a bill would have been approved and sent to the full Senate if the two had been able to get together. Three liberal Democrats on the subcommittee—Mondale, Eagleton, and Hughes—refused to co-sponsor the Kennedy bill because of the conflict. Those three votes would have made the difference.

Kennedy concedes most of the charges made against him in this episode. "Gaylord hasn't got the legislative committee. Now that's happened to me, too. That's the way it goes around here." An aide to Kennedy said, "We just did to Nelson what Gale McGee did to us on voter registration by mail. Kennedy introduced that, but McGee, who is chairman of the Post Office and Civil Service Committee, took it over." After the confrontation, Kennedy and Nelson worked out an agreement under which *two* drug bills would be reported out of the subcommittee in the next Congress, one with Kennedy's name on it and one with Nelson's. As of midsummer 1975 that was still pending.

Everything Kennedy did in connection with health legislation in the 1970s was accorded a secondary priority to national health insurance. The unspoken assumption in every staff meeting on drugs or HMOs or the war on cancer or malpractice or human experimentation or whatever was, "We don't do anything that will hurt us on health insurance." The goal of national health insurance was in Kennedy's mind when he discussed health legislation with other senators, with health experts in and out of government. It was as elusive a goal in the 1970s, as it turned out, as it had been in the 1940s, the only time previously federal officeholders made a serious attempt to enact it; but with Kennedy in the lead, the effort came considerably closer. There are some who believe the effort came within a scalpel's edge of achievement.

President Truman had led the first fight for a national health-care system covering all medical bills for the whole population, financed by a Social Security tax. He sought enabling legislation in 1945, 1947, 1949, and 1950. He never came close. The American Medical Association mounted an expensive and sophisticated lobbying effort that overcame the President and in effect killed the debate for nearly twenty years. National health insurance was branded socialized medicine, an epithet to many Americans. When Kennedy became chairman of the Health Subcommittee in 1971, the only federal programs related to health insurance were Medicare, Social Security-financed insurance for the elderly, and Medicaid, a program operated in conjunction with the states which paid the health care bills of the poor.

In 1968 a new organization had begun to think in terms of creating a public opinion in favor of the old Social Security-financed, cradle-to-grave health-insurance program for the entire population, young as well as old, rich as well as poor. Walter Reuther of the United Auto Workers was the organizer of the effort. He told friends that no matter who won the 1968 presidential election, it was clear that national health insurance was not going to get a very high priority. In January 1969, Reuther sent Max Fine, a UAW official who had formerly worked for the Kennedy and Johnson administrations on Medicare, to open a Washington office. It was decided to set up a Committee for National Health Insurance—one hundred leading citizens. Representative Martha Griffiths of Michigan UAW territory—was asked to introduce the comprehensive bill. Among the few senators asked to serve on the committee were Yarborough, then chairman of the Health Subcommittee, and Kennedy. "There were other subcommittee Democrats senior to Kennedy," Fine said later, "but Kennedy got you exposure you couldn't get with anybody else."

In 1970, a Senate version of the Reuther committee's bill was introduced, with Kennedy, Yarborough, and thirteen other senators listed as sponsors. Close followers of the situation called the bill the Yarborough-Kennedy bill. The press called it the Kennedy bill. The subcommittee held several days' hearings on the legislation in September 1970, but this was mere showmanship. Since national health insurance was to be financed by a payroll tax, the legislation had to originate in the House Ways and Means Committee. In the Senate, the Finance Committee would have jurisdiction. But in 1970, Ways and Means chairman Wilbur Mills was totally uninterested, as was Finance chairman Russell Long. So it was up to Yarborough to provide the forum for the publicity needed to generate any pressure on Congress and the White House. President Nixon had referred to the demands of Reuther and others who were calling for health insurance as "knee-jerk." The AMA, sensing trouble ahead, testified at the hearings for what it termed a substitute for national health insurance: Medicredit, a system that would give taxpayers tax credits for buying health insurance from private firms. Clearly not the same thing.

Yarborough was defeated in his primary in 1970. What the press was calling the Kennedy bill became the Kennedy bill in fact in 1971. He became the chief sponsor and busiest worker for the bill. The challenge still seemed a very difficult one. Kennedy told his aides and colleagues in private that he believed a five-year effort lay ahead. There is some dispute about something else he was saying around 1969–70–71. Carey Parker, who was beginning his tour then as chief legislative aide, says it was always understood that health care was Kennedy's middle-class-white issue. He was becoming identified with the various minority groups— blacks, Chicanos, youths, the very poor. He needed something to show the great middle-working class he was on its side. And everybody has medical expenses. Dun Gifford, who was ending his tour as legislative aide when Kennedy took on leadership of the national-health-insurance crusade, on having Parker paraphrased to him, says heatedly he recalls no such thing. A pause for cooling off and recollection. "And even if that was the reason, it shows you what kind of politician Kennedy is. His idea of a safe, middle-class issue is the most controversial piece of legislation of the sort that is before us." Kennedy himself says he never recalled thinking of this fight as a gesture to the middle class. But after pointing out that "we *still* don't have it," he says he thinks it may have been "good politics" to work for it, "in the sense that being a good senator is good politics." Hard work on the cutting edge of social change is being a good senator to him.

In 1971 there was evidence that some sort of national health-insurance scheme might become law. Kennedy introduced the Committee for National Health Insurance bill. The CNHI bill, S.3, like its companion measure in the House, H.R.22, again introduced by Representative Griffiths, was becoming known as the Health Security Act. Its ingredients were the classic ones: a new Social Security tax plus some funds from general revenue to finance compulsory federal health insurance with universal coverage, all medical expenses 100 percent covered (with some limits on psychiatric, dental, nursing-home, and prescription-drugs payments), the program to be administered by a special board in HEW, national standards for physicians' controls on fees.

As 1971 began, even Nixon's knee jerked, or at least twitched a little. Health-care costs had soared the year before, and ahead loomed the presidential campaign in which the President then believed he would be running against Kennedy. He sent his own bill up to Congress. It wasn't much compared to the Health Security Act. It only required employers to provide health insurance for employees, a subsidy for small businesses to help pay for insurance, federal insurance for poor families. The Nixon plan would cost taxpayers $2.6 to $3 billion a year; Health Security, $60 billion. "Someone at the White House admitted to me they were playing political games with Kennedy," says Fine. "I can't tell you who."

The time seemed to be ripe for some sort of legislation. The AMA reintroduced Medicredit. The Health Insurance Association of America got a friendly senator to introduce a bill tailored to its liking. In the Senate Long decided to hold Finance Committee hearings. In the House Mills scheduled Ways and Means hearings. Kennedy stole a march on both with early hearings by the Health Subcommittee. Those ran from February into April. Long's hearings followed. Then Mills's. But all the principals were revealed to be far apart, seemingly too far for any meaningful compromise. Mills and Long were not then even committed to legislation of any sort. In 1971 it was assumed by all that without assistance from, or at least acquiescence by, Mills, there could be no bill. The year's hearings ended with no real movement. The promise of January seemed empty in December.

Then in June 1972 Kennedy and Mills surprised everyone by appearing together before the Democratic party platform committee and saying they had agreed in principle on a national health-insurance system. That was significant, but on two of the most significant aspects of the plan, financing and administration, they were still far apart. Mills was particularly opposed to a system that froze the insurance companies out of an administrative role. The Kennedy-Mills appearance turned out to be the beginning of an enterprise, not the end of it; the earliest stirrings, not final unity. The presidential election came and went. (Mills ran an ineffective campaign for the nomination.) Kennedy reintroduced S.3 in 1973. All the other old bills were back in the 93rd Congress's hoppers. And senators Long and Abraham Ribicoff had introduced a bill providing for federal assistance to the poor, aid to all victims of so-called catastrophic illnesses, those of enormous expense, plus federal oversight of private insurance features. The Health Subcommittee held hearings on the various bills in October. At year's end, President Nixon announced that he was going to ask Congress to enact a new Administration bill. When the bill was unveiled early in 1974, it proved to be surprisingly comprehensive. Mills put his name on it as a co-sponsor.

The new bill, labeled Comprehensive Health Insurance Plan, would make insurance available to Americans through three plans: an employee plan, paid for by employer and employee; an assisted plan for low-income workers or others not eligible for the first plan, with federal and state governments paying the part of the cost the covered individual could not afford; and an expanded Medicare program. On the question of cost of services to the worker, the Administration approach was particularly objectionable to Kennedy, labor, and the CNHI. An individual with an income of $7000 a year would have to pay the first $150 of a doctor's fees before his insurance picked up, then pay 25 percent of all costs after that, up to a maximum of $1050. The cardinal tenet of labor and other strong supporters of national health insurance was that from the first dollar to the last, there should be no out-of-pocket cost.

The apparent Mills-Nixon concord frightened some people supporting S.3, perhaps including Kennedy. The fear was that this bill could become law, dooming any real effort for the real thing for another twenty-five years. For Kennedy there may have been a personal and political element to this concern. He had committed himself to the issue as the decade began. He had provided the Reuther committee with the access to media it had desired. He had invested a great deal of senatorial time on the subject. He had invested a great deal of his large staff's time and energy to it. He had become identified in the public's imagination with the health-insurance issue. Now if there were to become a law without his support, *over his objections,* how would he look? I believe that this was a major element in his decision about what to do next.

What he did next was to consummate the marriage with Mills. He had been courting Mills for over a year. Beginning after the 1972 platform, he began meeting the Arkansan (in Mills's office) with some regularity. Mills was always alone. Kennedy always brought Stan Jones, and did most of the talking, expressing his desires and priorities. Mills expressed occasional objections, but kept his own desires regarding specifics to himself. There were six or eight of those meetings in 1973. When the Administration's new bill came out, Kennedy and Jones walked back over to the Capitol Ways and Means office to make a more-or-less last-ditch effort at compromise. This time William Fullerton of Mills's staff was there—standing outside the door. That was taken as a signal for Jones to stay outside, too. Kennedy and Mills met alone. They agreed on a bill.

The result dismayed the Committee for National Health Insurance. Kennedy had given in on two key features: (1) deductibles and co-insurance, and (2) insurance company administration. The Kennedy-Mills bill would require an individual to pay the first $150 a year in medical expenses out of his own pocket, then 25 percent of all further expenses up to $1000. Thus it was like the Administration bill. Insurance companies would serve as fiscal intermediaries between Social Security, which would collect the money for insurance premiums, and doctors and hospitals. Mills had gotten those concessions by agreeing to the broad principles of compulsory coverage and payroll taxation. The CNHI was dismayed, but neither surprised nor upset with Kennedy personally. He had warned the committee and other supporters of S.3 at a meeting of the Washington Health Security Action Coalition, a lobbying group, that he was getting ready to make concessions. "There is a ball game going on up there," he said at a meeting in downtown Washington just before Kennedy-Mills was announced. "And I'm going to be a part of that ball game. I don't want to be outside the park listening to the cheers and yells." A few in his audience muttered "sellout," but most respected the political decision, even if they disliked it. Max Fine, who was at the meeting, says, "Kennedy implied that it would be a setback for *him* if the Senate passed a bill which he had not drafted. We respect that. Kennedy was never deceitful or misleading. He had worked hard for us. He was one hundred percent. He got to be an expert on health insurance. He thought the committee would go along, and he thought Mills could deliver the necessary votes on Ways and Means. He was just wrong."

Kennedy *was* wrong. Mills couldn't quite get a solid majority on his Ways and Means in support of the Kennedy-Mills bill, or even of a further compromise he and Secretary Weinberger began working out. The bill died with the 93rd Congress. They had come close, but not close enough. If labor and the CNHI had supported Kennedy-Mills, it or a version with a slightly bigger compromise might well have become law. But by August, when the Ways and Means Committee began voting on the health-insurance proposals before it, the prospect of a very liberal 94th Congress was already enchanting supporters of S.3. They preferred to wait a year. The November elections, when a large number of leading House opponents of S.3 were defeated, provided further hope that it could become law.

On January 15, 1975, Kennedy reintroduced S.3. In April he pointedly reminded the CNHI that he had *not* reintroduced Kennedy-Mills. But the 94th Congress was quickly buffeted by a wave of national fears over the fiscal integrity of the existing Social Security program, by waves of demands for tax relief and tax reform, and by waves of successful Ford vetoes of expensive social programs. Clearly S.3 would have a tough time in 1975 and 1976. Kennedy often spoke in favor of it, but privately he was indicating to associates he would again go with a new version of the Kennedy-Mills bill including the deductible and co-insurance features that labor so strongly opposed, if he saw an opportunity to get it enacted. He was said to see that as a far more realistic expectation than enactment of the true national health-insurance plan he had spent five years in pursuit of.

15. MORE OR LESS
FOR MASSACHUSETTS

S enator for the young, senator for the poor, senator for the blacks, Indians, and Chicanos, senator for the dispossessed not only of America but of the world—that is how Edward Kennedy was perceived by himself and others by 1970, when it came time for him to seek reelection from the only constituency that counts to the man who signs the certificate of election. In 1962 that constituency had considered only one issue—Ted Kennedy himself. He was the issue. That was true again in 1964, when Kennedy was hurt in that plane crash. In 1970 Kennedy should have been held accountable for his stands on issues of national and world importance. He should have been asked to explain what he had and had not done to carry out that long-ago pledge to Do More for Massachusetts. But once again in 1970 the only issue was Ted Kennedy. And once again it was no contest.

It was literally no contest within the Democratic party. There was no challenge to his renomination. Republicans in the state had no realistic hopes of defeating him. Bay State Republicans thought there had to be a contest, nonetheless, if for no other reason than that it would look bad not even to enter a candidate. Also, in the view of such Republicans as Senator Edward Brooke, there were national issues that deserved to be debated in a rational, nonhysterical way, such as foreign policy, aid to state and local governments, the broad area of welfare. That was the year President Nixon sent Vice-president Agnew around the country attacking "radical liberals" with a bruising rhetoric that was offensive to many of the Republicans and independent voters who tended to support a Brooke in *his* election years. In October of 1969 Brooke was quoted as saying that Kennedy was unbeatable, and that the party should therefore nominate a "nonpolitical" opponent who would provide "a frank, honest, and intellectual discussion of the issues." Governor Francis Sargent, who would be up for reelection in 1970, favored a tougher opponent, Representative Silvio Conte. But Conte refused. So did Transportation secretary and former governor John Volpe. There was talk of nominating such nonpolitical stalwarts as Erwin Canham, editor of the *Christian Science Monitor*, Dr. Jean Mayer, the Harvard nutritionist who had organized the White House Conference on Food, Nutrition and Health in 1969, John Knowles, the ambitious and public-spirited director of Massachusetts General Hospital, and even Al Capp, the cartoonist. Capp did switch his registration from Independent to Republican (while Knowles was switching his from Republican to Democratic), but in the end the party had to turn to a little-known former state party chairman and Rockefeller man, Josiah Spaulding. Spaulding, a Boston lawyer, had announced his availability long before Chappaquiddick.

It was the tragic episode at Chappaquiddick and its immediate aftermath that made an otherwise noncontest a slightly dramatic race. Kennedy watchers in the state and the nation wanted to see if Kennedy's margin would fall below that of 1964. Should that happen, the argument could be made that Kennedy's appeal was not what it used to be. The White House showed a keen interest in seeing Kennedy messed up. Charles Colson and Murray Chotiner, President Nixon's most reknowned political in-fighters, reasoned that if Chappaquiddick should hurt—or *seem* to hurt—Kennedy in Massachusetts, where the Kennedy name was revered, it could be made an issue of later, if need be, outside of Massachusetts. President Nixon still felt that Kennedy, not the then front-running Edmund Muskie, would be his opponent in 1972. Colson and Chotiner tried to get the nomination for John J. McCarthy, who they felt would be more likely than Spaulding to "claw" Kennedy.

Kennedy took the potential for challenge seriously.

Registration was down in Massachusetts, particularly in Democratic areas. Polls showed Kennedy still popular within the party, but not among Republicans. Other Democratic officeholders in the state drew favorable ratings from a majority of Republicans in polling, but Kennedy in one poll made a 31–50 favorable-unfavorable showing. So he authorized an expensive registration effort, which had been discussed before Chappaquiddick, and began a heavy campaign schedule, spending four days a week in Washington to work in the Senate and two or three days in Massachusetts, where he put in fourteen-hour days campaigning. He invested heavily in time in the suburbs around Boston. His campaign began long before his formal announcement, which was delayed till June by continuing developments in the Chappaquiddick story: first the inquest report was delayed, then a grand jury investigation was begun. If there was no fear of losing to a Republican opponent, there was a fear of the combination of Chappaquiddick, lethargy, a strong Republican gubernatorial candidate heading the ticket, a slight case of un-Kennedy-like campaign ineptitude, and a slight case of low morale on the part of those aides and workers who felt that there was no real challenge with a 1972 presidential campaign ruled out (the 1970 campaign, they had hoped, would be a trial run, à la John Kennedy's reelection contest in 1958). Some of the fears seemed a little more serious after primary day in September, when 185,546 Democratic voters left the unopposed Kennedy's name on the ballot blank. That was more than a quarter of the turnout. Then 100,000 telegrams were sent out over Kennedy's name to registered voters telling them they had not voted—when many of them had.

In that primary Republicans chose Spaulding over McCarthy. Spaulding began his uphill fight against Kennedy by stressing first in speeches and then in his television spots that *he* would listen to Massachusetts voters, but that Kennedy was too busy being a national politician to do that.

Kennedy, who himself emphasized the truth of this in a fund-raising dinner at Hickory Hill late in September by announcing that his main campaign themes would be "end the war, end racism, end poverty," began to play the listening theme, too. Often he would say to audiences around the state that fall that he had had eight years in the Senate to express his views, and that he planned to continue expressing them, but that now he would like to listen to his audience. People would make little statements or, more frequently, ask questions. There was never a question about Chappaquiddick, and seldom a question about strictly local affairs. Usually the questions were about national issues—the war, health care, Social Security, those campus riots. On the war Kennedy consistently called for a prompt U.S. withdrawal, "lock, stock, and barrel," a posture that was probably more popular in Massachusetts than in the rest of the country, probably in large part because of Kennedy's insistent dovishness and criticism of the war's impact. As to the riots, Kennedy made it clear that he was sympathetic to the concerns of the rebellious students, but, significantly, his first five-minute television spot in the campaign was a filmed conversation among Kennedy and a group of construction workers in which the candidate criticized the rioters.

Local issues were, of course, on people's minds. In New England the approach of winter always brings to people's attention the high cost of heating fuel, which was expensive in part because only a limited amount of then cheap foreign oil was allowed to be imported. Both Kennedy and Spaulding were opposed to import quotas, but Spaulding, a Rockefeller man, had determined to do the manly thing and support his President, who was for the quotas.

Spaulding never really tried to make an issue out of Kennedy's Senate service. It may have been that his most telling issue was the charge that Kennedy would not debate him on the issues. At least, it was telling in Kennedy's mind, if not the collective mind of the voters. Spaulding characterized Kennedy as "a frail imitation" of his brothers, called him "the only member of this family who has been afraid to meet his opponent in debate." That was late in October. Twice thereafter the candidates did debate. Late on the afternoon of the 20th they met at the Bay Club on the thirty-sixth floor of a State Street skyscraper, with thirty businessmen but no reporters, and argued over a range of issues—

all of national rather than just local interest. And they agreed on most of them. The next day they met at Bridgewater State College, where they again agreed on most issues. Spaulding said Kennedy wasn't doing enough for New England industries. Kennedy said Spaulding was running on Nixon's record. It was a good-natured debate, with as much an air of the seminar as of the campaign trail. The candidates and the crowd were in a good humor. Spaulding said he didn't care who won, to the crowd's affectionate laughter. Spaulding was beginning to run out of money. It was a forlorn campaign. His campaign headquarters even caught on fire.

Kennedy, meanwhile, was confident. The polls showed him with a nearly two-to-one lead. Even if all the undecided voters supported Spaulding, he would win. He began cutting back on planned spending. (He still spent over a million dollars in the race.) But the obvious good humor at the Bridgewater State debate was not the only mood of the candidate. It was a solemn campaign most of all. Kennedy was no longer at heart the Celtic prince of that first campaign eight years before. Martin Nolan of the Boston *Globe* mused, "The absence of friction has helped transform Kennedy into something different. . . . Solemn, sound, and middle aged, homogenized into Saxbe, Schweiker, Proxmire or some other earnest, estimable Teutonic colleague. He is different now from the zesty campaigner of '62 or '64. The difference is that between compassion and passion." That was—and is—the crucial difference in Kennedy, I believe. Kennedy was compassionate where his brothers, and he himself, had once been passionate—and the voters of Massachusetts were more compassionate than passionate toward the third Senator Kennedy. For Kennedy not only the passion but the thrill was gone. He told William Honan of *The New York Times* that spring: "The events of recent years obviously weigh heavily. . . . It's a lot more difficult to work up the same enthusiasm as before. . . . I don't mean campaigning is without rewards. I meet people. There is great warmth, and it's always a pleasure to experience. But a lot of thrill, and the will, the sort of excitement is gone for me. I expect it to be gone forever." Was that just post-Chappaquiddick or postassassination malaise? I asked Kennedy about campaigning four years later—eleven years after John's death, six years after Bobby's death, five years after Mary Jo Kopechne's. Without a flicker of hesitation he said, "1962 was fun, but no campaign since then has been." A charge often leveled at "the Kennedys" is that they are too passionate, create too much excitement, surround serious politics with playful and distracting fun. Such critics who are also liberals dissatisfied with society and desirous of change might find in Ted Kennedy the kind of leader they prefer, a serious, somber, "Teutonic" senator interested in the high-priority items on the nation's list of needs.

Kennedy won with ease. He got 62.1 percent of the vote. His detractors pointed out that his total of 1,202,856 votes was considerably fewer than in 1964. His supporters pointed out that 1970 was not a presidential year, when there is a heavier vote, and that Kennedy's performance in 1970 compared favorably with that of other nationally known liberal Democratic senators running for reelection in a year in which the White House was trying hard to hurt all such. Senator Hubert Humphrey received 57.1 percent of the vote in Minnesota. Senator Edmund Muskie received 61.7 percent in Maine. Only Senator Henry Jackson of Washington had a walk-in; he got 82.4 percent of the vote in Washington (but he wasn't on the White House-Agnew list of radical liberals).

On election night Kennedy, Joan, and other members of the family and staff walked leisurely from campaign headquarters to the Parker House, to make a victory statement for television and friends and workers. Again, his theme was his national, not his state responsibilities.

> I look forward to my return to the United States Senate. I look forward to being a voice for peace in the U.S. Senate. As long as there are [the forty-three Americans] who were lost this past week in Vietnam, or the hundreds who were wounded or the thousands of South Vietnamese who were destroyed by this war, the first matter that exists for all Americans is the peaceful conclusion and resolution of that problem and the bringing home of American servicemen to this country where they belong. Secondly, in this country at a time when there are high government officials who are

placing race against race, youth against the old, the South against the North, that are playing to the fears and frustrations of the people within our society, to their deepest prejudices, I want to be a voice of reconciliation, a voice that appeals to the best within people, within our country, and I'll return to the U.S. Senate for that purpose. Finally, I will return to the U.S. Senate to give voice to the powerless groups that exist within our society. I'm not just talking [of] the hundreds and thousands and millions of members of minority groups, of the poor in this nation, I'm talking about the thousands of senior citizens who are unable to get into projects. I'm talking about the thousands of unemployed that I met on Massachusetts streets. I'm talking about the thousands of consumers that do not have a voice in the highest councils of government, and I want to be their voice in the United States Senate.

And, my friends, the people of Massachusetts would expect no less. We are the oldest of the states and come from the oldest part of the country. We are full of proud traditions and proud history. We pride ourselves on this. But most of all we are forward looking and a progressive state, and the people of Massachusetts expect me to be a progressive senator.

A progressive state expecting its senator to advocate progressive ideas? In 1970 that description did fit Massachusetts. (In November 1972 Massachusetts was the only state George McGovern won.) But it had not always been that way. As late as the late 1950s the Democratic party in Massachusetts was less liberal than its national counterpart. For generations it had been regarded as a machine for controlling patronage and winning favors, not responding to the needs of all the voters. John Kennedy took over control of the state party in 1956 when his candidate for state chairman, John (Pat) Lynch, defeated the McCormack candidate, William (Onions) Burke. But Kennedy stayed aloof from state party affairs in the next four years, his attention focused first on winning his own reelection by a large margin, then on winning the presidency. John Kennedy expected the right things, the liberal things from the party, but he did not give it the time and commitment it needed. Some argue that he turned it around to face in the right direction, but failed to give it a shove. His own view in 1960 was that it would not improve more until it was "badly beaten." It was beaten in that year's election, losing both the governor's and senator's races to Republicans. His presidential coattails were of no avail.

As 1962 and Ted Kennedy's first race approached, liberal, particularly academic, opposition was met with Kennedy promises to begin leading or pushing the state party in the direction John Kennedy had turned its face to. Robert Wood complained in 1961 that the party was still playing "nineteenth-century politics. The problem is to divide the spoils, not how to manage society." Kennedy told Wood and Sam Beer that he was prepared to work for a paid state party executive director, an advisory panel of experts from the universities, and a new emphasis on programs. Liberal programs, naturally. Kennedy also agreed to replacing the President's man, Pat Lynch, with a new chairman. He picked the replacement, Gerard F. Doherty.

Through the 1960s the Republicans controlled the governorship, except for two years. That made Kennedy the senior officeholder in the Democratic party, and as such he moved a considerable way toward assuming something of control of internal affairs and direction-setting, as well as controlling the patronage in 1963–68—or sharing it at times with John McCormack. Kennedy had it all while his brother was president. But less than two months after John Kennedy was assassinated, Ted, Doherty, and McCormack met in the Speaker's office in Washington for nearly an hour. They parted with a handshake and an agreement to share patronage in the future, and to continue in place all existing Kennedy appointments.

Because of his own campaigns it was 1966 before Ted Kennedy became a disinterested party leader in an election campaign. There was talk of his running even that year, for governor. The scenario went like this: Two Kennedys were one too many in the Senate; the Democratic party in Massachusetts could unite only behind Ted; only Ted could beat the incumbent governor John Volpe; only Ted could reform the party and cleanse its lingering nineteenth-century image. When Robert became president Ted would run again for his old Senate seat. This may have been only talk, but it was widespread in Massachusetts in late 1965 and early 1966, according to some memories.

Robert Kennedy told Massachusetts Democrats that

his brother would play a different role. He would select the nominee for governor. Robert's statement was half-jesting. "I want to assure all Massachusetts Democratic candidates that my brother Ted favors an open convention. That's a convention where the delegates fully consider all the possibilities, debate all their merits and then pick whomever Teddy selects," he said. In fact, that is the role many Democratic leaders wanted Kennedy to play. They were afraid that another factional fight like one that had occurred in 1964 would surely cost them the governorship again. Kennedy demurred, saying he didn't see the difference between leadership and dictatorship (and, apparently, also not seeing how it would help *him* to step forcefully into the fight). He was chided in the national press for staying aloof. In response to that, perhaps, Kennedy then tentatively tried to suggest a "balanced" ticket for the Democrats, but got nowhere, probably because he wasn't insistent enough. He stayed away from the convention, but kept a direct phone line between there and 3 Charles River Square. Delegates objected to his aloofness. "Kennedy has a China policy. It's a shame he doesn't have one for Massachusetts," one said. Another delegate rushed to the platform to mock-announce Kennedy's arrival: "Here comes Teddy Kennedy—with Ed Brooke!" (the Republican senatorial candidate).

The Democrats went down to defeat again that fall. In 1970, Kennedy stayed even farther out of the picture, and again there was a bloody party fight and again a Republican victory all down the line (except in the Kennedy reelection Senate race). At one point the state chairman, David Harrison, asked Kennedy to take a stand behind one of the Democrats seeking the gubernatorial nomination. "How can I?" he replied. "Maurice Donahue is a friend of mine. Kenny O'Donnell was a friend of my brother, and Kevin White's a good Democrat." He stayed out in 1974, too, when the Democrats finally won the state house back after twelve years. The two main contenders for the Democratic gubernatorial nomination that year were Michael Dukakis and Robert Quinn. Both sought Kennedy's help in a tough primary fight. Some "Kennedy people" turned up in both camps, but Kennedy stayed out till after Dukakis won. Then he made several appearances for the ticket (which was "balanced" at last), helping to raise money at two Columbus Day affairs after first making the principal and most effective speech at a unity party in late September. "He really turned the audience on," a Democrat who worked for Quinn said of that affair.

But Kennedy's aloofness from party nomination battles did not mean he did not have an impact on both personalities and policies in Massachusetts democracy. He can claim the major share of the credit for turning it into the liberal, activist, twentieth-century party it is today. He made his contributions in several ways. To begin with, in 1966, after the Republican victory, Kennedy brought in a new state chairman, Lester Hyman, a Rhode Islander then working in Washington, with instructions to make the party a programmatic one. Kennedy had a Democratic Advisory Council set up to help with programs. This drew heavily on the Cambridge academic community. Its members included John Kenneth Galbraith, Daniel P. Moynihan, Jerome Wiesner, James McGregor Burns, and General James M. Gavin, and editor Robert Manning. Kennedy also suggested the establishment of a 500 Club, the 50 members of which paid $500 a year apiece for off-the-record meetings with national political celebrities. The $25,000 was used to pay for research and newsletters and other housekeeping. Between the paid staff and the advisers, the party soon came up with the programmatic approach that had been lacking. By the end of 1967, the party's leaders, Hyman, House Speaker Robert Quinn, and Senate President Maurice Donahue, were ready to announce an eighteen-point "party program for 1968." It was a good, standard, liberal package, with proposals for reform in the areas of civil rights, consumerism, campaign finance, gun control.

Just at this point, the whole thing blew apart. The 1968 presidential campaign exploded. Hyman was a Johnson supporter. Many other Massachusetts Democrats sided with challenger Eugene McCarthy. Then Robert Kennedy announced. Ted lost interest in state party affairs, devoting all his attention to his brother's race, then retreating into political isolation of sorts when Robert was assassinated, and never really coming out of it in the way local reformers expected. "But," says Robert Wood, "we now [1975] have a

programmatic state legislature and government. I don't say
Ted gets the credit for that, but he did his duty, and he did
get the thing started in the right direction."

Kennedy selected the successor to Hyman, state representative David E. Harrison, at the end of 1968, but his
interest in or commitment to the day-to-day workings of the
party structure would never again be at the levels they were
in 1967. In 1971, when Harrison wanted out, Kennedy intervened in order to prevent what was shaping up to be a
disastrous fight between the more or less liberal and conservative wings of the party. The liberal, newer members of
the party favored Representative John Buckley. The old-line
Democrats wanted Representative George Sacco. Kennedy
called leaders in both factions to a meeting at 3 Charles
River Square. A participant says of that meeting: "Kennedy
could have said 'I want Mickey Mouse' and they would have
gone along. Nobody wants to cross Kennedy if possible. But
he made it clear that he wanted *them* to come up with the
compromise." Some journalists said this was Kennedy's way
of playing it safe. Buckley was the logical candidate for
Kennedy. But another view more flattering to Kennedy is
that he genuinely believed the party would be stronger if its
wings began to compromise in such fights, rather than having solutions imposed.

The party leaders agreed on a temporary chairman,
state treasurer Robert Crane, who was later replaced by
state representative Charles Flaherty. Kennedy could have
vetoed Flaherty, but so could other leading Democrats in
the state. Flaherty is undoubtedly less of a "Kennedy man"
than any party chairman since John Kennedy's man defeated John McCormack's man in 1956. Furthermore, since
Democrats won the governorship in 1974, for the first time
since 1964 Edward Kennedy is not the sole and indisputable
titular leader of the Massachusetts Democratic party.

Kennedy's impact on the party is still enormous. He
has made other contributions to its rampant liberalism that
are of greater importance than his role as party chieftain. He
has championed all the liberal issues in the United States
Senate. He has thus attracted men and women of like mind
to active participation in party affairs, as candidates, contributors, or workers. Kennedy also has lent his staff and

other resources to "the Kennedy guy" in many political subdivisions. As a result, according to those journalists and politicians who know the Massachusetts political scene intimately, there are a number of officeholders in the state today who would follow Kennedy's lead on most issues, if he asked them to, as well as on political questions. "He doesn't often do that," says one who fits the description of a "Kennedy man" in the state legislature. "Except where his own interest is involved, he follows a policy of benign neglect." He really doesn't have to ask. The Kennedy men, the Kennedy guys who have benefited from their association with him, think the way he does on most issues. They don't have to be asked.

The man who was elected to the Senate to "Do More for Massachusetts" has had his successes and failures in the past fourteen years. Mostly, it has lately seemed, he has had his failures. He has not been very good at pork barrelism.* Thanks to President John Kennedy, Massachusetts did get the National Aeronautics and Space Administration's Electronics Research Center in Cambridge, one of the great, tasty pieces of pork of the 1960s. Even with the President and the President's senatorial brother supporting Massachusetts on this, it took a fight in Congress, with the House of Representatives initially blocking the project. The President's moon program and the growing defense budget also meant prosperity for Massachusetts. The sophisticated electronics engineering firms that had been growing up around Boston's circumferential Route 128 since the 1950s were a national resource that any president would turn to in the 1960s. Through the Kennedy and Johnson administrations, the federal money poured in. There were some 30 industrial parks and 700 firms along 128. Neal Peirce in his study of Massachusetts as a "megastate" called the defense-space related spending of the decade eastern Massachusetts's "greatest economic boom of its history."

*On occasion he has opposed pork-barrel spending in the state. He once sponsored an amendment to block a federal urban renewal project that would have destroyed a 200-year-old landmark. He has also opposed the enlargement of Logan Airport in Boston.

How much of this was attributable to the state's only Democratic senator is hard to say. Probably not too much. Kennedy was an active worker for jobs for his state. He had one notable success in December 1963, when he and speaker John McCormack prevailed on Defense Secretary Robert McNamara to keep the Boston Naval Shipyard at Charleston open. This came at a time when the government was closing a number of shipyards, including the historic one in Brooklyn. By most accounts the Boston yard was more obsolete than some that were closed, and was kept open only for political reasons. Four months later McNamara announced that he was closing the Watertown Arsenal, abolishing 1841 jobs. Kennedy got only a few hours' notice that this was to be done. But it was not until 1969 that the recession hit. By then Kennedy was the Democratic senator in a Republican regime. The first thing to go was, symbolically, the Electronics Research Center, which had a $17-million-dollar payroll and $25 million worth of contracts when the end came. In the next two years, 10,000 engineers and scientists lost jobs along 128, and at least that many nonprofessional employees were also laid off. Unemployment in eastern Massachusetts soared above the national rate and stayed there into 1975. Otis Air Force Base on Cape Cod, with 1500 jobs, was closed; Westover Air Force Base in Chicopee, with a $50-million payroll, was closed; the Chelsea Naval Hospital was closed. And most symbolically of all, the Boston Naval Shipyard, reprieved when there was a Democratic president in the White House, was closed. The announcement of that came early in 1973, and was viewed widely as the state's reward for voting for Senator McGovern. Over 5000 jobs were involved at the shipyard.

Lobbyists for special interests in Massachusetts and New England give Kennedy good marks generally for his work for constituents. So do other New England politicians and staff in Washington. But he has a special weakness: his national reputation and the need to keep that alive. When he first came to Washington, New England senators worked together as a group. The effort had been started by John Kennedy. "Ted Kennedy was cooperative and interested," recalls a staff member for another New England senator, "and he saw to it that his staff took a reasonably active interest in our work. We were mostly working on behalf of cheaper oil and to assist the textile and shoe industries. Most of the senators tended to be parochial. Kennedy was even then building a national constituency, so we noticed that he didn't invest as much time as some of his colleagues. I have often heard that Kennedy was always one for undercutting other senators, for taking good issues away, but I never noticed any of that then. We appreciated the fact that he was always willing to dramatize a local issue with a floor speech or a press release. His staff was well informed on local issues. At that time, at least, his reputation for servicing constituents was good, too."

The senatorial group eventually disbanded, but in 1971, Massachusetts representative Michael Harrington began working to create a new New England congressional caucus. What came into being in 1973 was a group composed of House members from the region. Senators were asked to be involved, but for the most part they have not been. "Senators already have the visibility," explains a staff member. "The purpose of the caucus is partly to provide representatives with some visibility of their own." Kennedy has attended a few of the caucus meetings, apparently about as many as any New England senator. More than his colleague Ed Brooke. When someone not familiar with Massachusetts politics and government begins making inquiries in this area, soon and often he hears this statement: "Kennedy is a pretty good senator for constituents—particularly compared to the other Massachusetts senator." Senator Brooke has the reputation of being a little lazy, or at least unproductive. Whether the reputation is deserved or not, it exists, and works to the advantage of Senator Kennedy.

Probably because he is a Republican and because the administration since 1969 has been Republican, Brooke is regarded by many in Massachusetts as the senator the company president goes to when he has a problem with government. Once during the Johnson Administration Kennedy sponsored a seminar in Washington for Massachusetts mayors and selectmen to learn how to get more federal aid. Kennedy proposed a similar seminar during the Nixon Administration, but the local officials, wise in the way of partisanship, turned him down. So

Kennedy asked Brooke to co-sponsor the program with him. "Kennedy, not Brooke, is regarded by the little guy in the state as the senator to write or call if he loses his Social Security check," the legislative assistant to a Massachusetts representative says. Ed Brooke is a liberal Republican, but he is still a Republican—"a black Yankee" one irreverent Massachusetts Irishman has called him—and for that reason he is generally regarded in the state as the senator more responsive to middle-class and upper-class problems, while the Democrat Kennedy is popularly believed to be more responsive to the working-class man and woman. "Kennedy's staff in Boston and in Washington is very good with case work and other constituent problems," in the view of a former aide to a Massachusetts representative. "That became noticeable after Chappaquiddick. Kennedy must have given orders to concentrate on reelection in 1970. The reason I think he is running for reelection in 1976 and not for President is that I noticed this again starting last year [1974]."

I noticed the same thing in 1975. On June 18 I sat with Kennedy at Washington National Airport while he waited for a flight to Boston. He was absolutely bone tired. He was in no mood for answering questions posed by a journalist. He was in no mood even for gestures of good will from tourists. "God bless you, senator," a young man said in a New England twang as Kennedy entered the airport. He ignored him. Others who made similar comments got similar brush-offs. I am told this is unusual for Kennedy. He didn't seem uncomfortable, or aloof, just exhausted. (He did seem uncomfortable when an attractive young blonde woman in a see-through blouse fell in step with him and began describing a dream she had had the night before about Kennedy and California governor Edmund Brown, Jr. "Well, I was in good company," he said with a forced smile, and stepped up his pace.) Kennedy told me he had been to Boston on the 16th and returned on the 17th. Before that he had flown up and back on the 14th and 15th. On the 13th he had flown up that day and back that night. He had gone up on the 9th and come back to Washington on the 10th. On the 5th he had flown up and back. These were all working trips. "The more you do the year before an election, the less you have to do election year," he said.

"Are you worried?" I asked.

"Well, this busing thing has hurt. Then my stand on abortion is not acceptable to a significant number of Catholics. The doctors and medical schools are very angry. And all this publicity about my national prospects doesn't help. That is hurting Muskie, you know, and it didn't do George McGovern any good last year."

On one notable occasion Kennedy found himself opposed on a pet project by Brooke and traditionally Republican real-estate developers and landowners *and* by traditionally Democratic members of the construction trades. The project was the "preservation and conservation" of Martha's Vineyard, Nantucket, and the Elizabeth islands. Conservation in general has been an appealing idea to Kennedy. He has championed, unsuccessfully so far, federal legislation that would limit development in the Berkshire Mountains area of Massachusetts and in the Connecticut Valley in Massachusetts and Connecticut. He and House Majority Leader Thomas O'Neill successfully championed legislation that authorizes federal funds for advertising and repairing historic structures in Boston, which their bill joined together as the Boston National Historical Park: Faneuil Hall, Paul Revere House, Old State House, Old North Church, Old South Meeting House, Bunker and Breeds hills, and Charlestown Navy Yard. That bill became law in 1974, after failing once in the previous Congress. In mid-1975, however, still no federal funds had been appropriated, nor was the Ford Administration in favor of spending money on such projects.

The islands bill was a major enterprise on Kennedy's part. He grew up around Cape Cod and the nearby islands. He has remained a sailor all his life. He has a deep attachment for the physical beauty of the region, and resents what he regards as the suburbanization and despoilment of the islands. John Kennedy had gotten Congress to create the Cape Cod National Seashore in 1961. That was the first national park to be acquired largely by condemnation of privately owned land. Ted Kennedy thought at first to try simply to add the islands of Nantucket Sound to the Cape Cod National Seashore. "He told me when he started this," said aide Dun Gifford, "that John Kennedy always had it in mind to go ahead on this, that the Cape Cod Seashore was only the first part. That wasn't *the* reason Ted did it, but it was *a* reason." In 1971 Kennedy introduced legislation to study the possibility of adding the islands to the national park. Then in April 1972 he said he had decided that was not practical, and proposed establishing a Nantucket Sound Islands Trust Commission which would control development on the islands. Four land classifications would be established: "forever wild," which could never be built on; "scenic preservation lands," where "intensity of development should not be increased over what it currently is"; and "town" and "county" lands, where development would be left up to the local governments.

The problem with the plan from many islands residents' point of view was that it gave the federal government more authority than local governments retained. Developers who wanted to put up more condominiums, workers who wanted to build them, and landowners who wanted to see the value of their land increased all opposed the idea. The All-Island Selectmen's Association voted unanimously in April to ask Kennedy to withdraw his legislation. The association said such a law would depress the construction industry, and went on to attack Kennedy personally: "[His] legislation . . . is a cold-blooded violation of the principle the senator had pledged to uphold when he took his oath of office. It deprives the people of Martha's Vineyard and other proposed trust territories the right of equal protection under the laws of the United States. It is an unreasonable seizure." Later that month Gifford went to a meeting of 500 islands residents in Edgartown to explain Kennedy's proposal. He was jeered and booed. The following month a new group of residents announced they would take Kennedy to court if he didn't withdraw his bill. Late in May, after an hour-long meeting with Nantucket officials in the John F. Kennedy Federal Office Building in Boston, Kennedy announced he would not press for his legislation. However, he did not withdraw it. In July he introduced amendments meeting some but not all of the local opponents' demands. The legislation still was silently opposed by Senator Brooke, however, and because of that Kennedy knew it was not realistic to think he could get it enacted into law. Brooke's principal objection was that local officials could be overridden by federal officials. The state legislature took the same view, and in March 1973 passed a resolution asking the new

Congress elected the previous November to scrap the Kennedy plan. That same month Kennedy began circulating a copy of a revised bill around the state, which still did not really meet the objections of the most outspoken islanders. In July Kennedy and senators Alan Bible and Bennett Johnston of the Interior Committee came to Nantucket and Martha's Vineyard for hearings on Kennedy's proposal. Senator Brooke made public his theretofore private objections. "Too harsh a penalty for our island ailments," he authorized a spokesman to say. Governor Francis Sargent endorsed the need for some federal bill, but not Kennedy's. Some debate was not so polite. A Chamber of Commerce official likened Kennedy to Mussolini.

Kennedy and his aides then began a series of meetings with Brooke, Sargent, and Representative Gerry Studds, whose district included the islands. Agreement was finally reached in which local officials would have more control of local development than in the original Kennedy versions of the bill. A parallel state law was to be enacted that would ensure that. Brooke announced his support of the compromise in 1974, but a busy Congress never got around to acting. As this is written (summer 1975), the expectation is that the 94th Congress will approve the legislation.

In many states the fact that a senator's most publicized involvement in federal-state relations was one in which a great many residents were opposed to the point of outrage would be regarded as an indication that the senator was in political trouble. So, too, would the fact that so much of his time was being devoted to non-state-related enterprises. Considering that Kennedy also has the problems his probusing stand has caused him, it would seem that a number of ambitious politicians would be planning to run against him in 1976. Yet as of this writing, there is practically no talk of a serious challenge. Some Massachusetts journalists and politicians speculate that if in early 1976 it begins to look more likely that Kennedy may be drafted for a presidential run, something he ruled out publicly in September 1974, then a number of candidates in both parties may emerge. Kennedy said flatly before he took himself out of the presidential race that if he were a candidate for president, he would not seek an arrangement by which he would simultaneously be a candidate for reelection to the Senate.

16. GOVERNMENT
IN EXILE

I can tell you one thing, if Ted Kennedy ever became President, you wouldn't have a White House staff like the one you've got." The man speaking was a former member of the Kennedy senatorial office staff and the time was the spring of 1974. What he was referring to specifically was the then accepted theory that H.R. Haldeman and John Ehrlichman (1) had shielded President Nixon from contact with any other subordinates and (2) had themselves ordered or engaged in illegal activities. "Everybody reports directly to Kennedy, and he attracts the kind of people who wouldn't pull anything like that [gesturing toward a Watergate headline in the Washington *Post*]." These were not self-serving assessments. The man talking had not stayed on Kennedy's staff long. He had left under circumstances in which the question of did-he-jump-or-was-he-pushed? arose. Furthermore, he was talking off the record. I was surprised to hear him talk so positively about his tour of duty there and about his successors. A number of Senate staff men and women I had talked to previous to this interview had been extremely critical of "Kennedy staff." The general complaint was that Kennedy staff aides tended to be arrogant, tough, selfish (for the senator), more concerned with publicity (for the senator) than accomplishment, amateurs. In the year of interviewing that followed,

I found a fair amount of evidence to support this critical view.

But the weight of the evidence seemed to me to tip the scales heavily to the view of the unnamed staff man quoted first. Most of the people—senators, staff aides, lobbyists, journalists—I asked about this in the course of a year agreed.

The purpose of what follows is not to assess the Kennedy staff, however, but merely to describe it, and to point out what a large and professional resource a senior senator like Kennedy has at his disposal.

The first point the anonymous ex-staff-member made about the senator's accessibility is something you hear about over and over when talking to present or former Kennedy staff. Apparently no one on his staff who has any sort of substantive responsibilities ever has trouble getting to see him personally or, on less urgent matters, getting a memorandum before his eyes. No senior staff man rations Kennedy's time or filters out staff reports. No pyramid. Paul Kirk, who is presently Kennedy's chief political staff assistant, describes the office organization chart as a circle, with all staff members on its perimeter dealing directly with the senator at its center. And, of course, dealing with each other. Those memoranda are all read, it would appear. Kennedy's take-home briefcase is a joke around the office. "It weighs a ton," one secretary laughed. It weighs a ton when he brings it back the next morning, too, with each memo scratched up with "Yes," "No," "See me," and other evidence that Kennedy has spent an hour or two or three reading and digesting.

Kennedy gets as much or more education in face-to-face briefings, conversations, telephone calls. I attended a staff briefing session that was probably typical late one June afternoon, a day before Federal Energy Administration officials were scheduled to testify before the Administrative Practice Subcommittee. Kennedy lounged behind his desk, tie undone, hair mussed from a nervous, tired running of his fingers through it. His coat was a mass of wrinkles on his desk top. Three subcommittee aides, Thomas Susman, James Michie, and Kenneth Kaufman, peppered him with suggested questions. There were briefing books and brown file folders everywhere, on the desk, on the floor, on a table. An empty jug of cranberry cocktail and a litter of styrofoam cups testified to a long session, as did the stifling blue haze of smoke from Kennedy's cigarillos, Susman's cigars, and Michie's cigarettes.

Kaufman proposed that Zarb be asked why large oil companies were paying less in fines than small companies. No, Kennedy said. "He'll just say the small firms don't have as large and as good accounting departments." Kaufman contended it was not that, it was that FEA's procedures were not adequate to deal with Exxon and other giants. Michie broke in to make another point. Kennedy had placed himself in the role of Frank Zarb, the FEA chief. Each point the staff men made, Kennedy would reply as he imagined Zarb might. "This just proves the big companies are obeying the law." Each Kennedy answer led to further refinement of the proposed questions, or to facts from briefing books that would allow Kennedy to rebut the anticipated answers. Zarb was put on the defensive the next day, was unable to obfuscate, as bureaucrats so often do, and conceded that oil pricing procedures might not have been monitored as carefully as they should have been. He promised to correct the deficiencies.

Kennedy staff people are seldom career Hill types. Like any other large institution, the Senate could hardly work without these career professionals. In Mike Mansfield's phrase, the Senate has become "a gray flannel organization," and it needs its senior and veteran bureaucrats. But it also needs its ambitious, restless sojourners, and it is to such people that Kennedy has consistently turned during his first fourteen years in the Senate. John Culver, his first press secretary, stayed only a little over a year, then returned home to Iowa to run successfully for the House of Representatives. (He later was elected to the Senate.) Milton Gwirtzman, his first legislative assistant, had been in that job for Senator Ben Smith. He left Kennedy in early 1964 for a highly successful law practice in Paris and Washington. David Burke was legislative assistant, then administrative assistant. He came late in 1964 and stayed a long six years, held in place first by the assassination of Robert Kennedy, then by Chappaquiddick, then by the 1970 election. He joined the

Dreyfus Fund in New York, to be replaced by Edward Martin, a former Boston newspaperman.* Dun Gifford spent three and a half years as a legislative assistant, then joined the Boston investment firm of Cabot, Cabot and Forbes as a partner. James Flug spent two years as a legislative assistant, then four years as chief counsel of the Administrative Practice and Procedure Subcommittee, before leaving the Hill to run the National Legal Aid and Defenders Society. Kennedy's current (1975) staff includes at least three members who have told him they may be leaving soon—Carey Parker, his principal legislative assistant who joined the staff at the end of 1969, Robert Hunter, who came in 1973, and Richard Drayne, his press secretary, who had been with him since 1966.

The above list is by no means complete, but the people on it are what other Senate staff people mean by "typical Kennedy staff men," I suspect, though they are by no means identical. Some similarities: Kennedy is oriented to Ivy League types, perhaps only because he is a Harvard man and Harvard is in his state. Culver was a Harvard football teammate. Gwirtzman is Harvard and Yale Law. Burke is a Tufts- (and University of Chicago)-trained economist. Gifford is Harvard and Harvard Law. Flug is too. Parker is Harvard Law. Flug and Parker, and Flug's successor at Administrative Practice, Thomas Susman, are also ex-Justice Department.

Flug's name was often mentioned by staff members of other senators when the subject of "Kennedy staff" arrogance and toughness came up. Flug just shrugged it off when I asked him to reply. I asked Dave Burke, who hired Flug, to comment. "Jimmy Flug *will* run over you—with his brain," he replied. "He'll argue you to death. And if you can't stand that, well, he's very brusque. That's just the way he is. It doesn't have anything to do with his working for Kennedy. He'd be brusque if he were working for Roman Hruska." Tough? "If by tough people mean realistic or that

*It was often said that the signal that Kennedy is running for president will come in the form of Burke's leaving Dreyfus to return to Kennedy's staff. In 1975 Burke left Dreyfus—to work for New York governor Hugh Carey.

old word pragmatic, well, I suppose Jimmy, and all the people around Ted Kennedy today, are that way. If you mean tough like these clowns Chuck Colson and Ehrlichman, and Haldeman—charade tough—they're not that way at all."

Despite what Burke says, if Jimmy Flug had worked for Roman Hruska he would have operated differently. Leaving personalities out of it, the fact is that *in general* a Kennedy staff man has more freedom and more authority than other Senate staff aides. Occasionally a Kennedy staff member will deal directly with another senator, rather than at the staff level. That is rare, but it happens. It doesn't happen the other way around nearly as often. Another way a Flug is different from a Hruska aide is access to outside sources of information. "I guess I could call up the chief economist at Brookings and get him," says Carey Parker, matter-of-factly. Most other legislative assistants on the Hill could not; in fact, some senators could not. Robert Hunter, the foreign-policy adviser to Senator Kennedy, says that when he wants to talk to the heaviest of heavyweights in the diplomatic and arms-control field, he gets right through. Part of this ready access is due, no doubt, to the cachet of the Kennedy name. Most of it, however, is due to the fact that those experts at the other end of the line know that Kennedy means business. If he is interested in a project he usually works hard at getting it accomplished, and he has a pretty good track record. The experts spare him and his staff time believing they will have an impact on policy. This, of course, in effect increases the size of Kennedy's staff. It's the old Kennedy story. Of Senator John Kennedy, it used to be said, "Other senators read the experts' books, John Kennedy talks to the experts who wrote the books."

Another resource for Ted Kennedy is ex-staff. "You never really break away," says Gwirtzman. Gwirtzman is a gifted writer. He is often called on to write a speech for Kennedy. He wrote the senator's eulogy to Robert Kennedy in 1968. He wrote the senator's Saturday Night Massacre speech in 1973. Kennedy regularly calls on Burke and Dun Gifford for advice and other assistance.

In 1969 Senator Edmund Muskie expressed a common resentment. He said if he had Kennedy money he would have Kennedy staff. Both Burke, who was then administrative assistant, and Edward Martin, the ex-Boston newspaperman who succeeded him, state flatly that *no* member of the staff has ever been subsidized by Kennedy, himself, or any family front while they were administrative assistants. However, Gwirtzman was paid $18,000 a year from the Park Agency (the family conduit) from the time he left the staff in 1964 until 1970 for writing speeches and giving advice. At least one other outside assistant was also so paid in that period.

By the end of 1970, however, there was really no need for Kennedy to think of subsidizing inside staff or hiring extra staff from the outside. His seniority and aggressive search for committee power had started him toward accumulation of a staff that by 1975 had become a formidable bureaucracy in itself. Some called it a government-in-exile. He was:

1. Chairman of the Subcommittee on Refugees and Escapees. This position allowed him to hire three professional employees. Dale de Haan, the chief counsel, had been a member of the staff since before Kennedy became chairman; he had an assistant, Jerry Tinker, listed as a consultant. The third professional staff position controlled by Kennedy was filled by Loretta Cubberly, who worked not for the subcommittee but for Kennedy personally, as assistant to the press secretary.

2. Chairman of the Subcommittee on Administrative Practice and Procedure. This position allowed him to hire seven professionals, including the chief counsel, Thomas Susman. Three of those (plus secretarial and clerical assistants) worked not for the subcommittee directly, but as legislative aides for the senator. Robert Bates handled the senator's civil-rights and gun-control bills; Robert Hunter was his foreign-policy adviser; Mark Schneider handled energy, amnesty, Chicanos, military matters.

   One of the professionals working for committee was investigator Walter Sullivan, another ex-Justice Department aide, who in 1975 was on loan to still another Kennedy subcommittee, the Health Subcommittee of the Labor and Public Welfare Committee.

3. As chairman of *that* subcommittee Kennedy had five professional jobs to fill. Stanley B. Jones and LeRoy Gold-

man were management specialists, Allan Fox was a lawyer, Dr. S. Philip Caper and Dr. Brian Biles were physicians. Kennedy also used a part-time consultant, Dr. Larry Horowitz. Horowitz had been a full-time staff member, specializing in the subcommittee's study of the drug industry, a study which continued after he left in 1974. It was to this work that Sheridan was on loan from Administrative Practice.

4. In addition to all the above, Kennedy was allotted one staff position as chairman of the little-publicized National Science Foundation Subcommittee of the Labor and Public Welfare Committee. Ann Strauss held that job.

All this is added to his regular Senate office staff in Washington and Boston. The budget for that in 1974 was approximately $500,000. Salaries for the professionals alone controlled by him on the three subcommittees came to nearly $400,000 annually. Senator Kennedy had a million-dollar-plus staff at his disposal, counting clerical and secretarial workers. And that was not all. In 1972 Congress created a new organization, the Office of Technology Assessment. Kennedy was a co-sponsor of the act. OTA was the fourth such agency created by Congress to help it with decision-making. The other ones were the General Accounting Office, the Congressional Research Service, and the Congressional Budget Office. The OTA's role was to "respond to . . . the needs of the House and Senate Committees for adequate, accurate, evaluated information; it is expected to provide expert and objective data and useful information concerning problems, questions and opportunities in areas of science and technology," in the words of Representative Charles Mosher, a member of the Senate-House Technology Assessment Board that oversees the OTA's operations. OTA had a budget of approximately $6 million in 1975, a full-time staff of 50, 100 consultants, and contract arrangements with a number of universities and research organizations. Its mandate was broad—and the chairman of the board in the 93rd Congress was Edward Kennedy. (The chairmanship shifts from Senate to House. In the 94th Congress, the chairman was Olin Teague of Texas.)

Jude Wanniski wrote in the *Wall Street Journal* in

1973 that OTA was a potential "Shadow Government" for Kennedy. He could foresee it becoming the sort of agency that could endorse "good technology" and censure "bad technology" in such a way that industries and universities would have to respond to it. Kennedy was able to put former Connecticut Representative Emilio Q. Daddario in as director of the OTA. Daddario had exhibited the same point of view as Kennedy in his technology-related votes in the House. He voted against both the SST and ABM, for example. There could be little doubt that OTA would be responsive to its board in a most direct way. Republican Representative Charles Mosher of Ohio, a member of the board, wrote to Speaker Carl Albert in 1975 summing up the OTA's first two years. He said, as if to chill any effort of Congress as a whole to try to direct OTA or set its priorities:

> An effective enterprise can have only one Board of Directors; in OTA, this function is vested exclusively in its Congressional Board. The Director of OTA is the chief executive officer of this enterprise. He can be effective in marshalling resources and executing the broad policies and decisions of the board only if he has sufficient authority and discretion. OTA's director must not be subjected to multiple lines of direction; he must be responsible solely to the Congressional Board. Members of the Board, particularly its chairman and vice-chairman, should insure that, having laid down broad policies, authority remains in the Director to execute these policies.

Clearly Kennedy had a great deal on his plate. He won his legislative subcommittee chairmanships in the nick of time, as it turned out. In 1970 Congress passed a legislative reform act that limited senators to one subcommittee chairmanship within the same committee. Thus Kennedy would have had to give up either Administrative Practice or Refugees—except that the new act "grandfathered" existing subcommittee chairmen. They could retain multiple chairmanships.

In 1975, Kennedy faced a challenge to his "imaginative" career as chairman of previously obscure subcommittees. The Washington *Post* ran a series of articles about the use and abuse of congressional committee staffs. Reporter Stephen Isaacs charged that Senator Henry Jackson was using some of his large staff to assist him in his presidential campaigning. Kennedy was singled out for the most criticism. The charge was that he was using such aides as Hunter, Bates, Schneider, and Cubberly for personal, i.e., legislative and political, assistance, rather than assigning them strictly subcommittee chores. The series appeared on the eve of the Senate Rules Committee's hearings on funding committee and subcommittee operations. Chairman Howard Cannon, a Democrat, and Robert Griffin, a Republican, quizzed all chairmen about the various allegations in the *Post* series. They reserved their most penetrating questioning for Kennedy.

At one point Griffin raised the question of why any one senator should have a larger staff than any other. Kennedy replied, "Whether we like it or not, we have the divisions of power in the Congress. . . . The seniority system brings responsibilities and you have to discharge those responsibilities. I mean, I think that is the way our particular system functions and works. I mean, I do not think it is all perfect, but I think it is the best one around. . . . We are competing with a major executive office that has extraordinary kinds of resources . . . and we are constantly being challenged to represent our interests . . . in an important way. If I am going to be able to, in terms of a variety of different responsibilities that I have and being completely willing to be judged in the nature of performance, require the kind of expertise and the kind of knowledgeable people in this area, I make no apology for it."

I think in that rambling answer Kennedy was expressing the view that he does want a "shadow government," that he *needs* one, and that any legislator who pretends to national leadership is in the same boat. He sees a senior party leader with a national following as entitled to—obligated to —develop the resources that will allow him to stand up to the president of the United States, particularly when that president is of the other party. That business about seniority was not just an idle line, either. In 1975 Senator Mike Gravel introduced legislation that would insure that junior senators received extra staff assistance to help them meet their responsibilities on their committees. Fifty-two senators co-sponsored the proposal. But not Kennedy, although he later voted for a substitute proposal—that would give him one or two new aides.

What the Rules Committee had in mind was probably not the *Post* series, and certainly not the threat a Kennedy shadow-government apparatus posed to President Ford. Rather, Cannon and Griffin objected to Kennedy's relative power vis-à-vis other senators and his encroachments on their preserves. Griffin expressed shock at the fact that Kennedy's two Judiciary Committee subcommittees spent more money than the entire Appropriations Committee, the most powerful in the Senate, more than Agriculture, more than Armed Services, and even more than the equally imaginative Henry Jackson's Interior Committee. A number of senators object to this, Griffin went on, and they bring their objections to the Rules Committee. As for Cannon, he had a very personal reason for objecting to what Kennedy had been up to. Cannon was also chairman of the Aviation Subcommittee of the Senate Commerce Committee. That subcommittee had, in the eyes of Kennedy and his staff at Administrative Practice, stood idly by while airlines raised fares and arranged schedules in a way not responsive to the public (see Chapter 11). Even the Refugees Subcommittee was threatened, though there had been no complaints that it was stepping on any other committee's toes. Griffin said that technically the subcommittee was limited to inquiries regarding European refugees, yet had made its principal mark in the past decade in Asia. Kennedy sighed that if the Rules Committee really wanted to reform the system and end all jurisdictional overlaps (he mentioned that the Finance Committee often strayed over into areas his Health Subcommittee should logically have exclusive control of), he was game. But until that sort of root-and-branch reform came along, he would fight any attempt to penalize just him and his subcommittees.

In 1975 Kennedy won a victory in the internal maneuvering for "committee power" that is always going on in the Senate. Kennedy won a new and prestigious committee appointment—the Steering Committee named him to the Joint Economic Committee, a valuable plum in a period in which the complexities of the economy and energy were melding into one of the most glamorous issues before the country. A seat on the committee gave a senator an extra dimension, making him a participant in significant congressional decision-making, but more important, a certified expert—with credentials—to be invited to speak before prestigious groups and television cameras about this most basic political issue. Kennedy won the seat in a race with several liberal colleagues.

His membership on the Steering Committee was another source of power for Kennedy. Committee assignments are both rewards and punishments. New senators seeking new assignments and old senators seeking changes have to take into account the desires of the Steering Committee members on other legislative questions. That Kennedy is a Steering Committee member may weigh only a fraction of an ounce on Senator X's scale of decision on, say, a technical amendment to a health bill, but that fraction may tip the scale. It was the accumulation, and wise and constant use, of just such fractions of ounces of influence that made Richard Russell the power he was in his last two decades in the Senate.*

It is senseless to predict what the Senate will be like for a generation ahead, but it would appear that as the 1970s come to a close, we will have entered a period in which liberal Democrats will dominate the body's inner workings and substantive output. And it appears that if he elects or is forced to stay in the Senate, Ted Kennedy will be a dominant senior leader of whatever Northern and Western and liberal equivalent of the old Southern conservative club evolves.

*Russell was simultaneously on the Policy Committee, to which Kennedy now aspires. He is blocked off at present because John Pastore of Rhode Island holds the "New England seat."

17. ON THE
CUTTING EDGE

Could it be that all this time that we all have thought Kennedy was preparing himself in the Senate to be a good president, he has been preparing himself to be a great senator? That is at least a possibility. I asked Dun Gifford in 1974, before Kennedy announced he was not going to be a presidential candidate in 1976, if he could visualize Kennedy's spending twenty more years in the Senate. "Easily," he replied without hesitation. "I think he's quite comfortable with it now, for whatever reasons. He has a lot of influence in the Senate. One of my ways of looking at questions like that is to ask, 'As opposed to what? Spending his life in a law firm? Running the family business? Or perhaps running for President and winning or losing?' "

Would he be happy as Secretary of State, president of Harvard or of General Motors, or something like that? "My personal guess is that he would not be as happy. It's safe to say he likes what he's doing now. He likes being an elected public official. His whole life is geared to that. Everything he can remember is geared to that."

Dave Burke had another view in midsummer 1974. "I remember once when Ted had worked hard to get a certain health bill through Congress," he recalled. "He was very excited about it. He was telling everyone how much good it would do. How it would help people who hadn't been helped before. Then Nixon vetoed it. That reminded him how much the executive could do, and that really a senator is just a special pleader. I doubt if Kennedy wants to remain that.

"Also," Burke continued, "he has to be measured in his own mind with how the public perceives him relative to John Kennedy and Robert Kennedy. He feels pressure from people who say, 'Your brother was President of the United States; your other brother was the leader of a great crusade and candidate for President; and look at you, futzing around in the Senate.' I don't believe he will accept being just a senator."

Just a senator? A man with a unique perspective is Senator John Tunney of California. He knows the Senate from the inside, and he knows Ted Kennedy as well as, if not better than, any public official does. They were roommates in law school at the University of Virginia and have been close friends ever since. In 1963 Tunney visited Kennedy in Washington, and they talked about their futures over a four-day weekend. "He told me that he had decided his career was really going to be there. He urged me to seek a Senate career. He told me how he had established a really good relationship with members of the hierarchy, particularly the Southern members, which was perhaps not to be expected, considering their political views. But he indicated to me that you could really take the word of a Southern senator. That was not always the case of the body in general. Ted said once you got a commitment from a Southern senator, he would always be with you on that issue. Other senators might give you their word, then renege on it when it was to their best advantage to do so. All of this went into Ted's explanation to me of why he enjoyed being in the Senate. I got the sense that he wanted to make the Senate his career and that he thought a person could get an awful lot done in the Senate."

But that was 1963, with John Kennedy in his first term in the White House and Robert waiting ahead of Ted in the line of succession. Ted was a thirty-one-year-old freshman senator with ideas about the possibilities of the Senate but little knowledge of the reality of it. In 1974 a lot had changed, in the family, in the Senate, and in the nation. I asked Tunney that fall to comment on Burke's assessment, particularly the invidious comparison of Ted to John and Robert. Tunney didn't wait a second before answering. "I think there are others who would have Ted measure himself by that yardstick, and so that obviously has to be a part of his decision-making calculus. It has to be, because it is constantly being fed into him. But I think that the fact that he stays in the Senate and works hard at being a senator means he has evaluated it and rejected it. I'm not saying that it is not a matter that is not subject to constant revision and reevaluation, but at least at the moment in my view the Senate is a very good place for him to exist and to be creative. . . . I feel Ted feels that the Senate is a *very creative* place to be. I think he feels that the Senate is the place where a person can have a fulfilling lifetime career."

Has he said that to you?

"Yes. Yes, he has said it. Sometimes we have talked in general terms about how frustrating it is not to be able to get things done, and see changes made, and the fact that there's an inertia in the system which is so difficult to break through. But then we would say, 'Well, if you take a look at this job and contrast it with any other job, it comes out way on top. . . . I mean, where else could you be where you would be sitting at the focal point of world events.' I think he feels that this is about as good a job as a man could have. . . . Dave Burke's statement may be accurate in the sense that it's something which Ted has thought about, but I do not think it is accurate if you suggest that Ted has weighed all the factors and has decided to stay in the Senate and to accept himself as a failure. No, that's wrong. I think I'm in a better position to know that."

The man in the best position of all to know is Kennedy himself, and he was asked about it often in 1974 and 1975, usually in relation to whether he would run for president or seek reelection in 1976. He told George Will, the Washington *Post* columnist, that he could visualize himself serving happily in the Senate for another twenty years. He told Paul Duke of the Public Broadcasting Service: "I enjoy the work that I have in the Senate. I find, having been there now for twelve years, increasing responsibility, increasing opportunity to have some impact. So I enjoy that work . . . and [people] say, 'Well, you have to be spending all your time worrying about [being President]. I don't. I enjoy the work that I'm involved in and what I'm doing." He told me, when I asked him if he ever lies awake contemplating being sixty years old and a thirty-year senator, a crusty chairman: "I can see that, but I'm still young enough to see some life out in front of me in that respect. I mean, I don't have to make a decision yet."

Does it repel you to think of being, say, the liberal Dick Russell of the 1990s? I asked. "No," he said, very hesitantly. He began to talk about the short-range future. "I foresee myself always on the cutting edge of social issues and programs. I'd like to see a completion of a number of things I'm involved in. The most obvious is in the area of health. My seniority, which gives me some additional authority, but more importantly just the knowledge and awareness of how the Senate functions, is obviously sort of advantageous to me. Gives you a feeling that you pretty much know your way around." His view began to reach beyond the short range to the middle distance. The Senate is a place for patient men with long-term projects. He began to talk about "building blocks." One Indian-education bill he shepherded through the Senate five times before the House passed it, then the appropriation was cut, then Nixon impounded that. "Finally that money is going out now. You recall all these frustrations all the way through, but now the money is going out, and you look back and see that you are achieving something after all. That gives you some satisfactions that you don't really get in the short terms."

I do not know how to balance all that against Dave Burke's recollection of the Kennedy frustration at being a special pleader. I suppose Kennedy would rather be president than a senator. Paul Duke asked him point-blank. "Would you, deep down, like to be President?" and the entire answer was: "Yes."

Not long after that I interviewed Kennedy in his office. The interview took place in the late afternoon of a not very busy day. Kennedy was relaxed and in a good mood. He stretched out in a chair, coatless, lit up a black cigarillo, and reflected on his work in the Senate. I said to him, "You have always been a special representative of the young, the poor, the black, but in Richard Scammon's memorable phrase, the country is un-young, un-poor and un-black. If you were President of the United States, could you still show that much concern, pay them as much attention as you do in the Senate?"

He said, "Oh, I think you could get more done."

"Get more done? There wouldn't be the constraint of having to represent the white middle-class majority?"

"It doesn't have to be at the expense of those others," he said very matter-of-factly, puffing a cloud of smoke toward the ceiling. The passion you usually associate with a Kennedy talking about social injustice was not evident. We could have been in a graduate seminar. "I think that's what the problem has been," he went on.

"But you've said several times that you enjoyed being on the cutting edge of social change. The people of Massachusetts may be tolerant of a senator like that, but can a President be——"

"I think a lot more than they have been," he interrupted, still in a reflective, relaxed tone of voice. "A lot more than they have done. I start from the position that the American people respond best when they're challenged. Part of the great malaise during the Nixon period was that they were unchallenged. I think the country needs to be challenged to respond to the dream of America. My sense is that the people want to be asked to do something about energy. I think they want to be asked to do something about hunger. I think they want to be asked to do something about the economy. They want to be asked to do something. I think if they felt they were getting an even break on this, I think it is unlimited what they would be prepared to do." He sat up a little in his chair as he finished the sentence; some of the Kennedy fire flickered, but he was still subdued. Fire in ice.

I suppose if he stays in the Senate the rest of his career it will be as something of prisoner, a reluctant Senate grandee, like Russell after his failing bid for the presidency in 1952, like Taft after that same year saw his last hopes of the presidency bleached out in the sunshine of Eisenhower's grin. When his bid for the presidency was thwarted, Richard Russell turned to committee chairmanships and the secrets of the Senate's rules and rhythms to become one of the most influential men in the country for two decades. Suppose Kennedy were to be similarly thwarted and one day wake up to realize, along with the rest of us, that he had grown old in the Senate, and grown powerful. What would he be like? I think it is unlikely that he would become bitter and negative, as Russell became. Another senator of this age who became a powerful man, with a constituency that spread beyond his state and party, was Everett Dirksen. In his last years of power he became an odd burlesque of himself and of a senator of great influence. It is difficult to imagine Kennedy devolving to that.

Robert Taft in the Senate after 1952 is what I imagine Kennedy in the Senate after 1976 might be like. But one has to imagine what Taft would have been like. He was a prisoner of the Senate in his thirteen years there, only accepting it as his lot after his final presidential failure in 1952. He became his party's floor leader—and died. There are many similarities in his and Ted Kennedy's career. Some are not so apparent. Richard Russell used to marvel in recalling that Taft was a man ("the *only* man") who decided how to vote or take other senatorial action with no thought for the political consequence. Ted Kennedy is a political animal to a greater degree than even his brothers were. "Kennedy" and "calculation" go together in many people's mind. Yet there is a strong idealistic strain in Ted Kennedy, to the point of Taftian stubbornness. Kennedy told the *Globe's* Martin Nolan in October, 1973, "I have a particular view of the country and its needs, the direction that it can and should go into. It may very well be that that view may not be shared by the country or the party. I have strong views about these issues. My particular approach to the country may not be the one the country wants to move toward. And I'm not going to change my views or alter my position."

Senator John Tunney says Kennedy has always been the idealist in the family. "In law school we used to argue all the time. Ted always took the idealistic side." Tunney says of that summer 1963 visit to Washington, when "pragmatism" was the watchword of the New Frontier, Kennedy talked about his budding public career in terms of ideals, not ambitions, not accomplishment. Like Taft, Kennedy has that national constituency. Like Russell he has that sense of the Senate. Unlike both, he has almost instant access to the media and thus to the nation. There is no better lever of power than that.

Certainly Kennedy is on the threshhold of real power if he stays in the Senate. He could begin exercising it now. Consider this: In 1975 Kennedy led reform efforts to strengthen liberals on important committees. Washington *Post* Senate correspondent Spencer Rich reported:

> A quiet revolution is underway in the Senate . . . and Edward M. Kennedy is a key figure.
>
> The Massachusetts Democrat mustered a liberal coalition that dealt a terrific beating to conservatives when the party's Steering Committee handed out assignments recently.
>
> Demonstrating an ability and force long expected but never quite achieved before, Kennedy thoroughly studied the rules, traditions and mathematical formulas governing appointments by the nineteen-member Steering Committee.
>
> Then he proceeded to grab most of the juiciest new committee spots for liberals and freshmen.

Kennedy alone kept Senator James Allen off the Judiciary Committee, saw to it that James Abourezk of South Dakota got on instead, giving the committee a liberal majority. Kennedy worked with liberals like Senator Dick Clark of Iowa to put two freshmen liberals on the Armed Services Committee, two others on Foreign Relations, and two others on Finance.

Rich continued:

> "Kennedy utterly dominated the sessions. He had learned every nook and cranny of the rules we use for appointments," said a Kennedy nonadmirer.
>
> Kennedy's victory, in a personal sense, marks a milestone in his recovery from the Chappaquiddick incident and the embarrassment of his ouster by [Senator Robert] Byrd from the whip job in 1971, largely because he hadn't performed the whip function adequately.

But in a much larger sense, it is simply a part of a silent, almost unnoticed realignment of power relationships now going on in the Senate. . . .

For years the South and its inner Senate "club"— headed by the redoubtable Richard B. Russell (D-Ga.)—ruled the Senate, but now the old-line conservative Dixie legion has shrunk and many of the new Southern senators are liberals or moderates. Democratic liberals, though not in control of the Senate as a whole, are by far the biggest single bloc.

There is also the possibility that unlike almost every other powerful twentieth-century senator, Kennedy might become chairman of an important committee while still a young man. He could conceivably become chairman of the Judiciary Committee in 1977 and remain its chairman for a generation, into the twenty-first century. That is not an insignificant committee. It handles something like half the bills that become law. Ralph Nader has described it this way:

> If Congress . . . is the heart of our democracy, then the House and Senate Judiciary committees are its lifeblood. These committees provide perhaps the clearest measure of the success or failure of Congress in protecting and advancing the public good. If Congress is to assert itself as a vital organ of our political and moral life, as a counterweight to a presidency grown swollen with power, as an energetic and passionate advocate for long-ignored public interests, the Judiciary committees will have to play a leading role.

Kennedy is fourth senior on the committee now. But the Democrats in the House of Representatives have overthrown seniority as the single automatic criteria for chairmanships. They did that in 1975, after laying the groundwork in 1973 by agreeing to select chairmen by secret ballot. Senate Democrats in 1975, with an assist from Kennedy, laid the same groundwork. Beginning in 1977, they agreed, Senate chairmen will be chosen by secret vote. Immediate Capitol corridor gossip was to the effect that seventy-one-year-old Judiciary chairman James Eastland was one of two or three prime targets for ouster. Next senior on the committee is crusty old John McClellan, who is eighty years old and chairman of another committee. Next senior is the liberal Michigander, Phil Hart. Hart is a relatively youthful sixty-three, but he has announced he will retire after the 94th Congress. Even if he doesn't, Kennedy might be the caucus choice for chairman. It has been speculated that Hart might be brushed aside, if he doesn't retire. I asked Kennedy about those stories once, before Hart's announcement. He praised Hart, but he never really answered the question. I asked a member of Kennedy's staff. He said he believed there would be a challenge to Eastland in 1977, by Kennedy. Did that mean Kennedy would ask Hart to step aside, or shoulder him aside? "That wouldn't be necessary. If Hart stays in the Senate, he would defer to Kennedy. He would prefer Kennedy chairman, because he would think Kennedy could do a better job. He is an unusual man, an unusual senator." After Hart's announcement, I asked Kennedy about challenging Eastland. He answered only by saying that maybe Eastland wouldn't seek the chairmanship again in 1977.

Nader's comment about the need for legislative counterweights is a thought attracting increasing attention among political scientists. A number of students of democratic institutions fear that growing population and dwindling resources will lead to the sort of pressures that make decisive and swift decision-making popular. Only a strong executive can so act. To prevent such an executive from becoming a dictator, there have to be strong personalities in other branches of government, particularly the legislative. Such a personality would have to be of great stature and be effective at his job.

The loyal Dave Burke quotes some of that literature when he explains why he believes it is important for Kennedy to perform such a role, and why he believes Kennedy can be such a superb senator. A few weeks before Kennedy announced in September 1974 that he would not be a presidential candidate, not accept a draft, in 1976, Burke stressed in an interview his belief that Kennedy was frustrated in the Senate. After the announcement Burke stressed his belief that this country needs a senator who is effective (because of brains, hard work, seniority) inside Congress, who can almost (by his glamour) command the media to give him access to the nation, who has a national constituency (the poor, the black, the young, the liberals, the longers for Camelot, etc.), and who is unawed by the White House (his brother used to live there). Burke had a long private talk with Kennedy on Labor Day weekend at Hyannis Port. That was when Kennedy made his decision to take himself out of the race. Whether Burke brought up the arguments regarding the need for this balance to a strong presidency, I don't know. I suspect so, though as Kennedy and Burke and Gifford and Carey Parker and almost any senator and senatorial aide will tell you, no one needs to tell Kennedy about the possibilities of the Senate.

I tend to believe Burke was right both times; that Kennedy wants to be a senator and wants to be president. Once Kennedy told me, "I've never been obsessed with the presidency, even though, because of a set of circumstances, it's always been a major factor in terms of my future plans. But in my own mind it has not been a major factor. I've never stayed awake contemplating the challenges of it or running for it. I have no consuming kind of passion for it. I have no lust for power. Jack obviously was planning to run for it in 1956. Bobby, I remember my father saying, 'What's Bobby going to do after this?' at every stage." So Ted Kennedy grew up in the Senate expecting to stay there, perhaps to *have* to stay there. By the time anyone said "What's Teddy going to do after this?" he was *settled* in the Senate. It was never just a stepping stone to him. If he left it, it would be with reluctance.

And if he left it, it is conceivable he would come back, even from the White House. One name on a silver cigar container John Culver gave Kennedy in 1963 is John Quincy Adams. The names are all the senators who had held the seat in the Senate Kennedy had just won. Adams went back to Congress after a term as president. I once started to ask Kennedy if he would do that. In leading up to the question, I asked him several others about the future. He answered each with some reluctance, I thought, increasingly so as the questions looked more and more years ahead. Finally he said, "In my family we have learned not to make long-range plans." We were sitting in his office at 431 Russell Office Building. The walls are a gallery of framed family memorabilia—a faded photographic portrait of Joseph P. Kennedy, Jr. . . . John Kennedy's dog tags . . . a teasing note from Robert Kennedy . . . several photographs of the Kennedy brothers together . . . a Christmas vacation theme by young Teddy, Edward M. Kennedy, Jr. . . . In such a setting, Ted Kennedy's answer effectively turned off that line of questioning.

Whatever the future holds for Kennedy, it is obvious that his years in the Senate have been as rewarding—even as pleasant—as they have been productive times for him. He once told an interviewer that he loved the actual physical presence of the Capitol. He once wrote to the children of Robert Kennedy in a book of remembrance that his special memories of Bobby included

> . . . touch football . . . ski trips . . . sailing trips off the beautiful coast of Maine. . . .
> But most of all I shall remember our walks through the park from the Senate floor to the Senate office building in every kind of weather. He would suggest that I speak at an early morning assembly at a high school here in Washington, urging students to stay in school and continue their studies. He would remind me to give wholehearted support to a fund-raiser to be held for Cesar Chavez' farmworkers. He would tell me of a recent trip to the Mississippi Delta, describing the extraordinary conditions of hunger, malnutrition and poverty he saw, and he would talk about the forgotten Indians in our country, and the injustices and indignities they suffered. Those moments of conversation as much as any speech he made revealed his deep feeling and passionate concern for the forgotten American. And no words can describe his purpose better than those words written by Tennyson of Ulysses, "How dull it is to pause, to make an end, to rust unburnished, not to shine in use as tho' to breathe were life!"

Ted Kennedy will have been in the Senate fourteen years when this term ends. That is a longer service than the tenure of John Quincy Adams and two other senators named on the cigar container: Henry Cabot Lodge, Jr., and John F. Kennedy. I believe any fair assessment of Ted Kennedy and

those senators made from today's perspective would conclude that his contribution to the nation has been greater
than theirs. Among other names engraved in the silver are
Daniel Webster, who served nineteen years, Charles
Sumner, who served twenty-three years, and Henry Cabot
Lodge, Sr., who served thirty-one years. It is illustrious company. Should Ted Kennedy's eventual total years of service
in the Senate approach theirs, it is not at all unlikely that
from the perspective of future historians, any fair assessment would conclude that his contribution to the nation
matched or exceeded theirs, even if he, like they, never rose
to the highest office the nation offers.

INDEX

LaVergne, TN USA
27 August 2009
156130LV00003B/5/P